THE BOLSHEVIKS
and other plays

MIKHAIL SHATROV

Mikhail Shatrov was born in 1932 into a family of active Bolsheviks – his father was executed during Stalin's 'Great Purge' of 1936–38, and his mother spent many years in prison and exile. Shatrov's uncle, Alexei Rykov, became Chairman of the *Sovnarkom* (the Soviet 'cabinet') on Lenin's death, and was killed in 1938 together with Bukharin and other leading Bolsheviks.

Shatrov graduated from the Institute of Mines in Moscow in 1956. His political plays include: *In the Name of the Revolution* (Moscow Young People's Theatre, 1957), *A Day of Silence* (premiered Leningrad, 1965), *The Sixth of July* (premiere at the Moscow Arts Theatre in 1966), *Blue Horses on Red Grass* (Komsomol Theatre, 1979), *The Dictatorship of Conscience* (Komsomol Theatre, 1986).

Mikhail Shatrov is the author of the film *The Sixth of July* and the four-part film *Sketches for a Portrait*.

Michael Glenny was born in 1927. He studied Russian at Oxford, and has taught at the Universities of Bristol, Birmingham and Southern Illinois. He has translated over 40 books and plays and has made numerous visits to Russia where he has studied the Russian Theatre at first hand.

In the same series

Stars in the Morning Sky

New Soviet Plays
introduced by Michael Glenny

Alexander Chervinsky *Heart of a Dog*
Alexander Galin *Stars in the Morning Sky*
Alexander Gelman *A Man with Connections*
Grigory Gorin *Forget Herostratus!*
Ludmila Petrushevskaya *Three Girls in Blue*

MIKHAIL SHATROV

THE BOLSHEVIKS
and other plays

Translated and introduced by
Michael Glenny

THE PEACE OF BREST-LITOVSK
THE BOLSHEVIKS
ONWARD, ONWARD, ONWARD!

NICK HERN BOOKS

A division of Walker Books Limited

A Nick Hern Book

The Bolsheviks and other plays first published in 1990 as an original paperback by Nick Hern Books, a division of Walker Books Limited, 87 Vauxhall Walk, London SE11 5HJ

The Peace of Brest-Litovsk © 1987 by Mikhail Shatrov
Copyright in this translation © 1988 by Michael Glenny

The Bolsheviks © 1985 by Mikhail Shatrov
Copyright in this translation © 1989 by Michael Glenny

Onward, Onward, Onward! © 1988 by Mikhail Shatrov
Copyright in this translation © 1988 by Michael Glenny

Introduction copyright © 1990 by Michael Glenny

Set in ITC New Baskerville by BookEns, Saffron Walden, Essex
Printed by Richard Clay Ltd, Bungay, Suffolk

British Library Cataloguing in Publication Data

Shatrov, Mikhail, 1932–
  The Bolsheviks and other plays.
  I. Title
  891.72'44

ISBN 1-85459-036-7

Caution
All rights whatsoever in these plays are strictly reserved. Requests to reproduce the text in whole or in part should be addressed to the publisher. Application for performance by professionals in any medium should be addressed to the author's sole agent, Michael Imison Playwrights Limited, 28 Almeida Street, London N1 1TD; amateurs and students wishing to perform or give public readings of any or all of these plays must apply for a licence before rehearsals begin to Nick Hern Books, 87 Vauxhall Walk, London SE11 5HJ; and for stock and amateur rights in the United States of America application should be made to the Dramatic Publishing Company, P.O. Box 109, Woodstock, Illinois 60098.

Contents

Introduction	page vi
The Peace of Brest-Litovsk	1
The Bolsheviks	81
Onward, Onward, Onward!	159

Introduction

Novels, poems and plays built around historical characters but carrying a political message for modern times have traditionally suffered heavily from official disapproval in Russia. As with so much else in Russian literature, it started with Pushkin: his brilliant chronicle-play *Boris Godunov*, based on Shakespearean models and written in 1825, was not performed until 1870 – thirty-three years after the death of its author, Russia's greatest poet. Soviet playwrights who tackle this genre, of which Mikhail Shatrov is an outstanding practitioner, must wonder at times whether anything ever changes in Russia: the first of the plays in this collection *The Peace of Brest-Litovsk*, had to wait twenty-six years before it could be performed in a Soviet theatre. The thought that one is in the distinguished company of Pushkin may be some consolation – but not much.

Mikhail Filippovich Marshak (Shatrov is an adopted name) was born in 1932 into a family which then belonged to the Soviet Union's intellectual and political elite. His mother's brother was Alexei Rykov, one of the leaders of the Soviet Communist Party and a successor of Lenin as chairman of the Council of People's Commissars or *Sovnarkom* (the Soviet 'cabinet'). But when Mikhail Filippovich was only six years old, his uncle Alexei was among the most prominent victims of Stalin's 'Great Purge' of 1936–38; degraded and humiliated in one of the infamous show-trials of those years, Rykov was executed along with most of the Bolshevik 'Old Guard' who had made the October Revolution of 1917. Altogether thirty of Shatrov's relatives died in those years, including his father, while his mother was incarcerated for years in a Gulag prison-camp, thanks to Stalin's barbarous policy of imprisoning or killing any adults connected by family ties to victims of the Purge. Young though he was, the trauma of this massacre of his family left a profound mark on Shatrov's personality and is not the least of the factors which later influenced his work as a playwright. This emerges with great force in the last and most recently written of the plays in this volume – *Onward, Onward, Onward!* – where, in a timeless, limbo-like 'world beyond the grave', Stalin is arraigned and condemned by his erstwhile victims and by Lenin for his blood-lust and his betrayal of the ideals and aims of the Revolution.

Plays and films with political themes were not a favourite genre with Soviet dramatists during the quarter-century of Stalin's absolute rule (1928-1953), being too fraught with possible danger for the author. Those works that were written tended to contain blatant distortions of fact dictated (sometimes literally) by Stalin, in order to exaggerate his own role in events and to present him as Lenin's closest confidant and legitimate successor. The 'Lenin trilogy' of films, made in the 1930s and scripted by Alexei Kapler, were classic examples of the kind – although even this did not save Kapler, too, from becoming one of Stalin's victims. A less tainted (and theatrically more enduring) set of plays on Lenin was written by Nikolai Pogodin (1900-1962), and they are to some extent Shatrov's models for his treatment of this theme. Pogodin, however, avoids going very deeply into the serious political issues of the time: he was more concerned with projecting an attractive image of Lenin's personality – above all his concern for the 'little man', for ordinary people in danger of being ground between the millstones of revolution.

There is something of Pogodin in Shatrov's approach; wherever appropriate, Shatrov brings out the considerate, courteous side of Lenin's nature in his dealings with individuals. But Shatrov's real contribution to the 'Leniniana' genre has been to plunge into his hero's role in the political crises of the revolutionary years. This is a riskier but also a more truthful and authentic way of portraying Lenin 'in the round', a man who was above all a politician to the marrow of his bones.

This approach has involved Shatrov in a great deal of research on primary materials – not always easy in a country where, until very recently, access to documentary sources has been difficult and restricted, even for compliant Party-line historians. In the late 1980s, with travel abroad made easier by Gorbachov's liberalising policies, Shatrov has taken the opportunity to sidestep the watchdogs who still stand guard over Soviet archives by undertaking research in Western documentary collections, including Britain's Public Record Office (for a new play dealing with Stalin and Churchill), and in the unrivalled holdings of Russian archive material that are kept in the Hoover Institute at the University of Stanford, California.

This drive to get at the truth about the formative years of the Soviet state is now shared by journalists, novelists, historians and other writers, and to some extent Shatrov is now one of many of the 'truth-tellers' of *glasnost*; but he has no rivals as a playwright in putting some of the crucial events of Soviet history into vivid dramatic form.

Trained to be a mining engineer, Mikhail Shatrov saw his first play – entitled *Clean Hands* – given a successful production in 1955 at the Moscow Young People's Theatre, when he was only twenty-three and in his final year at the Moscow Institute of Mines. As a result, he abandoned an intended career in mining for the life of a professional playwright. Since then he has written a new play every two or three years and is today one of the Soviet Union's most successful and respected dramatists. Shatrov's name has been especially connected with two kinds of plays, usually written with a distinct political tinge that has more than once got him into trouble with the censor: on contemporary social issues, especially those affecting young people; and, as exemplified by the three plays in the present volume, on the personality, career and political legacy of Lenin. His first 'Lenin' play, *In the Name of the Revolution*, was produced in 1957, also at the Moscow Young People's Theatre. The next, *A Day of Silence*, was premiered in Leningrad in 1965. Since then this subject has been the almost exclusive inspiration for his work, which now amounts to nine plays in which Lenin (even when off-stage all the time, as in *The Bolsheviks*) is the central pivot of them all.

Too often in the past, Soviet novels, plays and films of this kind have suffered badly from being mere slabs of congealed ideology or (when Lenin was the subject) saccharine hagiography. Shatrov stands out among his contemporaries because he does not write the sort of simplistic propaganda pieces that have been churned out to order by too many Soviet authors in the past, either to push current Party policy or to reinforce officially approved (and usually false) conceptions of historical figures either as ikons or as evil buffoons.

The Peace of Brest-Litovsk
The victor nations of the First World War have not always properly appreciated the extent to which that conflict was, above all, the greatest revolution in history. The Hohenzollern, Habsburg, Romanov and Ottoman empires were destroyed, and the first to collapse under the unprecedented strains of all-out modern war was the vast realm of the Romanovs. From the abdication of Nicholas II in March 1917 until the Bolshevik Revolution in November (or 25th October according to the unreformed Julian Calendar then used in Russia, hence the 'October' Revolution), Russia limped along as a lame-duck

belligerent, although already effectively defeated by Germany. The chief reason for the success of the Bolsheviks' seizure of power was their promise of 'Peace, Land and Bread' to the hungry, war-weary and demoralised Russian people – and above all to the peasants, who made up 95% of the huge but inefficient Russian army. To retain their precarious hold on power, the Bolsheviks then had to keep that promise – otherwise, if they failed to satisfy the expectations they had aroused among the mass of the peasantry, they would be swept away by a wave of elemental frustration and anger. Thus one of the first actions of Lenin's revolutionary government was to sue for peace with the enemy (Germany, Austria-Hungary, Bulgaria and Turkey), and in early December 1917 an armistice was signed as the prelude to negotiations for a formal peace treaty.

This is the situation at the start of the play, the action of which – allowing for some necessary compression and abridgement of detail – recounts with fair accuracy the interior politics that lay behind the tense, fluctuating course of the peace negotiations, as seen from the standpoint of the Bolshevik Central Committee. Coming so soon after the euphoria created among the Bolshevik leadership by the success of the actual revolution – which had been a comparatively bloodless walkover – the Brest-Litovsk wrangle was a crisis of the first magnitude. This was partly because failure to sign a treaty would mean the Germans simply marching into Russia, taking what they wanted and tipping the shaky Bolshevik regime into what Trotsky (in another context) called 'the dustbin of history'; and partly because the issue revealed that the Bolshevik Party – not to mention Russia as a whole – was deeply divided along ideological and emotional lines at the thought of capitulating to the demands of triumphant German imperialism. It must also be remembered that in late 1917 and early 1918 – when the Eastern Front had collapsed; when there were signs of mutiny in the French army; when Britain was within three weeks of starvation, thanks to the U-boat blockade; and when America's entry into the war did not look like being militarily decisive – it seemed distinctly possible that Germany and Austria-Hungary might well win the war.

These are the harsh realities which provide Shatrov with the material for intrinsic, ready-made drama. His skill as a playwright lies in the way that, from an overwhelming mass of documentary material, he has selected, juxtaposed and articulated within a three-hour time-span the pressures which caused Lenin's insistence on peace to be such a desperate, all-out struggle.

Shatrov's construction of a telling drama from historical

material is one aspect of this play which a non-Soviet audience is capable of perceiving and appreciating to the full. But there is another and highly significant dimension to it which may escape audiences or readers unless their attention is drawn to it. This is Shatrov's inclusion in the cast of the characters not only of Trotsky but also of Bukharin, Zinoviev and Stalin. It is not only that the first three were made 'unpersons', and hence unmentionable, by Stalin's fiat fifty years ago, with all the rewriting of history and scrupulous falsification of printed and photographic records which that entailed; but also the ban on these men, which even Khrushchev's de-Stalinizing reforms failed to remove, has over the years created such a holy, theological awe about these anathematised figures that on the few occasions when their names have been allowed into print (mostly in works of pseudo-history), it has only been in order to subject these phantoms to hysterical abuse.

In this play, Shatrov has not only restored Trotsky, Bukharin and Zinoviev to the roles they actually played in the historical events (though Zinoviev has a comparatively minor part); he has taken the process of restoration much further. In the case of Bukharin, the author goes a long way towards depicting the reality of the feelings that existed between Lenin and Bukharin, which had a strong emotional foundation in both men, and which (especially for the childless Lenin) in some degree functioned as a surrogate father-son relationship. Even though Bukharin opposes Lenin *politically* to the very end of the Brest-Litovsk episode, and Lenin has harsh words to say about Bukharin at the political level, Shatrov's writing leaves us in no doubt that the emotional ties between them were strong enough to survive even this rift – which, in view of Lenin's usual utter rejection of those who opposed him, was something so uncharacteristic as to be most remarkable.

In his treatment of Trotsky, Shatrov is perhaps not quite so 'revisionist'. This may be because for dramatic reasons he needed a fairly marked degree of conflict between Lenin and Trotsky, or because he judged it still too early to portray Trotsky wholly sympathetically. To have produced him on stage at all was enough of a bombshell. It is, of course, factually true that Trotsky's break-off of the Brest-Litovsk peace talks with his formula of 'No peace, no war' did indeed provoke the Germans to renew their advance into Russia, and thus went counter to Lenin's own consistently maintained policy that the peace *must* be signed, in order to prevent Russia being forced to accept much harsher terms – which duly happened. Yet it must also be said that Shatrov does Trotsky considerable justice: he states Trotsky's arguments for his policy quite clearly, and this in itself is also a major innovation.

Almost as interesting (though much sketchier) is the way in which Shatrov portrays Stalin: he is made out to be a devious trimmer, and in more than one passage in the play he provokes Lenin's anger and contempt. This tallies with the views on Stalin that Lenin later expressed in his 'Political Testament', when he urged the Party never to let Stalin attain the leadership – advice which unfortunately was never taken, in large measure because Stalin had the document suppressed during his lifetime.

In the form and structure of the play, Shatrov is striving to do two things: he proposes the use of more or less naturalistic methods in the acting-space at the front of the stage, in order to get across the quite meaty factual material of the political arguments, while also turning to more Brechtian techniques in his cabaret turns and his 'ampitheatre' set. The latter provides a flexible, kaleidoscopic setting in which to summon up the social, political and military forces that represent the different outside pressures that were being exerted on, or were offering support to, the politicians in their urgent conclaves.

The Bolsheviks

Shatrov has given this play the true, formal lineaments of Greek tragedy – unity of time, place and action – with results which, in a staging as good as its original production by Oleg Yefremov at Moscow's Sovremennik Theatre in 1966, can be exciting and very moving. The place and time are the Kremlin in Moscow during the few hours of the evening and night of 30–31 August 1918, when Lenin, the genius of the revolution, having survived imprisonment, exile and previous attempts on his life, is struck down by a would-be assassin. History does not provide playwrights with many scenarios for tragedy of such epic proportions – and in this case with the rare twist of a happy ending. It is a sign of Shatrov's dramatic skill that he elects to bring out the full, shocking implications of this near-catastrophe by focusing, in penetrating detail, on the effect that it has on Lenin's closest colleagues and family. By this means – keeping the central character off-stage throughout the play – the author achieves two results with maximum economy: he subjects his on-stage characters to a supreme test; and through that process he illuminates the nature and power of the stricken leader with an effect greater, perhaps, than he attains in other plays by having that leader appear before us. An earlier Russian play – which was to some extent a model for Shatrov – in which the author uses

xii INTRODUCTION

the same device of the unseen great man dying in the next room, is Mikhail Bulgakov's tragedy on the death of Pushkin, first performed in 1943.

Aside from the clear, indeed classic drama of suspense inherent in the situation Shatrov has chosen, there are two strands of subtext in this play which, for Russian audiences, are even more important than the overt narrative, gripping though this is. The first strand is the fact that the joyful relief at Lenin's survival was comparatively short-lived: the traumatic consequences of his wounds (one of the three bullets was never extracted) so shortened his life that he lived for only another five and a half years, and for long periods of that time he was reduced to a state of bedridden paralysis, partly deprived of the power of speech. Lenin died at the age of fifty-three (a year younger than the age at which Gorbachov in 1985 succeeded to Lenin's position), at a time when the fledgling Soviet state was still in dire need of his leadership.

But the second strand – the full, shattering, though unspoken impact of this play – lies elsewhere: it is the fact that, as the People's Commissars under Sverdlov's chairmanship debate the question of throwing overboard all ethical, legal and political restraints to protect Bolshevik rule by unleashing a 'red terror' against its opponents, the Russian audience realises, with a cold shiver running down its collective spine, that it is witnessing a replay of what was perhaps the single most fateful, ominous moment in the short but blood-soaked history of the Soviet Union. For that decision of the Council of People's Commissars (*Sovnarkom*), made in a moment of dire crisis as a temporary measure, was the statute (never revoked) which simultaneously created the *Gulag* and sanctioned the Soviet state's arbitrary use of unbridled violence. It was the precedent that enabled Stalin, ten years after Lenin's death, to unleash *his* reign of terror – an unimaginable act of policy that encompassed the deaths, at a conservative estimate, of 20 million people in Stalin's calculated assault on his own citizens, a massacre which makes Robespierre and Hitler look like timid amateurs. *This* is what lies in the collective memory of Soviet playgoers as they watch Shatrov's restaging of the enactment of a law that abolished law. The Russian audience's reaction to that production has lodged in my memory as the most powerful, electrifying theatrical event that I have ever experienced. This, surely, is what 'political theatre' is all about.

Onward, Onward, Onward!
The Peace of Brest-Litovsk was written during the 'Khrushchev Thaw' in 1962, the same year that saw the publication of Solzhenitsyn's

One Day in the Life of Ivan Denisovich, a shattering denunciation of the inhumanity of Stalin's prison-camps that was allowed into print on Khrushchev's personal insistence. Yet it was typical of the partial and arbitrary nature of liberalisation under the often unpredictable Khrushchev that Shatrov's play about the Brest-Litovsk crisis remained banned. The reason for this was the fact that Trotsky is one of its leading characters. Khrushchev and his fellow-members of the Soviet leadership at the time were still under the psychological spell of Stalin's branding of Trotsky as a cross between the Devil Incarnate and the Invisible Man. They could not make the leap over the irrational mental barrier that made it impossible to accept the stage representation of Trotsky's real historical role, even though Brest-Litovsk was an episode that hardly redounded to Trotsky's credit.

The choice of subject for Shatrov's next play, *The Bolsheviks*, was more fortunate, in that it deals with an episode in which neither Trotsky nor Stalin were directly involved. Indeed, that choice may not have been entirely due to chance; a factual consideration – the absence from Moscow on 30 August 1918 of both Trotsky and Stalin – no doubt played a part in Shatrov's selection of that particular event as the framework for his play; it absolved him from the need to observe authenticity by introducing those two contentious characters into the cast, when to have done so would have doomed the play to being banned, as had happened three years previously with *The Peace of Brest-Litovsk*. But that consideration does not bear directly on the quality of the writing. What matters is that the format of *verismo* in *The Bolsheviks* is most effective in conveying a telling account, in all its moral complexity, of a very touchy matter: the fateful moment at which, in self-defence during the early months of its existence, the first Soviet government effectively put the state apparatus above its own laws.

Written in 1987, two years into Gorbachov's era of *glasnost*, *Onward, Onward, Onward!* is the first result of Shatrov's partial liberation from the convention of 'documentary' drama, even though its protagonists are historical characters who rehearse actual past events and quote from their own speeches or writings. The method of letting Lenin's political opponents state their cases, begun in *The Peace of Brest-Litovsk* and used in somewhat muted fashion in *The Bolsheviks*, is deployed much more boldly in *Onward, Onward, Onward!*, especially since some of their more prophetic criticisms of Lenin and the Bolshevik Party have turned out to be devastatingly correct.

Thus after the two pre-*glasnost* plays, which are essentially illustrations of certain aspects of Lenin's character and policies (albeit with subtexts of wider import), in *Onward, Onward, Onward!* Shatrov moves into freer dramatic forms in order to conduct a straight political debate in which, to a degree unprecedented in Soviet drama, a spade is called a spade and the argument eventually focuses on Shatrov's real topic in this play: an indictment of Stalin's monstrous misrule. While no one today can dispute that Stalin was a bloodstained tyrant, in the West it is still a matter of debate as to whether, on the one hand, the horror of Stalin's reign really was a terrible aberration from Lenin's principles, or whether, in fact, Stalin really was (as he himself claimed) Lenin's true successor and only took to their logical conclusion the political forms and ideas bequeathed to him by Lenin. Amid the arguments on this topic which are now also being voiced in the Soviet Union, Shatrov firmly adopts the first of these two views, of which *Onward, Onward, Onward!* is so far his most explicit declaration in dramatic form.

Paradoxically this play, at the time of writing (October 1989), has had very little exposure on the Soviet stage. Aside from a couple of productions in relatively small provincial theatres, it has hardly been seen by the theatre-going public. Above all, it has not so far been performed in either Leningrad or Moscow, where a play must have a showing in order to make an impact on its intended audience: the intelligentsia, who are overwhelmingly concentrated in Russia's past and present capitals. Due to the centralisation of cultural life, which parallels the concentration of Soviet political power at the centre, it is the playgoers of these two cities who must be reached if the full effect of this work is to be felt in its true theatrical dimension.

It has, though, already made a considerable impact through publication of the script in one of the chief mouthpieces of *glasnost*, the boldly liberalising literary magazine *Znamya* ('The Banner'), in its issue of January 1988. This alone, together with a spate of press reviews in the following months, evoked a storm of response in the form of readers' letters to *Znamya* and other publications. These were divided more or less equally between fierce attacks on the author for his 'unacceptable' (read 'blasphemous') subverting of the hoary mythology which for so long has been fed to the Soviet population in the guise of 'history', and – on the other hand – heartfelt praise for Shatrov as the 'champion of *perestroika*'. If the printed text alone can arouse such passions, its eventual appearance on stage will doubtless produce a correspondingly more powerful effect.

Michael Glenny

THE PEACE OF BREST-LITOVSK

Characters

Male

LENIN
SVERDLOV
BUKHARIN
TROTSKY
DZIERZINSKI
LOMOV
ZINOVIEV
URITSKY
STALIN

COL. ROBINS (U.S.)

POET
LATVIAN
ORATOR
1st TELEGRAPHIST
2nd TELEGRAPHIST
GENERAL SAMOILO
GENERAL BONCH-BRUYEVICH
SOLDIER FROM BREST-LITOVSK
MAN IN WHITE TIE AND TAILCOAT
COMMISSAR
OFFICER
GERMAN GENERAL
WORKER
SAILOR

REFUGEE
SOLDIER
GORKY
BLOK
SIDORENKO
SUKHANOV
STROYEV

AVDEYEV
AKULOV
KARAKHAN
STEINBERG
MARTOV
YENUKIDZE
DAN
LUNACHARSKY
GORBOV
SOKOLNIKOV
JOFFE
FABRICIUS
RYAZANOV
KAMKOV
MURANOV
BUBNOV
ARTYOM
KRESTINSKY

Female

KRUPSKAYA
KOLLONTAI
INESSA ARMAND
LUKINA
WIDOW
KAKHOVSKAYA
SPIRIDONOVA
STASOVA

Non-speaking parts

SMALL BOY
FOUR FEMALE DANCERS

Chorus

Workers, peasants, soldiers, townspeople, politicians and writers.

The Peace of Brest-Litovsk was first performed in Great Britain by the Vakhtangov Theatre Company at the Lyric Theatre, Hammersmith, on 15 February 1989. The cast was as follows:

ORATOR	Maxim Sukhanov
SIDORENKO	Sergei Makovetsky
WIDOW	Natalia Moleva
LENIN	Mikhail Ulyanov
DZIERZINSKI	Evgeniy Shersnyov
BUKHARIN	Alexander Philipenko
STALIN	Vladimir Koval
SVERDLOV	Vladimir Ivanov
LOMOV	Alexander Pavlov
INESSA ARMAND	Irina Kupchenko
KRUPSKAYA	Alla Parfanjak
TROTSKY	Vasily Lanovoy
'FORMER PEOPLE'	Alexander Galevsky
	Lydia Konstantinova

Directed by Robert Sturua
Designed by Georgi Alexi-Meskhishvili
Music by Guia Kancheli

Performed in Russian, the play was accompanied by a live simultaneous translation based on the translation printed here and spoken by Frances de la Tour and Alan Rickman.

Translator's note

The set, as described by the author, consists of a tiered, semi-circular amphitheatre fitted with plain wooden benches, in front of which is the main acting space, which can be divided into two or more smaller acting areas. These are picked out and identified by means of lighting, a few pieces of appropriate furniture, and minimal props. The semicircle of tiered benches seats the CHORUS, i.e. the whole cast, from which the various principal characters either descend into the acting space to perform or stand up and speak from their places in the amphitheatre. From the start, the convention is established that the characters in the acting space at stage level and those above them on the benches can hear each other. Each act consists, in effect, of a series of fairly short scenes, the beginnings and ends of which are not usually demarcated by conventional scene changes, although such changes – minimal though they are – have to occur; while the author clearly wants the progression of scenes to be as smooth and unobtrusive as possible, he does not go into detail and in his first stage direction for a scene-change he specifically leaves questions of staging to the director and designer.

ACT ONE

Scene One

Petrograd, December 31st 1917. The Volkovo Cemetery. Deep snow. A funeral is in progress. Red flags, lowered, with bows of black crepe at the top of each staff. A small brass band. The sobbing WIDOW. *Members of the* CHORUS, *among them* LENIN, DZIERZINSKI, BUKHARIN *and* STALIN, *with heads bared, surround the grave. An* ORATOR *steps forward.*

ORATOR *(in a tragic, breaking voice)*. Our comrade's life was brought to an untimely end by a criminal's bullet. The newspapers are full of the news from Brest-Litovsk, where the hour approaches when a just, democratic peace will be signed! Rifles are being thrust into the ground by their bayonets, hands are reaching out for the promised land: socialism! But you, Stepan, will not be with us . . .

The WIDOW *sobs, and is comforted by those near her.*

We shall never forget your short but inspiring life, your courage during the July days, when you helped the leaders of the proletariat to escape, and we shall not forget the part you played in the victorious October Revolution. Farewell, dear friend, may the earth rest lightly upon you. We shall say goodbye to you for the last time . . .

The moment comes for the mourners to pay their last respects. The WIDOW *straightens up, sweeps them all with her gaze; suddenly the air is shattered by her piercing scream.*

WIDOW. So you came! He won't get up and walk to your orders any more! You no longer have any power over him! He is mine now, mine! You promised everything, told us how wonderful everything would be – 'there'll be bread, there'll be no more killing . . .' In the other world, I suppose? Just like the priests used to say! All just words – words to fool us! God, what use is all that claptrap to me now? *(Sobs.)* Aren't you ashamed?

Haven't you got a conscience, any of you? You've taken away our breadwinner . . . you've taken nearly everything . . . So take all I have left – take my son too. Go on, take him! (*Pushes her young* SON, *standing beside her, so that he falls at the feet of the Bolshevik leaders.*) Curse you – all of you!

Someone signals to the brass band, which strikes up a funeral march and drowns out the WIDOW's *curses. Another* WOMAN *bursts into tears. The coffin is lowered into the grave. As the music finishes, the sobbing* WIDOW *is led away. Slowly the mourners disperse.* LENIN, DZIERZINSKI, BUKHARIN *and* STALIN *come forward to the front of the stage.*

DZIERZINSKI (*speaks with a marked Polish accent*). Her nerves are shattered, poor woman.

STALIN. That speaker! Why did he have to talk like that and upset the poor woman?

BUKHARIN. He should have understood her feelings.

LENIN (*after a pause*). The point is, one must always pay up when one's I.O.U.'s fall due. One must always meet one's I.O.U.'s (*To his companions.*) Don't wait for me. My mother lives not far from here; I haven't seen her for a long time. Then I'll go straight to the teletype room.

DZIERZINSKI. The Sovnarkom is meeting at nine, then at midnight we'll see in the New Year.

LENIN. I'll be there on time. (*Exits.*)

Blackout.

Interlude One

The lights come on again to reveal a backdrop that is a collage of bright, cartoon-like episodes of the revolutionary events of 1917, in front of which stands a steeply-tiered, semicircular amphitheatre fitted with plain wooden benches; these are being filled as members of the CHORUS *mount the aisles between the benches and take their places . . . At stage level, just forward of either wing of the amphitheatre, two* TELEGRAPHISTS *each set up a Hughes teletype machine. Last to occupy their seats are* DZIERZINSKI, STALIN *and* BUKHARIN. *All is ready. Tense silence. Throughout the action, the* CHORUS *in the amphitheatre will intently follow everything that happens in the acting-space below, just as Russia and the whole world*

ACT ONE 3

followed the events in Petrograd and Brest-Litovsk, where, in the first months of 1918, the fate of the revolution was being decided. We hear the sharp sound of a breaking string.

Scene Two

LENIN *strides briskly on to the acting-space from stage left, crosses over to the* TELEGRAPHIST *at stage right, shakes him by the hand and starts to dictate a message.*

LENIN (*dictates*). 'To all branches of the Bolshevik Party; to all Soviets; to all Soldiers' committees at army and regimental level: The Decree on Peace, passed by the Second Congress of Soviets, has shown all nations the way to end the war on the basis of a democratic peace without annexations or reparations. The British, French and American bourgeoisie have not accepted our offer, and have even refused to discuss a general peace. That being so, we have been obliged to enter into separate negotiations with Germany, while leaving the door open for the Entente countries to join the negotiations. Germany, victorious on the Eastern Front, agreed to the principles of a democratic peace – without annexations or reparations – but only on condition that those principles are observed by the Entente Powers. On 27th December, however, having finally realised that the Entente will not join the negotiations, the German delegation, throwing aside all fine phrases about a democratic peace, has begun to talk to us in the language of victors. They have presented us, in categorical form, with the following demands: we are to accept the German seizure of Poland, Lithuania and a part of Byelorussia; we are to withdraw our troops from Estonia and Latvia; we are to evacuate the Ukraine; and we are to pay Germany reparations of three hundred million roubles. Otherwise, they will renew the war. You are requested to discuss this situation, sound out the opinion of the masses, put forward your proposals and communicate them to us. Signed: Ulyanov-Lenin, Chairman, Council of People's Commissars.' (*To the* TELEGRAPHIST.) Thank you. (*Sits down in his seat in the* CHORUS.)

MAXIM GORKY *stands up in his place in the* CHORUS.

GORKY. I am an old Russian writer. My name is Maxim Gorky. This is what I would like to say to you . . . If the Bolshevik leaders were to reject the offer of this shameful peace, all democratic opinion would support them, but this is not going to happen. Russia will be handed over to the Germans to plunder, so that they – the Bolsheviks – can stay in power and take part in this, which has always been their aim.

A member of the CHORUS, *the poet* ALEXANDER BLOK, *jumps to his feet.*

GORKY (*continuing*). As we know, one of the favourite and most loudly-proclaimed slogans of our home-grown revolutionaries has been: 'Expropriate the expropriators'! And they are going to do it – in the most remarkable and artistic fashion! There is no doubt that history will describe Russia's plundering of herself in the most heart-rending terms. They – the Bolsheviks and their German masters – will plunder and sell our churches, our palaces, our guns and our rifles. It is a unique proposal, and we can be proud that nothing like it has ever happened before, even during the French Revolution.

BLOK (*passionately*). My name is Alexander Blok. When the people take back what has been stolen from it over centuries, I find nothing wrong in the expropriation of the expropriators! When all around people are crying: 'It's the end of civilisation!' – I laugh! Why are the peasants knocking holes in an ancient cathedral? Because for a hundred years that cathedral housed a fat, belching priest, who took bribes and sold vodka. Why are they shitting in the beloved, beautiful mansions of our country gentry? Because it was there that peasant girls were raped and beaten. Do you really think a revolution is a poetic idyll? That a creative force never destroys anything in its path? That the long-awaited reckoning between oppressed and oppressors will be painless and bloodless?

GORKY (*sarcastically*). So we fought the autocracy of scoundrels and swindlers to exchange it for the autocracy of savages, did we?

Spotlights pick out LENIN's *office in the Smolny Institute. As they continue to listen to the polemics between* GORKY *and* BLOK, *the members of the Council of People's Commissars (Sovnarkom) come down from their places in the amphitheatre and assemble around the table.*

BLOK. There – you see?! With all their passionate spite, Russian intellectuals have been piling up logs, kindling and shavings. Then when it all suddenly bursts into flames – all that those intellectuals can do is run around screaming: 'Help, help! Fire! We'll all be burnt!'

GORKY. This contempt for intellectuals, which we often hear now, is typical of the intellectuals themselves. You won't find it among the peasants, because the only 'intellectuals' they ever knew were the dedicated country doctor or the village schoolteacher; nor among the workers, who owed their political education to intellectuals. It's an attitude that's wrong and dangerous. It destroys not only the intellectuals' own self-respect, but it destroys respect for their historic role. The intellectual is the sweating carthorse of history, who pulls the waggon of progress forward . . .

BLOK. I am convinced that the sacred duty of the Russian intelligentsia is to hear the music of revolution, which is literally shaking the very air, and not to pick out a few individual false notes in the magnificent sound of the orchestra.

GORKY (*grimly*). Even so, sooner or later we're all going to have to take off our rose-tinted spectacles and see what is really happening.

BLOK. And I see that our intellectuals are incapable of perceiving the greatness of the October Revolution behind its ugly features, which are few and could have been much worse – and that's shameful! (*To the auditorium.*) I want all of us to see that greatness.

BLOK *and* GORKY *sit down.*

Scene Three

STALIN. I think Gorky's a has-been. Still, let him say what he likes. The revolution hasn't time to regret its mistakes or to bury its dead.

BUKHARIN. No so fast, Koba. We have to stand by Gorky, otherwise we may throw out things of great value.

STALIN. Gorky valuable?! If we stay in power, we'll find plenty of others. We have a saying in Georgia: if there's no dog in the house, you must teach the cat to bark.

BUKHARIN. All right, but wouldn't it be better to get a dog?

STALIN. No, Nikolai, I object to your soft-hearted attitude. It's time that ex-proletarian writer was dead and buried. We shouldn't harbour any illusions. And I thought Mr Blok could have come on a lot stronger.

BUKHARIN. Oh, come now – don't you realise what it means to hear a symbolist poet say what he was saying?

SVERDLOV. I bought a beautiful edition of Blok the other day. What poetry!

STALIN. Why haven't I got one too? Would you lend it to me?

BUKHARIN (*To* SVERDLOV). You'd better give it to him altogether, Yakov. Koba can't bear not having something that someone else has.

STALIN. I want to know everything. Sverdlov's my witness – when he and I were serving out our exile in Siberia, there was no time to spare for culture.

BUKHARIN. You should have read when you were in high school.

STALIN (*smiles, spreading his hands*). I never went to high school. When I was in that seminary, and later, I preferred reading Marx. And when you were in solitary, even Marx was better than nothing. Some people go to school, others are self-taught. I was self-taught, and not ashamed of it.

Enter ALEXANDRA KOLLONTAI.

KOLLONTAI. I'm not late, am I? It's such a wonderful New Year's eve – they're dancing waltzes and polkas in the assembly hall, everyone's so happy and excited. I haven't seen Smolny in this mood for so long . . . not since the day after the October Revolution . . . How time flies . . . This our sixty-eighth day in power. Congratulations, everybody!

BUKHARIN. Don't interrupt, Alexandra Mikhailovna. Koba and I are discussing the relative merits of a seminary education over high school . . . By the way, talking of high schools: nine o'clock one morning, knock on my office door. 'Come in'. Enter an elderly gentleman of about seventy. Familiar face, but I couldn't place him. 'Are you Bukharin, editor of *Pravda*?' – 'I am.' – 'I've read your paper a couple of times, and I want to ask you one question. Are you the Bukharin who was a pupil at High School No. 1 in Moscow?' – 'Yes, I am.' – 'I now see why your newspaper and your whole gang of ruffians is leading

Russia to destruction: you had all the makings of it when you were in my school.' My mouth dropped open – it was my old headmaster! The old monster was still going strong!

STALIN. What did you do at that school?

BUKHARIN. I planted some revolutionary pamphlets in the staff common-room. He assembled the whole school, called me out for all to see and said to me: 'I don't want your feet in here any more!' So I did a handstand and walked out of the hall on my hands. All the other teachers have since died, but *he* survived.

STALIN. Oh dear, such a good start and such a feeble ending: you couldn't think of a good answer to the headmaster.

BUKHARIN. I could today!

STALIN (*winking to the others around him*). That's because you can't walk on your hands any longer. It's a fact, and facts are awkward things.

BUKHARIN. Want a bet?

STALIN. Done. Bet you can't go two paces. But where?

BUKHARIN. Here – now.

KOLLONTAI (*laughing*). You're members of a government now, comrades. It's undignified. (*To* STALIN.) Don't tease him, Koba, take him at his word . . .

STALIN. Never. Like Bukharin says – I'm jealous of anyone who can do more than I can, and I want to learn. Walking on my hands is one thing I can't do. I need to complete my revolutionary education.

BUKHARIN. If you lose, I bet you won't pay up. Right, Alexandra Mikhailovna is our witness.

KOLLONTAI. Lenin's coming.

BUKHARIN. Right, let's go. (*Stands on his hands and walks off on them, accompanied by* STALIN.)

LENIN (*coming down to the acting-space from his place in the amphitheatre*). They're waltzing in the assembly hall. And at the front too, believe it or not. I've just had the news from Dvinsk: our troops are fraternising with the Germans and dancing in no-man's-land. there you have it – the first waltzes of 1918.

The telephone rings; SVERDLOV *picks it up. Re-enter* BUKHARIN *and* STALIN.

8 THE PEACE OF BREST-LITOVSK

KOLLONTAI. Who won?

STALIN. We won't tell you. Let the historians answer that question.

LENIN. Whatever they say, it'll be a lie.

DZIERZINSKI (*from the wings*). All the very best for 1918, comrades. And for the sixty-ninth day of our existence. That's only two days less than the Paris Commune lasted.

LENIN (*smiling*). Dzierzinski's keeping count . . . I confess I've been keeping count, too . . .

SVERDLOV (*at the telephone*). Comrades, the Left S-Rs are having a special meeting of their Central Committee. They're discussing the German demands, and it's lasting longer than they thought. They apologise and ask us to postpone the session of the Sovnarkom until tomorrow.

LENIN. We agree, especially as it's nearly the New Year.

BUKHARIN (*looking at his watch*). Yes, only a few minutes now.

LENIN. Well, comrades . . .

All draw close to LENIN.

LENIN. Before wishing you well, I should like to wish that you do fewer stupid things in the new year than you did in the past year.

The People's Commissars murmur, laugh, whisper to each other.

That's firstly . . . Secondly . . . (*Pause*.) Somebody said something very interesting to me today. I've been haunted by it all day. A woman reproached me with not keeping our promises, with not paying our I.O.U.'s. It even depressed me a little. That's how we lose our support. We can lose *anything* but not the people's trust. The people's trust is, if you like, our Party's working capital. Kiev, the Donbass, Riga – we can give them all away, but not the people's trust . . . We must *never* forget that . . . We promised the people to do everything for peace . . . Have we? Of course I'm convinced that war will not be an eternal curse. Modern technology is making war more and more destructive. The time will come when war will be so destructive that it becomes an impossibility. War will mean universal death. Mankind will have to choose.

KOLLONTAI. We will give mankind the benefit of the doubt.

ACT ONE 9

LENIN. Indeed, we must. Meanwhile . . . (*A clock strikes midnight.*) A happy New Year, comrades!

Blackout.

Interlude Two

A crashing musical phrase is heard from off-stage. Instantly the amphitheatre is brightly lit to reveal it bristling with bayonets. The **CHORUS** *is transformed into a mass of grey-coated Russian soldiery deserting from the front line. Benches have been pushed together to form the roof of a railway freight waggon, packed with troops. Singing a wild, fierce song, the armed mob, seething with hatred and menace, pours down the aisles towards the auditorium as the tempo and volume of the music grows faster and louder . . . until it suddenly stops and the mob freezes. Blackout.*

Scene Four

Spotlight on a corner of the acting-space, revealing LENIN, *his overcoat slung over his shoulders. Glancing now and again at his watch, he is obviously waiting for somebody. Enter* LENIN's *wife,* NADEZHDA KRUPSKAYA, *with a newspaper.*

KRUPSKAYA. Have you seen Gorky's newspaper? He's written a long leader: Bolshevism is a threat to culture. And he's signed it.

LENIN (*angrily*). And I suppose a million peasants with rifles in their hands isn't a threat to culture. Does he think the Constituent Assembly can control such anarchy? *We* can control it, though – provided we don't do anything stupid . . .

KRUPSKAYA. Going out? At this hour?

LENIN. My head's splitting and I want a breath of air. Bukharin's coming with me. Want to come too?

KRUPSKAYA. I'm tired. Don't keep him out too long. If his wife wakes and calls for him, she'll worry if he's not there.

LENIN. How is she?

KRUPSKAYA. How d'you think, Volodya? She's bedridden for life, and so young – how would *you* feel?

LENIN. What do the doctors say?

KRUPSKAYA. No hope. He's not only her husband – he's her nanny and nurse as well . . . they're both so brave . . .

LENIN. We must think how we can help . . . Let's go and see her one day soon. Remind me.

KRUPSKAYA. Yes, I will . . . Here comes Nikolai Ivanych. (*Exit*.)

Scene Five

Enter BUKHARIN.

BUKHARIN. Sorry, I was held up at the *Pravda* offices. Flood of letters. Massive protest against the German terms. They all add up to the same thing – we cannot sign on those terms. They insist on a revolutionary war.

LENIN. If only we had as many regiments as we have paper resolutions . . . Won't you freeze to death in that short jacket?

BUKHARIN. I'm used to it.

LENIN. Well, what do *you* think? How are we going to grasp this nettle?

BUKHARIN. Not much choice. A humiliating peace – or a revolutionary war, which is bound to start with a series of severe defeats . . . We need to count up the pluses and minuses.

LENIN. Count them, then.

BUKHARIN. A shameful separate peace. We abandon our international obligations as socialists. Why? Because the German capitalist machine is falling apart while it's running at full speed, and we choose this moment to negotiate with it, which means keeping it going if we sign a peace treaty with it.

LENIN. Falling apart, is it? Really?

BUKHARIN. Look, Vladimir Ilyich, can't you see what is obvious to the naked eye?

LENIN. Revolution in Germany? I don't see it. So when do you think that revolution will start?

BUKHARIN. I'm sure this winter and spring will see the total collapse of German capitalism – provided, of course, we give it a push.

LENIN. But *when*? Nikolai Ivanych, tell me the date when revolution will break out in Berlin. I'm a practical man, I need to work out my tactics – an exact date, please!

BUKHARIN. I'm not saying there'll be a revolution there tomorrow, but I'm sure it won't be long now.

LENIN. Can you guarantee that in four or five weeks there'll be a revolution in Germany? Can you? You can't. Unfortunately, Nikolai Ivanych, all this is like reading tea-leaves. A game. And if my analysis of the situation in Germany is more correct, then a revolution is maturing there but not ripe yet and it's impossible to predict its date. What then? I realise that this assumption – revolution tomorrow – underlies your tactical thinking. But can one plan one's tactics on such dubious assumptions? You'd be the first to laugh me out of court if I . . .

BUKHARIN. Even so, there'll come a day when I say to you: 'Vladimir Ilyich – there is a revolution in Berlin!' Then we shall see how you feel and whether you can look us in the face!

LENIN. I shall be the happiest of men.

BUKHARIN. Then why . . .

LENIN. Emotion is no help to us at a moment like this. Let's hear your minuses.

BUKHARIN. Certainly. A peace will help Kaiser Wilhelm to gun down the growing German revolution – which, in your own words, is maturing. He'll take a couple of divisions from the Russian front and hurl them against his working class. And he'll stuff the mouths of the restless middle classes with Russian bread.

LENIN. Now those are serious considerations. We must bear them in mind . . . (*Suddenly.*) All right – what happens if we start fighting again but there is *no* German revolution? It'll mean curtains for us.

BUKHARIN. Can't you see that our revolutionary war will hit Germany so hard that instead of the day after tomorrow, the revolution will break out there *tomorrow*? All the Germans need is one good push, and our revolutionary war could be just that push. It's our duty – can't you see that?

LENIN. Marx and Engels said: 'The victorious proletariat cannot force their happy condition on another people without thereby undermining their own victory.' Socialism cannot be imposed by external force, Nikolai Ivanych, and we must never forget it. Otherwise we shall come to a total break with Marxism. We shall lose sight of the true nature of revolution if we make it depend on a blow from outside. We will always help and collaborate with revolutionary movements, but they must grow out of their own specific origins. No, we're not going to give anyone a push! (*Pause.*) You're all pregnant with world revolution . . .

BUKHARIN. I won't deny it. We are. And we know who the father is. It's you, Vladimir Ilyich.

LENIN (*roars with laughter*). Yes, I'll admit to that! Look, Nikolai Ivanych, I'm hoping for a revolution in Germany, and I live for the world revolution too . . . And at this moment there is just one overriding question: how can we help it to come about?

BUKHARIN. I am convinced that without immediate support from a revolution in a West European country, we won't hold out for a year.

LENIN. Obviously we don't see eye to eye over certain things. Are you so sure we can't hold out on our own? You and I argued about this before we took power. I happen to think we can not only start creating socialism in Russia but can make a great success of it – provided we go about it the right way: *that's* where the trick lies . . . So let's go on. A revolutionary war, you say? Who will do the fighting?

BUKHARIN. We have no army now, that's a fact, but it will grow out of partisan detachments, it will grow of its own accord out of the fighting.

LENIN (*unable to restrain himself; sharply*). At what price?

BUKHARIN. Any price! But in exchange we shall have acted honestly in the eyes of the whole world and our own. Honesty and a clear conscience – the greatest things a revolutionary can wish for!

LENIN. But shall we have acted honestly towards our people, who have entrusted their lives to us – not abstractions, not empty words and phrases but their real, living flesh and blood? Was the revolution made for people – or people for the revolution? Do we serve the people or do they serve us?

ACT ONE 13

BUKHARIN. Have you already made up your mind? Are you certain?

LENIN. Oh, come now! My head is still buzzing with unanswered questions.

A group of people, surrounding an injured, ragged man, comes down from the CHORUS *towards* LENIN *and* BUKHARIN.

VOICES. Comrade Lenin! Comrade Bukharin!

WORKER. Comrade Lenin . . . look, this comrade's come all the way from Lithuania . . . refugee . . . things are bad there . . .

REFUGEE (*continuing the story he has been telling*). . . . they drove them all to a ravine . . . and machine-gunned them . . . the whole organisation, seventeen men . . . and the Germans wouldn't let us bury them till three days later. Don't leave us in the lurch, comrades! If the Germans stay in the Ukraine and Lithuania, we're done for. We all belong to the same Party – don't abandon us! There are dozens of workers in prison, waiting their turn . . . they'll kill them. They'll top the lot before long – they've put up gallows everywhere. Don't you realise what they're like? Comrades! Help us! Don't ditch us, brothers!

BUKHARIN. Get a grip on yourself, comrade. No need to panic. Come to the *Pravda* offices. We'll print your story tomorrow. Come along . . . (*To* LENIN.) There's real, living flesh and blood in the Ukraine and Latvia, too, Vladimir Ilyich. And they're waiting. (*Exit with* REFUGEE *and others from the* CHORUS).

Interlude Three

LENIN *is left alone, in silent thought, on the acting-space. A spotlight falls on a* SOLDIER *in the amphitheatre, who reads out a letter.*

SOLDIER. To Lenin, Smolny Institute, Petrograd: Dear comrade Lenin and other People's Commissars. We beg you to make peace soon, because we soldiers can't put up with it much longer, we can't bear the cold and hunger in the trenches any more. What's more, our people back home write to say that they're dying of starvation, so the soldiers have decided to a man: come what may, we're not staying here any longer, we want to go home. Make peace, any sort of peace, and if you don't do it by the end of January we'll go home anyway – or worse, we'll march on Petrograd, throw out your government and put in one that'll make peace. We beg you, comrade Lenin, to do all you can to make peace, and if your enemies kill you, the memory of you will live for ever, like Jesus Christ. Give us peace! Give us peace! We don't need anything else. Signed for me and my comrades – Sharonov.

Scene Six

While the **SOLDIER** *is reading out his letter, the acting-space is turned into the canteen in the Smolny Institute, the government building: small tables and bentwood chairs; a long queue of people disappearing into the wings. From the wings upstage others emerge, each carrying a couple of sandwiches and a glass of tea. They sit down, quickly eat their breakfast and go off.*

As **LENIN** *stands listening to the* **SOLDIER**, *he is approached by* **SVERDLOV**; *they greet acquaintances and join the queue.*

LENIN (*to* SVERDLOV). Has there been any response to our request for views on Brest-Litovsk?

SVERDLOV. An absolute flood. The overwhelming majority reject the German terms and insist on a revolutionary war. Admittedly, these are mostly the views of the local Party committees.

LENIN. I see. We need to sound out the rank and file, too.

SIDORENKO (*entering from the wings. To* LENIN). Vladimir Ilyich, can I bring your breakfast to your office?

LENIN. Kind of you, but this is my only chance to see our comrades. Thanks all the same. (*To* SVERDLOV.) Have you been over to the Bukharins lately?

SVERDLOV. I was there yesterday. Brought two specialists to see her.

LENIN. And?

SVERDLOV. They can't do anything. The prognosis is total paralysis.

LENIN. Does she know that?

SVERDLOV. She's guessed it.

LENIN. And what about him?

SVERDLOV. Bad. Very nervy, and loses his temper if you ask him a question.

LENIN. How can we help?

They go off into the wings. Enter, upstage, carrying their tea and sandwiches, DZIERZINSKI, BUKHARIN, KOLLONTAI *and* LOMOV. *They sit down at a table on the forestage.* SIDORENKO *finishes his breakfast and exits.*

LOMOV. If Nikolai (*Nods at* BUKHARIN.) understood him rightly and he's inclined to sign a peace, it will cause such a crisis . . . It means total capitulation. The workers won't understand why we did it.

BUKHARIN. And to that he'll say to you: 'If it was the right thing to do, we'll explain it honestly – and they'll understand.'

LOMOV. Understand our appeasement of the Germans? And what were we saying yesterday? 'It's the peoples of the world against the governments of the world'.

BUKHARIN. That may have been right yesterday, but not today. It's too simplistic.

LOMOV. I'm sorry, I can't agree. You can say that about almost anything, but not about Marxism.

BUKHARIN. You would immediately hear him retort: 'Yes – about Marxism above all! Marx can no longer develop Marxism any further, so we must do it for him.'

LOMOV. Just a minute – do you *agree* with Lenin?

BUKHARIN. We have to consider every serious argument, for and against.

DZIERZINSKI. Comrades, I can't believe it. After all we've been through, after so much bloodshed, to stand by and watch the barons and the landowners take over again in Poland, Lithuania and the Ukraine? Watch them destroy the Soviets? Watch them hang our comrades? I'd rather put a bullet in my head! But perhaps you misunderstood him, Nikolai? Perhaps he didn't make himself clear?

Enter LENIN *and* SVERDLOV; *they sit down at another table.*

KOLLONTAI *(noticing* LENIN*)*. Ask him.

LOMOV *(to* KOLLONTAI*)*. Don't wind him up. *(To* DZIERZINSKI.*)* Felix, don't do it.

But DZIERZINSKI *has already jumped up and is striding over to* LENIN*'s table.*

DZIERZINSKI *(very agitated)*. Vladimir Ilyich, they're saying that you're inclined to accept the German terms. If so – you're making a mistake!

LENIN. I'm thinking, Felix. I'm weighing up the pros and cons.

DZIERZINSKI. But I hope you won't take such a vital decision without discussing it in the Central Committee?

LENIN. Of course I won't.

DZIERZINSKI. Thank you. *(Returns to his table.)* Nikolai was right. I couldn't believe it. It would be the greatest error.

KOLLONTAI *(To* DZIERZINSKI*)*. Calm down. Look, your hands are shaking. He's thinking it over – there's still hope.

LOMOV. No, he's made up his mind. Look how calm he is.

BUKHARIN. It's always like that – utter calm on his face, a storm raging inside. I'll bet he didn't sleep last night. It was exactly like this in 1914, when I went to see him in Poronino and told him quite specifically that Roman Malinovsky was a police spy. The old man wouldn't believe me, but he was very reserved . . . As well he might have been: the leader of the Bolshevik deputies in the Duma, Central Committee member – a police agent . . . Enough to shake anyone. But he didn't show it. Put me to bed in an upstairs room, but stayed out on the verandah himself. Paced up and down, up and down, all night long, stopping for a moment then starting up again. I couldn't sleep, heard it all. Next morning he was neatly dressed, clean-shaven. Only his face looked ill, bags under his eyes – like now. But all the usual self-confident gestures, cheerful laughter: 'Sleep well? Ha-ha-ha . . . Tea? Bread and butter? Shall we go for a walk?' And all the time such a grim look in his eyes. But try and show him sympathy, and he'd bite your head off. So we know what that calm look means.

Exeunt LENIN *and* SVERDLOV, *having finished their breakfast.*

KOLLONTAI. The Party won't accept a peace treaty on the Germans' terms. Great as Lenin may be, we've got heads on our shoulders too. And we are just as responsible for the revolution as he is. So cheer up! We have common sense on our side – and a majority in the Central Committee.

BUKHARIN. But we must get the local Party branches lined up behind us before the C.C. meeting starts. The old man won't go against the united Party. (*To* LOMOV.) Georgii, go to Moscow, round up all our supporters and bring back a toughly-worded resolution . . .

Enter SIDORENKO.

SIDORENKO. Has comrade Lenin gone?

KOLLANTAI. A moment ago. What's the matter?

SIDORENKO. A soldier . . . just arrived from Brest-Litovsk . . . personal letter from Trotsky . . .

Scene Seven

A spotlight falls on the amphitheatre and picks out TROTSKY, *leader of the Russian delegation to the peace talks at Brest-Litovsk.*

The canteen disappears, to be replaced by LENIN's *office.* LENIN *is seated at his desk, reading* TROTSKY's *letter, while the* SOLDIER *from Brest-Litovsk sits to one side.*

TROTSKY (*reads out letter*). 'Dear Vladimir Ilyich, I am sending my proposals to you by a courier who will pass through the front lines. It is absolutely clear to me that we are no longer capable of fighting. But can the Germans fight either? Can they advance and attack a revolution which, let us assume, announces that the war is over? Should we not try to put the German working class and the German army to the test: on the one hand the Russian Revolution, which declares the war to be over, and on the other – Kaiser Wilhelm's government ordering them to shoot at that revolution? I am profoundly convinced this will be the spark that sets off the powder-keg of the German revolution, without which we cannot last out the year, just as we cannot hold on without revolutions in France, Britain and America. All this motivates my proposal to make the following political gesture: in reply to a German ultimatum we announce that we are stopping the war and demobilising the army but will not sign an extortionate peace. No peace, no war! If the

German generals cannot get their army to move against us – of which I am convinced – that means revolution in Germany and a colossal victory for us, with boundless consequences. If they *do* manage to strike at us, we can always capitulate at an early stage. If you agree, reply by telegram with the phrase: 'Plan approved; put into effect.'

TROTSKY *sits down.*

Having read the letter, LENIN *puts it aside and turns to the* SOLDIER.

LENIN. Thank you. So what happened when you crossed the front line?

SOLDIER. I crawled across no-man's-land and shouted: 'Hey, lads, don't shoot – I'm one of yours!' Silence, no answer. I dropped into a trench – empty. I went down a communication trench to the second line – no one. I saw a field-gun near a wood. Went up to it – all in working order, but no one there either. Alongside were the wheel-tracks of another gun. Leading towards the German trenches. Then I found out that the gunners, before they left, had sold three guns to the Germans and left one behind. I found the gun-crews a mile away – just getting ready to push off home. Nobody paid me any attention. Well, they formed up, the sergeant made a speech, even burst into tears, saying the army was breaking up and anyone who wanted to leave could drop his rifle and go.

LENIN. And did they?

SOLDIER. Not one. They all took their rifles with them . . . Then a Bolshevik made a speech, trying to persuade them not to go, so as not to leave the front wide open. But they wouldn't listen. They marched to the station, took over a train by force, and I went with 'em. That's how I got here.

LENIN. Tell me, why are the troops going home against orders? Deserting the front line, selling their guns . . . Why didn't they listen to the Bolshevik? The Bolsheviks have always been on the troops' side, so why did they go against the Bolsheviks' advice?

SOLDIER (*sincerely*). But what have the Bolsheviks ever done for us? Made promises, that's all . . .

LENIN. What about land? Haven't they given you land? Have you read the Decree on Land?

SOLDIER. Here it is! (*Pulls a folded leaflet out of an inside pocket.*) But what use is your decree to me, out there at the front? It's not even big enough to wipe your arse with . . .

LENIN. But haven't we given you the right to your own land? What you've always wanted . . .

SOLDIER. Yes, but if a man stays in the trenches, the only right he's got is to six feet of earth – under the ground. And we had that right under Kerensky . . .

LENIN. Even so, you can't just abandon the front line because you feel like it. Couldn't you have waited for orders?

SOLDIER. We're tired of waiting, comrade Lenin. Anyway, you can't call it a front line. Not a living soul for five miles either side of you . . . And there's more than enough for the men to do at home. It'll be time to sow soon, got to get ready, got to be on the spot to get a bit of land from that decree of yours . . . (*Carefully folds up the decree and puts it back into his pocket.*) When I can touch *my* piece of land with my own hand, *then* I'll tell you whether or not the Bolsheviks have given us land, comrade Lenin.

LENIN (*watching with interest as the* SOLDIER *puts the Decree away*). I understand. Well, thank you very much. Goodbye.

Both stand and shake hands. The SOLDIER *salutes and exits.*

LENIN (*picks up the telephone*). Commissar of Nationalities, please . . . Hello. Where's Stalin? . . . when he comes, tell him this: the Rada, the new government of the Ukraine, is going behind the backs of our delegates at Brest-Litovsk and holding talks with the Germans. Today or tomorrow they may sign a separate peace and give the whole Ukraine over to the Germans. I need some urgent information on Ukrainian affairs, and I want Stalin to report on them. As soon as he comes, tell him to go at once to the teletype room. I'll be there.

Scene Eight

LENIN *crosses over from his office to the* TELEGRAPHIST *at stage right.* TROTSKY *goes to the* TELEGRAPHIST *at stage left. Both machines start humming and clattering.*

TROTSKY (*dictates*). 'Trotsky asks Lenin whether he has received the letter sent by courier. Letter requires immediate answer.

Reply should consist of either "approved" or "not approved".'

LENIN (*dictates*). 'Lenin here. Your letter only just received. Stalin not available, so have not been able to show it to him yet. Your plan strikes me as debatable. Could you postpone tabling it until the special session of the Central Executive Committee has voted on it here? As soon as Stalin returns, will show him your letter. Lenin.'

TROTSKY (*dictates*). 'We will try and delay tabling your decision until we hear from you. Please hurry. Ukrainian delegation is clearly pursuing treacherous policy. Discussion of my plan in Central Executive Committee undesirable, as it may be leaked before I can put it to Germans. Trotsky.'

LENIN (*dictates*). 'To Trotsky. Must consult Stalin first before giving you an answer. Lenin.'

TROTSKY (*dictates*). 'Waiting. Trotsky.'

The spotlights on the teletypes go out. STALIN, *in greatcoat and fur hat, enters* LENIN's *office, where* SIDORENKO *is waiting for him.*

SIDORENKO. Comrade Stalin! At last! Comrade Lenin is at the teletype, he wants you to go there at once . . .

STALIN. In a moment . . . (*Sits down.*) Just let me get my breath back. Long enough to smoke a pipe . . . (*Lights his pipe.*) Right, now tell me – only don't hurry and try to remember every detail . . . I need to know everything. Only then can I give Lenin the right advice.

SIDORENKO. Yes, well . . .

Telephone rings; SIDORENKO *picks it up and listens.*

SIDORENKO. It's comrade Lenin. He's been ringing every ten minutes.

STALIN. Tell him not to worry. Say I haven't come yet, but I'm expected any minute.

SIDORENKO. Very good . . . He hasn't come yet, but he's expected any minute now . . . Very good, I'll tell him . . . (*Puts down the receiver.*) As soon as you arrive, you're to go straight to the teletype room. Comrade Lenin is on the line to Trotsky, and . . .

STALIN. I'm waiting.

SIDORENKO. Yes, well, as I said, nothing special . . . Only a rumour that comrade Lenin wants to sign a peace treaty at once, on the German terms.

STALIN. Significant rumour. What's the reaction?

SIDORENKO. Bukharin, Dzierzinski, Lomov and Kollontai are furious. Sverdlov supports Lenin.

STALIN. How reliable is that rumour?

SIDORENKO. Hard to say . . .

STALIN. And Trotsky?

SIDORENKO. I don't know.

Telephone rings.

STALIN (*nods towards the telephone*). Tell him I'm on my way . . . (*Going off.*) Find out what Smilga and Bubnov think. (*Exit.*)

SIDORENKO. Right. (*Picks up receiver.*) He's on his way to the teletype room . . .

Spotlights pick out the two teletypes, at which TROTSKY *stands stage left;* LENIN *is stage right, listening to the report given by* STALIN, *who uses the stem of his pipe to point to a map of the Ukraine.*

STALIN. In effect, a civil war is raging in the Ukraine. A Bolshevik government of a Soviet Ukraine has been set up in Kharkov, which is already in control of the situation. Power is slipping away from the Rada in Kiev by the hour.

The teletype machine starts to hum and click.

TELEGRAPHIST (*To* LENIN). The line's working.

LENIN (*dictates to* TELEGRAPHIST). 'Stalin now with me. He and I are conferring and will shortly give you our joint answer.'

STALIN (*continuing his report*). Those are the facts, and facts are obstinate things. Given that the Kiev Rada is on its deathbed and is not a serious political force; that it is holding its own talks at Brest-Litovsk behind our back – I suggest we have nothing more to do with the so-called Rada but fight it ruthlessly until the Ukrainian Soviets are in total control.

LENIN. Now read that. (*Hands him* TROTSKY's *letter.*) The soldier who brought it had some most interesting information. Even so, I think Trotsky must break off the negotiations, come here, and we'll discuss the whole situation.

STALIN (*returning the letter*). I agree with you. I'm still not clear about it all, but even without going into detail I simply trust you, Vladimir Ilyich.

LENIN. I don't want you to trust me. I want you to *understand* me.

STALIN. I'll try, Vladimir Ilyich, and I apologise for using the wrong word.

LENIN (*dictates to* TELEGRAPHIST). 'To Trotsky: Please call for a break in talks and return Petrograd. Lenin. Stalin.'

Interlude Four

With a flash and a crashing chord the amphitheatre and acting-space are turned into a cabaret, patronised by the seedy remnants of Russia's bourgeoisie. Enter MAN IN WHITE TIE AND TAILS.

MAN IN WHITE TIE AND TAILS. Good evening, ladies and gentlemen! Petrograd's night-life continues to flourish, despite the little temporary misunderstanding last October, which some people thought was a revolution. Once more we open the doors of our decadent but ever-popular cabaret, 'The Red Light'! A chord, please, maestro! . . . (*Confidingly*.) Between you and me, ladies and gentlemen, the only reason why we got permission to re-open was because the gentlemen – sorry, the comrades! – in city hall were so thrilled by the *colour* of our light. Give them their head, and there'll soon be red lights all over Russia. However, *we* don't fancy too much competition, and we're hoping ours will remain the only one . . . Of course, if you're bored here, you can always go next door, where a great new proletarian art-form is being born. Here's the advertisement in today's paper: 'The Cultural Section of the Workers' Soviet present the first proletarian play in the "Red Star" club: "Money Doesn't Bring Happiness", and the one-act farce "Rising Prices".' So you have a choice, ladies and gentlemen! I call you that, and not 'Ex-ladies and ex-gentlemen', as the so-called 'comrades' sometimes do. But seriously, what is the historical paradox of our time, my friends? It's that the most comradely comrades, the Bolshevik leaders, are all ex-gentlemen! . . . We start our programme with a question that concerns us all – did time stop on the 25th of October, 1917?

A carpet representing a huge clock-face has appeared in the acting-space, on which the figures 12, 3, 6 and 9 are formed by four female DANCERS *in skimpy costumes. As a tune with a 'tick-tock' rhythm starts to play, the 'figures' gradually come alive and the* DANCERS *perform a suggestive dance as they sing this song:*

DANCERS. There stood on a high place, right over the fireplace,
    A clock with a beautiful chime.
    Its owner had vanished, was hounded and banished,
    To take his old clock he'd no time.
    The shipping's at anchor, the factories are bankrupt –
    Socialism is with us – hurray!
    But still on a high place, above that old fireplace,
    The clock keeps on ticking away.

    Ding-dong, ding-dong, bing-bong, bing-bong,
    Tick-tock, tick-tock, tick-tock –
    For oh! disaster – the Reds are master
    And times have changed – tick-tock!

    Oh, last year a school-girl, I now am a call-girl,
    My body I cheerfully sell –
    'Cos when I undress I am proud to confess I
    Am socially useful as well!
    Come soldiers, come sailors, come tinkers, come tailors,
    The time now has come to unite!
    All classes are one now, you too can have fun now,
    So come up to my place tonight!

    Ding-dong, ding-dong, bing-bong, bing-bong,
    Tick-tock, tick-tock, tick-tock,
    Once you were oppressed – now just get undressed:
    The time to come has come!

MAN IN WHITE TIE. But everyone now knows that time is running out for the *comrades*. Take your partners for the tango!

Enter TROTSKY, *making his way through the dancing couples.* LENIN *comes to meet him, and they make their way to* LENIN's *office.*

Scene Nine

As TROTSKY *takes off his coat, etc., the dancers tango away into the wings.* LENIN *takes his place behind his desk;* TROTSKY *sits down.*

LENIN. Your idea of a political gesture sounds too risky to me.

Our revolution is now the most important thing in the world. We must secure it at all costs.

TROTSKY. Very well – here's another argument: the British and French press are making us out to be nothing but German agents. The story goes like this: as soon as the Bolsheviks come to power, they sign a highly unfavourable peace treaty. And why? Because they are German agents, of course . . . Then Germany removes her troops from the Russian front and throws them against the British and French. You can imagine the effect this will have on working-class opinion in Western Europe. How will we look in their eyes? And how much easier it will then be for the Entente Powers to intervene against us, because it will be seen as an attack on the German spies who have seized power in Russia. That being so, the workers in the West will do nothing to stop that intervention. But by announcing 'no peace, no war' we shall give working-class Europe clear, unambiguous proof of the hostility between us and the Kaiser's government.

LENIN. You are absolutely right about the French and British workers. What worries me is something else: what about Volokolamsk? What will our Russian peasant say? I would like to satisfy both of them, but it seems we have to choose . . . At this moment the Russian peasant is more important.

TROTSKY. Is that where Bukharin gets his expression 'a peasants' peace'?

LENIN. Perhaps . . . Bukharin, by the way, has become the leader of a whole faction; they're fiercely militant. On the one hand, they're taking this stand because they're young . . .

TROTSKY. And intelligent people can do stupid things, especially when they're young. But that is a right, as Heine said, which should not be abused.

LENIN. He's only twenty-nine.

TROTSKY. I thought he was younger. You're too indulgent to him, Vladimir Ilyich. I've already noticed you have a very soft spot for young Bukharin . . .

LENIN. No one can accuse me of giving way on important issues for *that* sort of reason. But as for being indulgent . . . We're all comrades, after all, in the same Party . . . Although I admit there's nothing more painful than quarrels between close colleagues . . . (*Pause.*) All right, let's say we accept your plan:

we refuse to sign a treaty, we disband the army – and the Germans simply laugh at us and start advancing again. What then?

TROTSKY. We sign the treaty under duress, and the myth about our behind-the-scenes dealings with the Kaiser is exploded. The working-class of all the world will support us.

LENIN. And if that happens you won't back the call for a revolutionary war?

TROTSKY. Indeed I will not. On my word of honour.

LENIN. But *you* may not be able to sign that treaty. This German beast moves fast. I can foresee a scenario like this: a series of crushing defeats will force Russia to sign a treaty on far more extortionate terms than the present ones . . . But it won't be you who signs that treaty. After the first defeats, the peasant army will turn its bayonets against us and overthrow our government. The treaty will be signed by a bourgeois government – or something even worse.

TROTSKY. I fully understand you, and I'd be glad to support you. But I'll never forgive myself if we don't at least try this experiment. With one skilful tactical move we may win everything!

LENIN. You can do experiments in laboratories, but in real life they can be too costly . . . Aren't you forgetting that the subjects of your experiment are people . . . living souls . . . *our* people? . . . Look – you are certain the Germans won't advance. What is that certainty based on? On your intuition, that's all. What hard evidence is there behind that phrase of yours? None . . . In other words, it's nothing more than a phrase. You can't build a policy on phrases. 'No peace, no war' – it sounds good, it's tempting . . . On the other hand, it could mean we were deliberately allowing the Germans to march into the very heart of the country. Have you thought of that?

TROTSKY. But the German revolution . . .

LENIN. And if it doesn't happen? What then?

TROTSKY. Oh, Vladimir Ilyich – if, if, if . . .

LENIN. But we *must* think of those 'ifs'. Tactics are a complicated business, I tell you . . . If you can't retreat and adapt when necessary, if you're not ready to crawl on your belly in the mud if need be, then you're not a revolutionary but a windbag. I don't like these peace terms either, but there's no other way. And we've got to save Russia from disaster, it's our duty . . .

TROTSKY. I'm very sorry that once again you and I disagree over tactics.

LENIN. Oh come on, why try and hide the truth? Our disagreement goes far beyond mere tactics.

TROTSKY. Time will show who's right.

LENIN. It's too risky, Lev Davidych.

TROTSKY. But why? Why? Don't you see? The international aims of our revolution oblige us . . .

LENIN. Oblige us to do one thing only: to create socialism, but in fact, and not just on paper. So far, socialism only exists in books; we've got to make it a reality, and history has given us this chance. The world needs a shining example. Its significance will be enormous. And if we fail that will be equally significant: people will reject socialism. So therefore, when defining our international duty, I shall always judge it by how far we have created socialism in Russia. Seen from that angle, what do we need today – peace or war? Peace – always. We can never initiate a war, because war is not in the nature of socialism. I don't count defence – that is merely a response that is forced upon us. Peace – always. And now especially. Just tell me – how will a war against the Kaiser help us to create socialism, given the millions of problems that face us at this moment?

TROTSKY. The Party leadership meets in an hour. Let's test our points of view on them.

LENIN. I quite agree. I have prepared my arguments in favour of signing a treaty at once.

TROTSKY. After you will come Bukharin with his idea of a revolutionary war, and then I'll speak.

Interlude Five

A spotlight falls on the amphitheatre and picks out a **WORKER**, *who stands up and reads out a letter:*

WORKER. 'To Sverdlov, Central Executive Committee, Petrograd. The workers of the Surgansk iron-ore mines protest against the shameful peace terms and demand that we wage a revolutionary war against the Germans. Motion passed unanimously. Signed: Martynov, Chairman, Soviet of Workers' Deputies.' (*Exit*.)

Full lighting is switched on to the amphitheatre revealing that it is empty. Everyone has gone to the Party meeting to debate the peace-treaty issue. Sound of a door opening off stage SVERDLOV's *voice is heard:*

VOICE OF SVERDLOV. Our meeting must shortly close: all those who wished to speak have had their say. Three main points of view have emerged. We shall now proceed to take the vote. I would remind comrades that this voting is merely to establish the approximate strength with which those views are held. The decisive vote remains to be taken by the Central Committee, which meets tomorrow. Those who intend to support Lenin's position, raise your hands, please . . .

Silence; the off-stage 'open door' is heard to shut. Enter LENIN, *who sits down dejectedly on a bench.*

Scene Ten

The off-stage door is heard to open and close. A moment later, enter INESSA ARMAND.

INESSA A.. Vladimir – are you unwell?

LENIN. No . . . I simply couldn't stand it . . . Those hostile, uncomprehending looks . . . It was like talking to a brick wall. They listened, but didn't hear. You voted against me too.

INESSA A.. For once, yes. But you're wrong about the looks being hostile. They were showing pain – pain for you. Sapronov expressed the mood best: 'He'll change his mind, and join us. And we couldn't have a better army commander'.

LENIN. No, I was on the rostrum and I saw them – hostile, totally alienated.

INESSA A.. I could have bitten off my tongue, I was so upset.

LENIN. Didn't I convince even you?

INESSA A.. Remember your last letter to me? I was moved to tears by your devotion and selfless friendship. Our friendship demands the truth and nothing but the truth . . . Vladimir, you're not the man you were before October 1917. Before, you were a revolutionary: the firebrand, always keeping up the pressure, *'on s'engage, et puis on voit'*. But now? A cautious little shopkeeper, afraid of your own shadow, always calculating how to increase your capital and keep your virginity. When you and I and Nadya went for a walk round Smolny this morning, we watched a workers' detachment being formed. Remember how well they held themselves, what heroes they looked, what strength there was in those keen, well-drilled men? Well, you must try and draw on that strength and get back your old daring! It hurts me to see your face the colour of putty and bags under your eyes.

LENIN (*bitterly*). What you *didn't* notice was that there were only a dozen rifles for the whole detachment; that those men couldn't shoot and didn't know how to fight. What can their enthusiasm do against gunfire, their bare hands against modern weapons? Should I keep silent about that? . . . Remember the Bernese Oberland? There was a wonderful view across almost the whole of Switzerland, and on a clear day you and I could see Mont Blanc. What am I to do if I can now see, with equal clarity, what lies ahead of us if the Party opts for *your* view? Hold my tongue? Say nothing? Give no warning, just for fear of being in a minority?

INESSA A.. I'm not asking you to be silent, I'm asking you to listen to others.

LENIN. Listen to Trotsky?

INESSA A.. No. His speech was very eloquent, but just not realistic.

LENIN. To Bukharin, then?

INESSA A.. Look, Vladimir, almost the whole Party leadership is against you. Everybody sees signing a treaty on these terms as a betrayal, a stab in the back. It's like what Zinoviev and Kamenev did when they leaked our plans for last October.

LENIN. As bad as that?

INESSA A.. I doubt if anyone would dare to tell you, but that's what they're saying. In fact the very backbone of the Party is against you: Dzierzinski, Uritsky, Bukharin, Yakovleva, Kollontai, Pyatakov, Volodarsky, Radek . . . Can you doubt their sincerity and dedication? Last September and October, when you were arguing with the C.C. about the date of the uprising, *they* were the ones on your side, they supported you and showed their mettle on the day itself.

LENIN. Yes, they're very close comrades. I've worked with them for years and they've supported me at the worst moments . . . it's true.

INESSA A.. And who are you left with now? Zinoviev, who felt sick with fear at the very word 'uprising'. And Stalin, who's only with you because you're you. Is that what you want from us? Just because we believe in *you*? A new sort of papal infallibility?

LENIN. Inessa, you know quite well, that's not so. I want you to *understand* me.

INESSA A.. Then get moving – prove your point, find some new arguments. You managed to show me what a fool I was about that squad of workers!

LENIN *looks at* INESSA *and suddenly starts to laugh. The Party meeting has ended, and the participants are coming back to their places in the amphitheatre.*

INESSA A. (*to* KRUPSKAYA). Nadya, we're over here!

KRUPSKAYA. Bukharin got thirty-two votes, Trotsky – sixteen, and we got fifteen.

LENIN (*fully in control again*). Nadya, can we offer Inessa a glass of tea?

KRUPSKAYA. Joining us for tea? Aren't you afraid we'll try to get you to change your mind?

INESSA A.. He may try it on *us*!

LENIN. There's nothing I hate more than disagreement within the Party. Even so, the revolution is more important than our personal feelings.

KRUPSKAYA (*to* INESSA). I was remembering the Second Congress. (*To* LENIN.) Remember when we realised we simply couldn't go along with Martov and Zasulich? (*To* INESSA.) He and I sat up all night and shivered.

Scene Eleven

The acting-space turns into LENIN's *modest living-quarters in the Smolny Institute.* LENIN *and* INESSA ARMAND *sit down at the table, while* KRUPSKAYA *makes tea.*

KRUPSKAYA. I was at the Social Revolutionary Party's meeting this afternoon. It was very depressing. They won't hear of a peace treaty. It almost came to a fight . . . Only five of the older, more experienced members voted for signature. But they were drowned in a flood of indignant opposition . . .

INESSA A.. As was to be expected.

LENIN. It would be unnatural if a majority of the working class reacted otherwise. At this moment.

KRUPSKAYA. At this moment, you can't expect the workers to understand your arguments . . .

LENIN. Yes, and Bukharin knows it. He goes to their meetings. And today we all saw the mood of the Party leadership and the Petrograd committee.

KRUPSKAYA. But perhaps the bulk of the Party membership doesn't yet share that mood?

LENIN. True, it doesn't. But don't forget that the people at today's meeting are the cream of the Party. They are the ones who led the revolution to success in October. The mood . . . (*Pause.*) That's it! The *mood*! Of course! (*Laughs cheerfully.*) Of course! (*Chants in a sing-song.*) The moo-ood! The moo-ood! . . . The point is that the passing moods of a class may not correspond to the fundamental interests of that class. And I've always been primarily concerned with the fundamental interests. Why are the workers in this mood at the moment? (*Ticks off the points on his fingers.*) Illusions produced by the ease of their victory between November and January – right? Right! Gut protest against the Germans' arrogance and effrontery – right? Right! These are the moods reflected by Bukharin and his cronies. But the fact is that when faced with the crucial question – is Soviet power to survive or not – the workers will instantly come to their senses, while Bukharin, out of inertia, will go on playing his old tune.

INESSA A.. Not necessarily, Vladimir – you're being unfair to him.

ACT ONE 31

KRUPSKAYA. Not necessarily at all.

LENIN. Well, we shall see. At the moment they are accusing us of opportunism, deriving from a particular social source: the mass of soldiery, the smallholders, the peasants. No, dear comrades, we reflect the fundamental interests of the working class – who have, by the way, unbreakable links with the peasantry. A war now would mean a total break with the peasantry. When the peasant can bend down and touch the land which the revolution has given him, and if he is faced with the danger of losing that land – then he will defend it. Our 'leftists' tell us to leap over the stage of peasant ownership of land. If we were to do that, we'd break our necks.

INESSA A. (*to* KRUPSKAYA). Nadya, I now recognise your husband again and I'm going to get out of here before he pins me to the wall with his logic.

LENIN. Thank you, Inessa. You've been a great help to me.

Interlude Six

LOMOV *enters, goes to the teletype machine stage left, and dictates a message to the* TELEGRAPHIST.

LOMOV. 'To Central Committee, Bolshevik Party, Smolny Institute, Petrograd. Moscow regional bureau Bolshevik Party insists on immediate termination of peace negotiations with imperialist Germany also on cessation of all diplomatic relations with all state-licensed robbers of all countries.'

Scene Twelve

The acting-space becomes LENIN's *office. All is prepared for a session of the Bolshevik Party's Central Committee: chairs placed around the table, papers in readiness at each place. One by one the members of the Central Committee enter.*

DZIERZINSKI (*to* BUKHARIN). Are we the first?

BUKHARIN. The old man's in the ante-room with Makarov's dictionary, trying to calm himself by reading it. I've never seen him like this before.

DZIERZINSKI. I've been feeling terrible all day . . . I hate arguing with him.

KOLLONTAI. But he'd be the first to despise us if we blindly repeated everything he said.

BUKHARIN. Comrades, we're faced with a serious fight. In order not to be in a minority, I think we should support Trotsky's formula, since it will in any case lead to war.

LOMOV. I agree.

The Central Committee members take their seats around the table. Present are: LENIN *(Chairman);* SVERDLOV *(Deputy Chairman);* STASOVA *(Secretary);* LOMOV; URITSKY; KOLLONTAI; STALIN; BUKHARIN; TROTSKY; MURANOV; BUBNOV; ARTYOM; ZINOVIEV; KRESTINSKY; DZIERZINSKI.

SVERDLOV. Comrades, the agenda for today's meeting of the Central Committee is the question of the peace treaty. Are there any objections? . . . The agenda is therefore confirmed. I call on comrade Lenin to speak.

LENIN *(after a pause)*. Comrades, we Bolsheviks have never refused to defend the socialist fatherland. But the issue today is simply – *how* do we defend it? By war or by peace? We cannot wage war; you all know why not. A policy of 'revolutionary war' would, perhaps, satisfy the human need for clear, striking and vivid action, but it would bear no relation to the objective correlation of forces and physical factors. We are told that such a war would precipitate revolution in Germany. But Germany is still only pregnant with revolution, whereas we have given birth to a healthy baby – our socialist republic, which we can easily kill if we start a war. Granted, the peace treaty which we may sign will be an obscenity, but we need a breathing-space in which to enact social reforms, we need to consolidate our position, and for that we need time. Trotsky's proposal would be a political gesture to the world at large which would give *us* nothing, because it would open the way for the Germans to penetrate deep into Russia. In signing a peace treaty we shall, of course, betray Poland at her moment of self-determination, but we will save socialist Russia and consolidate what we have already achieved. We shall thereby also be making a turn to the right, which will take us through a political midden, but we have no choice. In signing a treaty we will show the whole world that while the imperialists continue to fight we have opted for a peaceful life in which to create socialism. The example of our socialist republic will be a living model for all peoples to follow, and its revolutionising effect world-wide will be colossal.

SVERDLOV. I call on comrade Bukharin.

BUKHARIN. Comrades, I believe the most correct position to be that of comrade Trotsky. In comrade Lenin's position I see two contradictions. Firstly, how can he say that he is in favour of defending ourselves? Defence presumes a war, does it not? It does. I've never heard of a situation in which peace might constitute defence. It doesn't add up. We must examine our problems from the wider, international angle. Comrade Lenin is mistaken in opposing a political gesture. Let the German army strike at us, let them advance another hundred miles or so: they will then be stopped by a revolution in Germany. The German Social Democrats don't want us to sign a peace treaty, because if we do we shall checkmate the struggle that they are waging inside Germany. By preserving our socialist republic and not lifting a finger to help the cause of revolution in Germany, we throw away our chances of support from the international workers' movement. That is the crux of the problem.

SVERDLOV. I call on comrade Trotsky.

TROTSKY. I think we must make a careful analysis of what will offer us the greatest advantage. To put all our efforts into waging war at this juncture is pure utopia. Therefore I regard the question of a revolutionary war as quite unrealistic. We must disband the army, but disbanding the army does not mean that we sign a peace treaty. By refusing to sign and by demobilising the army we will promote the revolutionary process. At the same time we show the German Social Democrats that we are *not* playing a part in a game secretly agreed in advance with the German government.

SVERDLOV. I call on comrade Stalin.

STALIN. Comrades, if we adopt the idea of a revolutionary war, we shall be playing into the hands of the imperialists. At the same time, comrade Trotsky's position is not one that will bring us success. There is no revolutionary movement in the West – there is no evidence for it – there is only a potential, and we cannot base our plans on mere potential.

Murmurs and movement among the members of the Central Committee.

STALIN. Our socialist reforms will encourage revolution in the West, but we need time to implement them. If we adopt comrade Trotsky's policy, we shall create the worst possible conditions for the workers' movement in the West, and I suggest we adopt comrade Lenin's proposal.

SVERDLOV. I call on comrade Zinoviev.

ZINOVIEV. Comrades, we are, of course, faced with performing a very difficult surgical operation, because a peace treaty will produce a wave of chauvinism in Germany and will for some time weaken the workers' movement everywhere in the West.

BUKHARIN. As I have always said!

ZINOVIEV. Not so fast . . . The alternative, however, is a different prospect – the destruction of our socialist republic. But comrade Trotsky's proposal is equally unacceptable, because General Hofmann's answer to it will be that since we haven't signed a peace treaty, we remain in a state of war with Germany. So why risk that experiment, when we know precisely how it will end?

LENIN. I request the right to intervene, comrades, in order to say that I disagree with certain of the remarks made by my supporters, Stalin and Zinoviev. There is not just a potential for revolution in the West, comrade Stalin, but a mass movement, though admittedly a revolution has not yet begun there . . . I don't agree with Zinoviev's view that if we sign a peace treaty we shall temporarily weaken any revolutionary movements in the West. There will, of course, be a whiff of chauvinism, but it will not hinder the German revolution. The nub of the matter is that there the revolution hasn't yet begun, whereas here it has produced a bawling, new-born infant. Yes, yes, comrade Kollontai – and if we now fail to say clearly that we agree to peace, we are finished.

KOLLONTAI. I appreciate your arguments, Vladimir Ilyich, but I completely disagree with you.

DZIERZINSKI. Signing a treaty means surrendering all we've won. I think comrade Lenin is doing, in concealed form, exactly what Kamenev and Zinoviev did last October. He claims that if we sign, we shall strengthen revolutionary forces in the West. We shall not. Comrade Lenin has told us repeatedly that our socialist republic rests on the support of the poorest peasants and the proletariat. We are the party of the proletariat and we should clearly realise that the proletariat will *not* go with us if we sign this treaty.

TROTSKY. In my opinion, comrades, it is obvious to almost all of us that to wage a revolutionary war is impossible. I move that we take a vote on the question: Are we prepared to issue the call to a revolutionary war?

SVERDLOV. A vote is called. Who is for it? . . . Bukharin and Lomov. Against? . . . Eleven.

LENIN. I move that we vote on the proposal to drag out the talks and postpone signature of a treaty for as long as possible.

SVERDLOV. A vote is called. Who is for the proposal? . . . Twelve. Against? . . . Only Lomov.

TROTSKY. In that case, I request that we vote on my formula: we stop the war, we do not sign a peace treaty and we demobilise the army.

SVERDLOV. A vote is called. Those in favour of that formula, please raise their hands.

TROTSKY, BUBNOV, BUKHARIN, DZIERZINSKI, KOLLONTAI, KRESTINSKY, LOMOV, STASOVA *and* **URITSKY** *raise their hands.*

For the proposal – nine. Against?

LENIN, SVERDLOV, ZINOVIEV, STALIN, ARTYOM *and* **MURANOV** *raise their hands.*

Against – six, but taking note of comrade Smilga's letter, in which he states that he is also against Trotsky's proposal, that makes seven votes. The Central Committee has therefore voted to accept comrade Trotsky's formula. There is no other business, comrades. I need hardly remind you to observe absolute secrecy over the decisions we have taken. That is all.

The Central Committee members get up from their places and leave the office. SVERDLOV *goes over to* LENIN *and sits down beside him.*

SVERDLOV. What are we going to do?

LENIN. What *can* we do?

SVERDLOV (*shrugging his shoulders*). I don't know. (*Stands up, paces back and forth.*) One thing's obvious: the Germans won't pay any attention to Trotsky's magic incantation; they'll attack, the remnants of our army will run away, and from running the government we'll have to go underground again. And when that happens it'll be no good you and I saying: 'We told you so!' It's not intentions that count in politics but results, they'll say – and they'll be right.

LENIN. So what do you suggest? Open conflict with a majority of the C.C.? Reveal all our cards to the Germans by showing them how divided we are? Impossible.

SVERDLOV. What *is* possible?

LENIN. Yakov Mikhailovich, if I knew I'd tell you . . . What do *you* suggest? I can see you've got some idea . . .

SVERDLOV. Exploit our chances within the C.C.

LENIN. What chances?

SVERDLOV. Trotsky. He's feeling a bit uncomfortable and he's hesitating. It wasn't by chance that he proposed stopping the call to a revolutionary war. It was a kind of gesture towards you. We should exploit Trotsky's wavering mood. Use your influence on him to make him sign the treaty.

LENIN. Is that realistic?

SVERDLOV. Absolutely. He'll be impressed if after your defeat you make a personal plea to him.

LENIN. But won't he go back on it later?

SVERDLOV. He may. And he may not.

LENIN (*after a pause*). I don't like it.

SVERDLOV. Who would!

LENIN. What about using the Congress of Soviets? It's the highest body in the state . . . The Bolshevik members must move a resolution at the Congress to give the Sovnarkom unrestricted powers to deal with the treaty question, but without going into any details . . .

SVERDLOV. It's an idea.

LENIN. And if the Bolshevik members, knowing our position, will still move that resolution and the Congress votes us those powers, then my talk with Trotsky will not be between two equal members of the C.C. – it'll be between me as head of the government and Trotsky as Commissar for Foreign Affairs – my subordinate.

ACT ONE   37

SVERDLOV. Yes, that sounds better.

LENIN. That way, we're not banking on Trotsky's hesitations but on a resolution of the Congress of Soviets. Then it'll be a political tactic and not a political intrigue.

SVERDLOV. I'll ask him to come and see you. (*Exit*.)

After a short pause, enter **TROTSKY**, *wearing an army greatcoat with a hood attached to the collar.*

TROTSKY. Your request was unexpected – I was just coming to say goodbye . . .

LENIN. History will not forgive us and we'll never forgive ourselves if we don't immediately protect the revolution against a possibly fatal blow. What you suggest will sound sensational, but we may have to pay too high a price for it.

TROTSKY. What about the vote in the C.C.?

LENIN. No serious revolutionary breaks Party discipline, even over a formality, if there aren't pressing reasons to do so. But anyone who hides behind Party discipline and tolerates a policy he knows to be disastrous is no revolutionary!

TROTSKY. I take your point. (*Pause*.) But on who's responsibility?

LENIN. I will take full responsiblity. Now please take note that I, as Chairman of the Council of People's Commissars, am giving you, as People's Commissar for Foreign Affairs, a categorical instruction that if the Germans present us with an ultimatum, you will sign the treaty. I am acting on the strength of a decision of the Congress of Soviets, which gives the Sovnarkom unrestricted powers to act in the matter of the peace treaty. After it has been signed, I am prepared to justify myself to any authoritative Party body.

TROTSKY. Good. I will carry out your instructions.

LENIN. This is the plan: hold out until a German ultimatum. Drag the talks out by every possible means and try to gain time, but after the ultimatum – we give in. Can I rely on you, comrade Trotsky?

TROTSKY. Yes, you can. Goodbye.

LENIN. Bon voyage.

Exit **TROTSKY**. **LENIN** *watches him go. Enter* **SVERDLOV**.

SVERDLOV. Did it work?

LENIN *nods.*

SVERDLOV. Will he keep his word?

LENIN (*shrugs his shoulders*). His past record for that is not good, but he gave it . . . I'd have preferred something more reliable, more certain . . . but beggars can't be choosers. Unfortunately . . .

SVERDLOV. Well, since words are ephemeral things anyway, while they're bluffing each other in Brest-Litovsk, we must do something about an army. Peace is fine, but an army's an army . . .

LENIN. I've already told Podvoisky that our anti-war attitude by no means absolves us from being ready for war. We must create a new army at once – a Red Army. Will you draft a decree?

Exit SVERDLOV. LENIN *goes over to the window and stares up at the night sky. Enter* KOLLONTAI.

LENIN. What stars there are tonight . . . Must be a sharp frost . . . (*To* KOLLONTAI.) Do you ever look up at a starry sky?

KOLLONTAI. Only at sea or in the country.

LENIN. At sea? Oh yes, of course, you went to America. When I was a young boy I could name all the constellations, but I'm starting to forget them. Did you want to see me?

KOLLONTAI. I promised the sailors of the Baltic Fleet that I'd bring you to one of their meetings. At any time to suit you. They keep reminding me.

LENIN. No, I won't go.

KOLLONTAI. Why not? You've always wanted to go to Kronstadt.

LENIN. Will they ask questions about the peace treaty?

KOLLONTAI. Of course!

LENIN. But I won't be able to put my views to them, because the C.C. voted against me!

KOLLONTAI. Can't you put the Central Committee's view?

LENIN. No. You must excuse me – I'm only human!

Curtain.

ACT TWO

Scene Fourteen

The Smolny canteen at the lunch-hour. A noisy, cheerful crowd that includes most of the Bolshevik leadership, many of whom are standing in a long queue. Enter LENIN.

LENIN. H'mm – what a crowd. I'd better come back later.

VOICE FROM QUEUE. The Left S-Rs will finish their committee meeting soon and then you won't be able to move in here. Better stay.

DZIERZINSKI. Come over here, Vladimir Ilyich – I've kept you a place in the queue.

LENIN. Have you really?

VOICES. Yes, he has . . . he has . . .

LENIN (*to* DZIERZINSKI). Thank you.

SVERDLOV, *having finished his lunch, comes over to* LENIN. *They move aside in order to talk.*

SVERDLOV. Radek arrived from Brest this morning. According to him, they're keeping to the agreement and dragging out the talks by every means. But it can't last more than a couple of days longer. Then the Germans will present an ultimatum.

LENIN. I see. And here?

SVERDLOV. Bukharin and his friends are cock-a-hoop, prancing around and grinning like madmen. They're just waiting for the talks to collapse and for us to be dragged into war.

LENIN. Well, well . . . And have they lifted a finger to prepare for a war?

SVERDLOV. Here's my draft of the decree to create a new army.

SVERDLOV *hands over a document, which* LENIN *studies intently.*

ZINOVIEV and STALIN get up from their table, continuing their conversation as they cross the stage.

STALIN. Let's be quite clear about this. Gorky says he cannot remain silent. Isn't he ashamed? After all, there was a time when he was quite a Bolshevik. And you notice he doesn't denounce *counter*-revolution but the revolution itself, which he once used to sigh for with every breath. Now that it's in danger, he curses it.

ZINOVIEV. It's those people around him – a gaggle of snivelling Mensheviks, like Sukhanov and Stroyev.

STALIN. And what's he – the Lamb of God? You're just finding excuses for him. Why bother? The Russian Revolution has toppled a lot of figures of authority – and more will follow, no matter who they may be. The revolution is strong because it has never been impressed by big names. It will either use them or consign them to oblivion if they won't learn from it and acknowledge it. Gorky will always be jealous of such real revolutionaries as Plekhanov, Kropotkin and Zasulich. Can't you see that when the whole world celebrates our revolution, the least welcome guest at the feast will be Gorky?

ZINOVIEV. You're an extremist, Koba, but here I agree with you . . . What do you say about the prospects at Brest-Litovsk?

STALIN. I think the best way out of this nasty situation is the middle road – Trotsky's proposal.

Exeunt STALIN and ZINOVIEV.

LENIN (*hearing STALIN's last remark, stares after him in disbelief, then turns to SVERDLOV*). Did you hear that? The best way out of this nasty situation is *Trotsky's* proposal?! A plan which may destroy the revolution? Why is he suddenly bowing to Trotsky? We need flexible minds, not flexible waists. Or is that a tactical 180-degree turn? . . . Why don't you say something?

SVERDLOV (*after a pause*). I know Stalin too well.

LENIN. So you're not surprised at him? Is that it?

SVERDLOV (*reluctantly*). Yes, it is.

LENIN. A result of the time you and he were in exile together?

SVERDLOV. Let's change the subject . . . I'm afraid I may not be objective.

LENIN. Nonsense! We're discussing the most serious matters and you start being coy . . .

SVERDLOV. It's to do with his character . . .

LENIN. Well, if politics are to depend so directly on our characters . . .

SVERDLOV. Please – don't . . . But it's not only a question of character. We've argued about this before: Stalin sees the Party as something like the Order of Teutonic Knights.

LENIN. The Party as – what?!

SVERDLOV. A closed order of warrior knights, with its hierarchy, its discipline, its own morality and philosophy.

LENIN. But that could lead to . . .

SVERDLOV. Precisely. Christianity succeeded by preaching love and mercy, but the Inquisition turned the same ideas into torture and death at the stake. To be honest, I don't think Stalin understands our position. He supports it, votes with us, but he doesn't understand.

LENIN (*smiling*). Oh well, we must make allowances for that self-taught education Stalin is so proud of.

SVERDLOV. We'll try to . . . We're going to see Bukharin's wife at four.

LENIN. Good. When I've had lunch, I'll come round and collect you. I must speak to Stalin.

Exit SVERDLOV. LENIN *advances to the forestage and addresses the auditorium, thinking aloud.*

LENIN. In concentrating on Brest-Litovsk, are we neglecting Petrograd, where the public is getting a daily dose of ultra-leftist propaganda from Bukharin & Co.? We can't ignore it. They speak – we stay silent. So the public judges *our* position from Bukharin's standpoint. So what can we rely on? On time, on events teaching people a lesson and changing their minds? Perhaps. If my analysis is right, the ground will slip from under Bukharin's feet . . . the mood will change in a matter of hours. We must watch out for any shifts in public opinion, on any tendency to shift . . . But am I so busy fighting Bukharin's views that I'm in danger of becoming a prisoner of my own? Perhaps I *shouldn't* keep silent? Perhaps I should speak up, argue, persuade, for all to hear? . . . That means swimming against the current. Not for the first time, though, and I don't mind it. But it also means showing our hand to the Germans. No. So long as the facts will change people's minds and Trotsky keeps his promise to sign, I must keep silent. Though there's nothing worse than silence when you're longing to shout aloud!

DZIERZINSKI's VOICE (*from the wings*). It's your turn now, Vladimir Ilyich!

LENIN. Coming!

Exit LENIN *through the wings, to return almost at once carrying a plate of* kasha *and a glass of tea. All the tables are occupied, except for a couple of free places at the table where* BUKHARIN, LOMOV *and* DZIERZINSKI *are sitting.*

DZIERZINSKI. Come and join us, Vladimir Ilyich.

There is nothing for it: LENIN *has to take a seat at their table. The mood is cheerful;* BUKHARIN *is telling jokes.*

BUKHARIN. A philosopher and a banker were arguing. The philosopher said: 'We owe a debt to life'. The banker corrected him: 'Life *is* debt'.

All laugh. KOLLONTAI *joins the table.*

LENIN. I'm surrounded by enemies, it seems.

BUKHARIN (*mischievously*). Come over to our side, then . . .

LENIN. But is there room for me?

BUKHARIN. We talk and think almost identically.

LENIN. True. We agree on nine-tenths. We only differ over three words, like the banker and the philosopher.

BUKHARIN. So we must define those nine-tenths, the common ground which neither you nor we would contest. Take this glass, for instance. (*Puts an empty glass in the middle of the table.*) What is it? Seen in one way it's a drinking-vessel, and in another – a glass cylinder. However much you and I may argue and swear at each other, it remains both a drinking-vessel and a glass cylinder. The same applies to Brest-Litovsk: it is both a deal with German imperialism *and* a blow at the German revolution.

LENIN (*laughing*). Since Bukharin has drawn the sword of dialectics, I must thank him for his choice of weapon, with which I have some skill, then pick up the gauntlet and explain the difference between dialectic and eclectic reasoning. *(Drinks the rest of his tea in one gulp and puts his glass on the table beside BUKHARIN's glass.)* There is a glass. It is indeed a drinking-vessel and a glass cylinder. But apart from those two qualities, it also has an infinite number of other aspects, characteristics, direct and mediated relationships with the rest of the world. Isn't that so, Felix Edmundovich?

DZIERZINSKI *(suspecting a trap; vaguely)*. Ye-es . . .

LENIN. One could, for instance, pick it up and throw it at someone . . . What do you think, Georgii Ippolitych?

LOMOV *(smiling)*. It's possible.

LENIN. You see? Bukharin's closest ally, comrade Lomov, thinks a glass can be a missile. And can it not be used to hold down a pile of paper? It can. Ergo, it is a paperweight. Can one put a butterfly into a glass? One can. And if it's made of Venetian glass, beautifully ornamented, it is a work of art, regardless of whether it's any use as a drinking-vessel or is cylindrical in shape. Do you agree, Alexandra Mikhailovna?

KOLLONTAI. I agree.

LENIN. You see? Kollontai agrees with me too. Let's go on. If I need a drink, I don't care whether or not it's made of glass or is a cylinder. The essential is that it isn't cracked and doesn't have a chipped rim on which I might cut my lip. But if I want to keep a butterfly in the glass, then I don't care if it is cracked or has a chipped rim. Formal logic – of which Bukharin and any well-educated person has a good grasp – only embraces formal definitions, only deals with what lies on the surface, with the normal and the obvious, and is limited to such categories. How did Bukharin pull off that classic example of eclectic definition? He took two characteristics and juxtaposed them at random – drinking-vessel and glass cylinder. But dialectical logic makes us go further. If you want to know the true nature of something, you must hold it, study it from all angles, see its connections and mediations, examine it in development, in movement, and so on. And now, if we approach both the glass and Brest-Litovsk from all those angles, we shall draw some very startling conclusions. But I don't want to deprive you all of the pleasure of trying that very entertaining experiment for yourselves. Thank you for an enjoyable lunch-hour. *Bon appétit.* *(Gets up and strides out of the canteen.)*

44 THE PEACE OF BREST-LITOVSK

DZIERZINSKI (*admiringly*). The Old Man is quite amazing! Brilliant!

All laugh delightedly. The acting-space is blacked out.

Interlude Seven

A spotlight falls on the amphitheatre and picks out MAXIM GORKY, *who stands up.*

GORKY. The Bolsheviks have the right to describe my behaviour in whatever terms they choose, but I must remind them that the many great qualities of the Russian people have never blinded me to their defects . . . Vileness must always be shown up, and if our peasants are brutes, we must say so . . . If a worker says: 'I'm a proletarian!' in the same repellent, class-conscious tone that a duke might say: 'I'm a nobleman!' – then that worker must be mercilessly ridiculed. Now that a part of the working class, encouraged by the Bolshevik 'comrades', is behaving like a superior caste and using violence and terror, I cannot side with that part of the working class. And when the despotism of the semi-literate masses celebrates its easy victory – thanks to which individual humans are being persecuted and oppressed exactly as before – I have no business to be at that feast. To me, citizen Stalin, that is no celebration. I react with extra suspicion and mistrust to a situation where power is held by someone who was but recently a slave: allowed to rule over his fellow-men, he will become the most ruthless despot.

GORKY *sits down. The spotlight picks out the poet* ALEXANDER BLOK.

BLOK. Everything that stems from illiteracy and lack of culture is repellent, even if explicable. And the slave-mentality of the Russian people is, in my view, the Russian Revolution's worst legacy from the past. 'To squeeze the slave out of people' – to quote Chekhov – is precisely what we want, what we've always dreamed of. We must help this to happen! It will, after all, be the fault of the Russian intelligentsia if the Bolsheviks have difficulty in doing this.

The spotlight is switched off.

Scene Fifteen

A part of the acting-space becomes BUKHARIN's *flat.* NADEZHDA LUKINA, BUKHARIN's *wife, sits propped up on a chaise-longue, her legs covered with a rug; she is 28 years old.* KRUPSKAYA *is sitting beside her.*

KRUPSKAYA. . . . You see, the Lafargues lived about twelve miles outside Paris. We cycled out to see them. They were old by then and retired, but they greeted us very kindly. Volodya sat down to talk to Lafargue about his book of philosophy and Laura took me for a walk in the park. I was terribly nervous – she was Marx's daughter, after all! – and I kept looking at her, trying to see his features in her. I was so tongue-tied that I talked absolute nonsense. She replied very sweetly, but it was hardly a conversation. When we came back, the philosophical discussion was in full flood. Laura nodded towards her husband and said to me: 'He'll soon prove how sincere his philosophical convictions are.' She and Paul exchanged a funny look, but it meant nothing to me at the time. But later . . . when they both died in a suicide pact – I realised the meaning of that look and her words . . . They were old, they had lost the strength needed for the struggle, and so . . . Their death hit Lenin very hard. He said to me: 'If one can no longer work for the Party, one must face the truth and die like the Lafargues.' Now, Nadya – don't cry. D'you think I didn't realise why you asked me about the Lafargues? There was nothing in common with you! Can you write?

LUKINA *nods.*

KRUPSKAYA. Run a discussion-group?

LUKINA *nods.*

KRUPSKAYA. Can you help Nikolai? Read his proofs? So what's the matter?

LUKINA. He's only twenty-nine . . . still young . . . and I'm a cripple . . . this illness has struck so suddenly . . . and it'll get worse . . . I'm afraid of being a burden to him . . . I start to argue with him about Brest-Litovsk, I do it on purpose to annoy and provoke him, but he's so understanding, he just laughs and teases me and says: 'Lenin's much harder on me than you are . . .'

KRUPSKAYA. Their arguments are terrible, I only hope they

don't part company for good . . . whenever they get together I always try to disappear, but I can't help hearing some of it . . .

LUKINA. And when he tries to laugh me out of it, all my determination just vanishes . . . And then, especially at night, the thought keeps hammering in my head – I'm a burden to him, but he simply won't accept it.

KRUPSKAYA. Listen, Nadya – you and I and our husbands were all brought up on the same principles, so how could he do otherwise than act according to his conscience?

Enter KOLLONTAI.

KOLLONTAI. They've chased me out of the kitchen, they want to do it all themselves.

LUKINA. Why are you going to such trouble?

KOLLONTAI. Hush, Nadezhda. We're preparing a feast. We've got hold of some English tea, some sugar, lemons, and even some biscuits. And what cooks! Three virtuosi – Lenin, Felix and Sverdlov. They've made such chaos in the kitchen – admittedly under my orders. Frankly I thought they'd never manage it and I wanted to throw them out, but they turned out to be very good.

KRUPSKAYA. I should think so too . . .

KOLLONTAI. Then Sverdlov assured me that he had a special, magic recipe for making tea. All three of them were laughing their heads off and chased me out.

Enter DZIERZINSKI, *singing a triumphal march, followed by* LENIN *and* SVERDLOV. *They are carrying a tray of tea-things, with which they lay the table and start serving tea.*

LUKINA. Oh, why all this, comrades? Nikolai and I have all we need . . .

LENIN. Nadya, I assure you – you've never drunk such delicious tea as this!

DZIERZINSKI. The whole secret is in how you get the water up to the critical temperature of 100 degrees.

LUKINA. You mean, when it starts to bubble?

SVERDLOV. Much simpler than that: we simply threw in more tea until it looked right.

ACT TWO 47

The sound of a door opening and closing is heard off-stage followed by footsteps running down a long corridor.

LUKINA *(frightened)*. It's him! Something's happened . . .

Enter BUKHARIN, *pale and out of breath, holding a sheaf of papers and teletype tape.*

BUKHARIN *(his voice breaking with emotion)*. Comrades! Vladimir Ilyich! In Germany! Revolution! *(Flings himself at* LENIN *and embraces him, weeping.)*

LENIN *(excited, reading from the telegrams)*. Austria and Germany . . . Mass strikes . . . A Soviet of Workers' Deputies formed in Berlin . . . in Vienna too . . . armed clashes on the streets of Berlin and Vienna . . . Yes, comrades, the revolution has begun there . . .

LUKINA *(pulls herself up to a sitting position; with great emotion, starts to sing the 'Internationale'.)*

Arise, ye starvelings from your slumbers,
Arise, ye prisoners of want . . .

All join in . . . the singing is picked up by the CHORUS *in the amphitheatre, red flags appear, all embrace and shout 'Hurrah!'*

BUKHARIN *(to the auditorium)*. The flames of world revolution are spreading! The German proletariat has risen! A Soviet formed in Berlin! Capitalism is doomed! The workers will triumph! Long live the international proletarian revolution! Long live the international Soviet republic! Workers of the world, unite!

KOLLONTAI *goes over to* LENIN.

KOLLONTAI. What fools we'd have looked if we had signed the treaty.

LENIN. Fools? We'd have had a breathing-space and the German revolution would have torn up that treaty.

KOLLONTAI. What do we do now?

LENIN. If the news is confirmed, tear up the treaty. Meanwhile, just in case it's not, we continue to spin out the talks.

KOLLONTAI. So was Bukharin right? Was his analysis of the situation in Germany more accurate than yours? Was his readiness to take a risk justified by circumstances?

LENIN. My dear Alexandra, even if the prediction of a German revolution starting today was Bukharin's, then it's not he who did it but the Lord God himself, thanks be to Him for such foresight! A revolution's no cause for self-congratulation. Have we put up statues to ourselves in Russia?

KOLLONTAI. But what do we *do*?

The lighting picks out LENIN'*s office.*

LENIN (*walking over to his office, continuing his conversation with* KOLLONTAI). . . . Karl Liebknecht has already answered that question: if circumstances change within twenty-four hours, then one's tactics change within twenty-four hours . . . (*Suddenly.*) Look – what if it isn't the revolution? What if it's just journalists' exaggeration? There is very little real, hard news . . .

KOLLONTAI. Do you really think that?

LENIN. No – the trouble is I've started to distrust even the news of real events. I mustn't do that!

KOLLONTAI. Calm yourself, Vladimir Ilyich . . .

LENIN. I can't: I know so very few facts . . .

Enter BUKHARIN, LOMOV *and* DZIERZINSKI.

LOMOV. The time has come to act. We must immediately break off negotiations at Brest and recommence military operations.

LENIN. To think the only way to help the German revolution must be war is the same as thinking the only way to a dictatorship of the proletariat is through an armed insurrection. We don't think that, do we?

DZIERZINSKI (*explodes*). While you're laughing at us and lecturing us on political science, the German revolution is being gunned down in Berlin while we might save it. We must act, not split hairs!

LENIN. Save it? How?

BUKHARIN. If necessary, at the cost of our own destruction.

LENIN. Yes, comrade Bukharin, you are absolutely right: *provided* there really is a revolution there and not just the first signs of one, which you and I have blown up out of all proportion! *If* this is a real uprising; *if* there is general civil war; *if* this is really the decisive battle; *if* the Germans really want and ask for our help! Answer me all those 'ifs', then you will all see what has to be done. But none of you *can* answer those 'ifs', because you're all as badly informed as I am. If you're determined to base a tactical plan on nothing but emotion, then don't come to me. Intervene just to pacify your conscience? No, I'm sorry; that way we won't save the German revolution, we'll only destroy our own. And our defeat will frighten the German proletariat off socialism, just as the dispersal of the Paris commune frightened off the English working class. Is that what you want? We have already been helping the German revolution and will in future – by our own example, by propaganda, fraternisation at the front, by publishing the secret treaties, and if necessary – with our blood!

KOLLONTAI. But isn't it necessary *now?*

LENIN *is silent.*

DZIERZINSKI. You're simply afraid of the risk. Politics isn't algebra – it's not just formulae, sometimes you have to take risks.

LENIN. Yes, I am afraid . . . I'll risk anything except the Russian Revolution.

Interlude Eight

TROTSKY *goes over to the teletype machine at stage left. The* TELEGRAPHIST *starts the machine.*

TROTSKY *(dictates).* 'To Lenin, Petrograd. Could not wire you earlier, due to breakdowns on the line purposely arranged by the Germans. Our press has grossly exaggerated the events in Germany. There is no revolution there, only a sharp swing in the mood, a shift, perhaps the beginnings of a revolution but that is all. All demonstrations etc. have been brutally suppressed. The military party has come to power in Germany, headed by Hindenburg and Ludendorff. The man now effectively in charge of these negotiations is General Hofmann, who this evening intends to present us with what amounts to an ultimatum. The enormous territorial demands, of which we informed you earlier, remain unchanged, and there will be a categorical demand for our reply. Please send me your views on the substance of the German ultimatum. We will give them our final answer this evening. It should be made known all over the world. Please take the necessary steps to ensure this. Trotsky.'

Scene Seventeen

In LENIN's *office, where* STALIN *and* SVERDLOV *have joined them; there is silence. All are reading the teletype tape with* TROTSKY's *message.*

BUKHARIN. If we had started fighting again, this wouldn't have happened. (*Exit.*)

No one reacts to BUKHARIN's *remark.* LENIN *watches him go. Exeunt* KOLLONTAI *and* LOMOV *in silence.* DZIERZINSKI *goes over to* LENIN.

DZIERZINSKI. Of course we couldn't have started fighting again. You are absolutely right. And although I don't agree with you over the other questions, there's no escaping the truth on that point.

LENIN (*after a pause*). Have you ever given thought to the problem that the most positive qualities – readiness to fight, burning hatred of the bourgeoisie, a sense of internationalism taken beyond a certain limit – may be turned, dialectically, into their very opposites?

DZIERZINSKI. I'll think about it.

LENIN. You were depressed about something yesterday. I didn't ask you what it was.

DZIERZINSKI. We arrested a burglar, the so-called 'Prince Eboli'. He had been robbing people's flats, using a false warrant. I ordered him to be shot. My first death sentence.

LENIN (*after a pause*). Felix Edmundovich, I have absolute faith in your competence in such matters.

DZIERZINSKI. Thank you (*Exit.*)

LENIN (*to* SVERDLOV). When Trotsky says 'our final answer', does he mean he'll sign?

SVERDLOV. Of course. Look, he's asking us to make it known world-wide. And he's asking for our views, to make sure our position hasn't changed since you last talked to him. There can be no doubt – he'll sign today. We've won, Vladimir Ilyich! Just think of what we'll be able to do now!

LENIN. Yes, you're right . . . (*Picks up the telephone receiver.*) Teletype room, please . . . Please open the line to Brest-Litovsk. We'll be with you shortly . . . Yes . . .

ACT TWO 51

STALIN (*to* SVERDLOV). So the Old Man stuck to his guns. And he was right. As I always say: if there's no dog in the house, you must teach the cat to bark.

SVERDLOV. That cat of yours, Koba, is turning into a whole philosophy. But the ancient Romans said: *Non omnia possumus* – we can't do everything, not everything is possible.

STALIN. You know I can't cap that one, so – 'Let this cup pass from my lips'!

LENIN (*replacing the telephone receiver*). We must be ready for Trotsky's telegram when it comes. I won't be going to bed; I'll wait by the teletype. (*To* SVERDLOV.) Have the radio station at Tsarskoye Selo broadcast it as soon as we get it. And we must hold up the morning papers, at any rate *Pravda* . . .

SVERDLOV. I'll see to that.

LENIN. Stalin and I will go to the teletype.

LENIN *and* STALIN *go over to the teletype machine at stage right.*

LENIN (*to* TELEGRAPHIST). Transmit the following, please: 'To Trotsky, Brest-Litovsk. You know our views. They have only been confirmed by recent events. Await your further news. Lenin.'

TROTSKY (*Enters, advances to the forestage and addresses the auditorium*). The session will shortly begin. So what is stopping me? There is the decision of the Central Committee, which I am bound to carry out. There is Lenin's categorical instruction, as chairman of the Sovnarkom, confirmed just now, which I am also bound to carry out. And there is my word of honour, given to him, that I would sign the treaty in the event of a German ultimatum. And there are today's latest events, on which I base my profound conviction that there is no need to sign the treaty, that the best course now is my formula of 'no peace, no war' . . . I gave him my word, but that was nearly two weeks ago. I am certain the Germans will not advance, will hear me out and accept it . . . They must now keep a large amount of troops in Berlin: strikes and demonstrations may break out at any moment . . . And we mustn't overlook the grandiose impression that my formula will make on mankind at large. No peace, no war! Excellent! It sounds like a slogan. It will go into every textbook of modern history. Revolution means a new kind of diplomacy directed at peoples and not at governments. No, I've made up my mind. (*Comes further forward on the stage.*) Members of the Brest-Litovsk peace conference! Gentlemen! The hour of decision has come. The peoples are asking when humanity's unprecedented orgy of self-destruction will cease, which was begun by the selfishness and lust for power of the ruling classes of Europe. When will this struggle to carve up the world cease? We no longer wish to take part in this purely imperialist war, in which the greed of the propertied classes is being paid for with human blood. Our attitude to the imperialism of both sides is equally intransigent and we are no longer willing to shed the blood of our soldiers in defence of the interests of one imperialist camp in its fight against the other. In expectation of the moment – which we hope will be soon – when the oppressed working classes of every country will seize power, as the workers of Russia have done, we are withdrawing our army and our whole people from this war. Our peasant soldiers will return to their ploughs, so that the land may be tilled this spring – the land which the revolution has taken away from the landowners and given to the peasants. Our worker soldiers will return to the factories, so as to produce not the weapons of destruction but the tools of constructive work and, together with the ploughmen, to build up a new, socialist economy. At the same time we announce that the conditions proposed to us by the governments of Germany and Austria-Hungary are in fundamental opposition to the interests of all peoples. We refuse to endorse the conditions which the German and Austro-Hungarian imperialist governments are writing with the sword on the bodies of living people. We cannot put the signatures of the Russian delegation to conditions which entail oppression, grief, hardship and misfortune for millions of human beings. The governments of Germany and Austria-Hungary want to rule the world and its peoples by right of conquest. Let them pursue that aim openly. We cannot sanction such violence . . . (*To* TELEGRAPHIST.) Comrade, please transmit this telegram to Petrograd. (*Hands over a telegram.*)

The two teletypes – transmitter and receiver – begin to work simultaneously.

TROTSKY (*reads out from a copy of his telegram*). 'Further to my previous communications, I have today handed to the joint delegation of the Central Powers the following written and signed statement: "In the name of the Government of the Russian Republic, the Council of People's Commissars hereby informs the governments and peoples of all hostile, allied and neutral countries that, while refusing to sign an annexationist treaty, Russia declares unilaterally the state of war between herself on the one hand and Germany, Austria-Hungary, Turkey and Bulgaria on the other to be terminated. Simultaneously the order for total demobilisation is being issued to the Russian forces on all fronts. Signed: L. Trotsky. A. Joffe. M. Pokrovsky. V. Karelin."'

LENIN (*crumpling the teletype tape in his hand; grimly*). Where is your word of honour now, comrade Trotsky?

Interlude Nine

Spotlights play on the amphitheatre. The **CHORUS** *is agitated and uneasy. Sporadic shouts of 'Peace! Peace!' A spotlight rests on* **GENERAL BONCH-BRUYEVICH**, *who stands up and reads out a telegram.*

GENERAL BONCH-BRUYEVICH. 'To Lenin, Smolny, Petrograd. The army has taken Trotsky's declaration as a *de facto* peace treaty. Krylenko's demobilisation order, which repeats Trotsky's announcement, has also been received. A state of confusion has thus arisen: the peace talks have been broken off, no accord has been reached, but the order refers to the war having ended and it decrees general demobilisation. A spontaneous demobilisation is already taking place. Considering that the army has effectively ceased to exist and that it is impossible to make any sense of the actions of the central government, I hereby inform you of the disbandment of the General Headquarters of the Commander-in-Chief and of my resignation from the post of Chief of Staff. Signed: General Bonch-Bruyevich.'

Scene Eighteen

LENIN *and* SVERDLOV *are in* LENIN's *office; they are later joined by* STALIN. *Enter* TROTSKY, *returned from Brest-Litovsk.*

TROTSKY. Comrade Lenin . . .

LENIN. We must now discuss what the government is to do next. Therefore, comrade Trotsky, please inform us . . .

TROTSKY. But the situation in Brest-Litovsk had evolved in such a way that no other action was possible. The workers of France and Britain now trust us absolutely and will not allow military intervention to be organised against us.

LENIN. Comrade Trotsky, both comrade Sverdlov and I realise that you were acting on certain premises. However, you might have refrained from playing what was, to put it mildly, a not entirely honest game with us and you might not have sent us your last telegram, in which you asked for our views, well knowing what you were going to do an hour later . . .

TROTSKY. Vladimir Ilyich!

LENIN. It was, well, how shall I put it? . . . less than decent. Such behaviour is intolerable, not only between fellow members of a government but in general . . . between people . . . to say nothing of whether it's proper between comrades in the Party – if, of course, they really *are* comrades.

TROTSKY. Vladimir Ilyich!

LENIN. However, that is just emotion. Only time will tell whether this was a tactical move of genius, as you think it is, or a showy gesture, effectively a betrayal of the interests of the revolution and a free gift to Kaiser Wilhelm and his generals, as I regard it.

TROTSKY. I remain convinced that we have successfully left the war . . . (*Exit*.)

SVERDLOV. Comrade Trotsky will have to report to the All-Russian Central Executive Committee of the Soviets . . . and they will then have to decide on it.

LENIN. He began so well at Brest-Litovsk. He made brilliant use of it as a forum for propaganda, and we were all with him in that. And now he has to shoot off at a tangent, slam the door, play to the gallery . . .

STALIN. Vladimir Ilyich, you yourself said that only time would give its verdict . . . Supposing Trotsky's move is successful?

LENIN. Exactly – 'supposing'. All we can do now is rely on that 'supposing'.

SVERDLOV. When Trotsky reports to the C.E.C. we'll move a resolution on these lines: 'Having heard and discussed the report of the peace delegation, the C.E.C. fully approves the actions of its delegates at Brest-Litovsk'.

STALIN. In that case he'll think he's won. Though if that happens, the word 'defeat' will have lost its meaning . . . Don Quixote also thought he had won when he was nearly battered to death by the windmills.

SVERDLOV. Two days ago you thought that Trotsky's proposal was the only way out of the crisis.

STALIN. That was a 'buffer' position in between the two extremes and I supported it up to a certain point because it might prevent the Party from splitting apart. But when Trotsky passed well beyond that point, I turned away from him.

LENIN. Right. (*To* SVERDLOV.) We will move a resolution on those lines. We have no choice. Formally, Trotsky carried out the decision of the Central Committee and the Sovnarkom. We will not inform either the Germans or the public of our disagreements. It will not help matters at this juncture.

Telephone rings.

Yes, speaking . . . Dismiss him at once! . . . No 'ifs' or 'buts'! . . . No, no! . . . Tell him I do not wish to speak to him! (*Replaces the receiver.*)

STALIN. What was that?

LENIN. My secretary – you know him, Sidorenko. Got drunk and went around shouting that he was Lenin's secretary.

STALIN. But is it worth getting so upset about it? You've gone quite pale.

LENIN. Yes, it is worth it. How I hate that disgusting attitude of 'servant' and 'master', the lowly and the élite. It's an obscenity that will go on dogging us for a long time to come, unless we deal with it firmly and once for all – and providing we don't perpetuate it ourselves.

Enter DZIERZINSKI *carrying a telegram which he silently places in front of* LENIN. *Enter* TROTSKY, *immediately behind* DZIERZINSKI. *A spotlight picks out* GENERAL SAMOILO *in the amphitheatre, who reads out.*

GENERAL SAMOILO. 'To Lenin and Trotsky, Smolny, Petrograd. Today at 1930 hours General Hofmann informed me officially that at noon on 18th February the armistice between Germany and the Russian Republic will expire and a state of war will recommence. Signed: General Samoilo, Military Adviser to the Russian Delegation, Brest-Litovsk.'

LENIN *starts to pace nervously up and down;* TROTSKY *watches him, expecting an outburst.*

SVERDLOV. I'll go and call the Central Committee together. (*Exit.*)

Exeunt DZIERZINSKI *and* STALIN.

LENIN. Well, we now know the result of your cherished experiment. Are you satisfied?

TROTSKY. No, the experiment is not yet complete. That telegram is just words. Wait and see whether Hofmann actually starts advancing.

LENIN. What d'you mean? (*Amazed, unable to believe his ears.*) You want to go *on* playing this game? That means losing Dvinsk, losing men, artillery . . . What's the use?

TROTSKY. Of course it implies certain losses. But it is essential that German troops should actually enter Russian territory on a war footing. The German, British and French workers must be aware of this – as a fact, not just as a threat . . .

LENIN. But you're now no longer dealing in abstract quantities but in real human lives! Do you realise that for every minute that you and I delay, people are paying for it in blood?

TROTSKY. Vladimir Ilyich, if you put it like that . . .

LENIN (*angrily*). I am purposely putting it like that! If you don't realise that any further provocation will destroy the revolution, then I do!

TROTSKY. Having started this experiment, we must see it through!

LENIN. *You* started this experiment, comrade Trotsky, *you* presented us with a *fait accompli*, although you gave me your word that you wouldn't – and now you refuse to see that your experiment is already over! You won't see it, despite the hard facts.

TROTSKY. I see no such facts.

LENIN (*holding out the telegram*). And what's this?

TROTSKY. Nothing but a piece of paper! Why d'you suppose we went through all that performance? Only an actual advance by the Germans will give us the real answer.

LENIN (*restraining himself*). All right. On your last visit here I asked you: 'And what if the Germans renew the war?' You replied: 'Then we'll be forced to sign the peace treaty.' What's stopping you from doing that now? Wounded self-esteem? Isn't it time we forgot about self-esteem, when the fate of millions is in our hands?

TROTSKY. Comrade Lenin, I shall ignore the tone of your remarks and remind you that we were not talking about a verbal ultimatum but about an actual advance by the German army.

LENIN. So you need casualties, do you? You won't believe in the reality of a German advance without them?

TROTSKY. Putting it like that is sheer demagogy!

LENIN. Putting it like that is laying bare the truth of the situation.

TROTSKY (*trying to avoid answering*). After all, why should we believe that telegram? I'm sure it's a German trick. I will immediately issue a protest by radio!

LENIN. You want to leave? All right . . . You and I have nothing more to say to each other. We shall, however, see what the Central Committee has to say.

Scene Nineteen

LENIN's *office. One by one the members of the Central Committee enter, sit down, and read* GENERAL SAMOILO's *telegram.*

SVERDLOV. Comrade Trotsky, have you read the decree on the creation of the Red Army? Comrade Lenin has requested me to ask all members of the C.C. for their comments or additions to the decree.

TROTSKY. Only one. (*Takes a copy of the decree out of his pocket.*) – You can't create an army without ultimate disciplinary sanctions. You can't lead a mass of people to their death unless the death penalty is available to the army command. We should always face the soldier with the choice of possible death from the front and certain death from the rear if he runs away.

SVERDLOV. We don't want to base our discipline on fear. But I'll pass your comment on to Vladimir Ilyich.

DZIERZINSKI. German aircraft have appeared over Dvinsk. An attack on Reval is expected. Four German divisions have been transferred from France to the Eastern Front. The Germans have broadcast a radio message claiming that they are defending the civilised countries against the infection from the East.

SVERDLOV. Comrades, I declare this session of the Central Committee open. I propose to limit the agenda to one question: Should we or should we not send a telegram agreeing to sign a peace treaty on yesterday's terms? Speakers should give us their arguments for one course or the other. Then we will take a vote. I call upon comrade Trotsky to speak against the despatch of such a telegram.

TROTSKY. Comrades, only now is the public beginning to digest what has been happening. To sign a peace treaty now would only bring chaos into our ranks. The same can be said of the Germans, who have supposed that we were only waiting for their ultimatum. They may have been counting on its psychological effect. We must wait and see what sort of impression it will make on the German working class. In Germany, the ending of the war on the Eastern Front was greeted with joy, and it is by no means impossible that a German attack on us will cause a serious popular eruption in Germany. I repeat: we must wait and see its effect, and *then* propose peace – provided the Germans themselves don't propose it first.

LENIN. I am in favour of sending the telegram at once, immediately, while there is still time. Enough of proposals, enough of fantasizing in a vacuum, we must base our thinking on reality, bitter though it is. The Germans are not advancing so much to acquire territory as to overthrow the Soviet government. Consider that. Delay now means death.

SVERDLOV. We will take a vote. In favour of sending a telegram? . . . Lenin, Sverdlov, Smilga, Zinoviev, Stasova, Sokolnikov. Six. Against? . . . Trotsky, Dzierzinski, Bukharin, Joffe, Uritsky, Lomov, Krestinsky. Seven. The proposal is rejected by a majority of one vote. We shall await the development of events.

LENIN. Which may well destroy us! (*Exit.*)

SVERDLOV. Comrades, I must ask you not to disperse. It is now midnight. As soon as the first telegrams arrive, we will immediately resume the session.

The C.C. members get up, gather in groups, conversing in low voices. Someone goes out and returns again. LENIN *advances to the forestage, where he is joined by* SVERDLOV.

LENIN (*to* SVERDLOV). Perhaps it's time to move? Appeal directly to the public and call a spade a spade. Irresponsibility is a game two can play at!

SVERDLOV. There is a Central Committee resolution . . .

LENIN. But maybe the moment has come when formal considerations don't count any more? You and I say nothing, we make no public speeches, and a policy we know to be disastrous is given official blessing by our names too. So shouldn't we tell them the real facts? No one would stop me! We'll go to the sailors, the soldiers, the workers – to the people! Let's appeal to the Party! The good of the revolution is the only law! I don't want people ever to say bitterly of us: Revolutionary hot air about a revolutionary war destroyed the Russian revolution!

SVERDLOV. Vladimir Ilyich . . .

Enter COLONEL ROBINS, *U.S. Agent.*

. . . the representative of the Allies – Colonel Robins.

LENIN. Yes, we have met – how d'you do, colonel. We are having a short recess, so we can talk. What can I do for you?

Exit SVERDLOV.

LENIN. Which language would you prefer to speak?

ROBINS. Forgive me, my Russian isn't . . .

LENIN. Good, we'll talk in English, but you mustn't judge me too severely. Pray proceed.

ROBINS. Does Trotsky's announcement mean that you have made peace with Germany? If not, to what extent could Allied aid play a role, if you decide to fight back?

LENIN. Last time, you told me you had advised your government to recognise us de facto. Have you had an answer?

ROBINS. Not yet. But it's my conviction, Mr Lenin, that such a step by the U.S. government would be the best for us all.

LENIN. I have no doubt that what you have just said expresses your personal opinion. But do your personal views coincide with the intentions of your government? Now I will answer your questions. So far there is no peace treaty with Germany. We have refused to sign the extortionate terms that are being forced on us by the German imperialists, and that is all. As to whether military operations will be renewed – you had better refer that question to the German general staff. Will your offer of aid play any part in our decisions? No, it will not. Our strategy will serve the interests of our revolution – and nothing else.

ROBINS. But what if the Germans renew the war?

LENIN. *Then* we will accept your aid. We will collaborate with the Allied governments, provided such collaboration has no political conditions. What's more, we are ready to extend that collaboration to economic matters in peace time. We believe this would be of mutual benefit to both sides.

ROBINS. Russia – what a market! But . . .

LENIN. Yes, there is a 'but'. It sometimes seems to me that all this talk of aid is simply a device to draw Russia back into the war against Germany, then to withhold the aid and thereby overthrow Soviet rule.

ROBINS. No, no, Mr Lenin! If military operations are renewed on the Eastern Front, we will supply you with *real* aid. And you wouldn't be fighting alone; you'd be supported by Britain, France, Italy and the U.S.A. – and that's not counting your own people. With cards like that, even a less experienced gambler than you could play the game and win.

LENIN (*pulls five sheets of paper out of his note-pad and holds them up, smiling*). I'm not a gambler, I'm a politician. But even if I were a gambler, I wouldn't sit down to play with a hand like this. Four of them are blank . . . (*Hands four sheets to* ROBINS.) They represent the Allied Powers' collaboration with us. Only one is real: the support of the workers and peasants of Russia. *That's* the one card we can rely on.

ROBINS (*putting the four pieces of paper into his pocket*). Mr Lenin, before the week is out I will bring these sheets of paper back to you – covered in words and figures. But I mustn't take up any more of your time . . .

ROBINS *and* LENIN *stand up and shake hands. Exit* ROBINS.

Interlude Ten

Spotlights on the amphitheatre pick out an ARMY COMMISSAR, *an* OFFICER *and a* BOLSHEVIK.

ARMY COMMISSAR (*reads out a telegram*). 'To Lenin and Krylenko, Smolny, Petrograd. German troops have begun to attack. Panic in Dvinsk. The army is running away, offering no resistance. Council of army commissars has decided to evacuate Dvinsk.'

OFFICER (*reads out a telegram*). 'To Lenin and Krylenko, Smolny. Units of Fifth Army retreating in disorder to Rezhitsa and Drissa. Twelfth Army, defending approaches to Petrograd, has mostly abandoned its positions and withdrawn to the rear.'

BOLSHEVIK (*reads out a telegram*). 'To Lenin and Krylenko, Smolny. Front line is melting away by the minute. Immediate peace essential at all costs. Signed: Myasnikov.'

Scene Twenty

The Central Committee members resume their places at the table, several members holding copies of the telegrams from the front.

TROTSKY. We must ask Berlin and Vienna – what exactly do they want?

LENIN. Can you still not see?

URITSKY. Waste of time. We must act at once. Right now, a 'wait and see' policy is the worst of all. We must either count in the votes of today's absentees, Artyom and Muranov, whose views are known, or else those in a minority must submit.

SVERDLOV. And what then – fight?

URITSKY. Yes.

LENIN (*bursts out*). The Central Committee has voted against a revolutionary war. Now that we have 'neither peace nor war', as Trotsky has seen fit to describe this interesting condition, some members, with the tacit consent of others, still want to draw us into precisely that so-called 'revolutionary war'. You cannot play with war! This game, comrade Trotsky, has led us up such a blind alley that the destruction of the revolution is inevitable if we continue to adopt your 'middle' position. We do not have so much as an hour to spare. Waiting any longer means throwing the Russian Revolution on to the scrap-heap! If we ask the Germans any more questions, as Trotsky suggests, that will just produce one more scrap of paper! That's not a policy! Offering to sign a treaty – that is a policy! We scribble away on paper while they seize towns, stores, rolling-stock – and our people die! By playing around with war now, we are handing over our revolution to the Germans! We could have signed a peace which in no way threatened the revolution. But we didn't. Now it's too late to put out feelers to the enemy, because it's obvious even to an infant that the Germans can and will advance.

SVERDLOV. Does that constitute your speech, Vladimir Ilyich?

LENIN. No, that was a reply to Uritsky. I shall make my speech at the end.

BUKHARIN. Comrades, all this talk about 'playing with war' is quite extraordinary. Events have developed exactly as we predicted. Yet we exhibit nothing but panic and confusion. We have always said the Russian Revolution must either defend itself or be destroyed . . .

LENIN. Yes – asphyxiated by revolutionary hot air!

BUKHARIN. Please, Vladimir Ilyich – I didn't interrupt you . . . There is no question of postponing the battle with world imperialism: they are now openly attacking us. Even if they take Petrograd, the workers will still resist them. We are far from having exhausted our possible support: we can induce the peasants, too, to turn on the Germans. We can do anything, if we simply stick to our original objective – world revolution. And it will lead us to victory.

SVERDLOV. I call on comrade Lenin.

LENIN *stands up, but for a long time says nothing.*

SVERDLOV. Vladimir Ilyich . . .?

LENIN. Worst of all is the fact that many of us are not paying heed to the real situation but seem, in spite of everything, to be sticking to our old positions. I made the mistake of thinking that the facts would in some measure influence people, make them at least think twice . . . What a hope! Once again Trotsky adopts a mid-way stance, suggests new prognoses – and yet the clock ticks on, counting out our last minutes. Bukharin, having mounted his hobby-horse – revolutionary war – apparently can't dismount. He doesn't care that the peasants don't want war and won't fight for us. But because Bukharin wants it – they'll fight! 'We can do anything . . .' he says; it will apparently cost us nothing, just like in that idiotic song: 'Bombs and shells don't scare the Russian soldier, he catches and chucks them over his shoulder!' . . . It's said that if we make peace, the Germans will seize Latvia and Estonia. Well, we'll give them up to save the life of the Russian revolution. They'll demand that we withdraw from Finland . . . All right, let them have revolutionary Finland.

Murmurs and rustling among the members of the Central Committee.

Yes, it will be a bitter pill, but we must swallow it. We will concede territory to the victor in order to gain time. If we give up Finland, Estonia and Latvia the revolution is not lost. If we lose the revolution, what will we gain that might help Finland's self-determination?

BUKHARIN. A clear conscience!

LENIN. We will gain the profound and justified conviction among the world proletariat that the Russian Revolution was led by blinkered fools, who bungled the main issue for the sake of a moral pose. That's all. Nothing else. I move that we send the Germans an immediate telegram agreeing to a peace treaty.

SVERDLOV. A vote will now be taken. Who is in favour of Lenin's proposal? . . . Lenin, Smilga, Sverdlov, Sokolnikov, Zinoviev, Stalingrad and Trotsky. Who is against it? . . . Bukharin, Uritsky, Lomov, Joffe, Krestinsky. For Lenin's proposal: Seven; against: five. Adding Dzierzinski's vote to those 'against' – six.

SVERDLOV. Stasova abstains. The motion is carried.

LENIN. Now the only question is – will the Germans accept. (*Exit.*)

Interlude Eleven

A spotlight falls on the amphitheatre and picks out a GERMAN GENERAL, *who stands up and reports.*

GERMAN GENERAL. Events are taking their course. The demoralisation of the Russian army is much greater than we supposed. No one wants to fight any more. Yesterday one German lieutenant and six soldiers took six hundred and thirty cossacks prisoner. Hundreds of guns, locomotives, railway waggons, several thousand prisoners and a dozen divisional headquarters were taken without a shot being fired. Today a Bolshevik courier arrived with their agreement to make peace. But we shall not stop until we reach Lake Peipus, the border between Estonia and Russia proper. (*Sits down*.)

The spotlight shifts from the GERMAN GENERAL *to* GORKY, SUKHANOV *and* STROYEV – *the editorial staff of* GORKY'*s newspaper* Novaya Zhizn *('New Life')*.

GORKY. Sukhanov, please read that last paragraph again. Listen to it, Stroyev.

SUKHANOV (*reads*). 'They could have risked losing the revolution – that would have meant destroying the body but leaving the spirit alive . . . Then defeat would not have been too terrible. But our rulers, in their blindness and panic, have not done what was their clear duty. History will not forgive them. We, however, are not interested in the verdict of the future but in saving the country. Soviet rule has proved itself bankrupt, and not only over the peace treaty: it has done everything possible to undermine all the gains of the revolution. The liquidation of the present government of ruin and shame and the substitution of a new government capable of defending the revolution must at once be put on the agenda by all democratically-minded citizens.'

STROYEV. Excellent!

GORKY (*shaking his head disapprovingly*). That sounds to me like an indirect call to overthrow the government.

SUKHANOV. Not indirect – direct.

GORKY. Worse still. Don't you think that's overdoing it?

SUKHANOV. It's the logical outcome of our position. And it's the only constructive platform for any party.

ACT TWO 65

GORKY. No, I disagree.

SUKHANOV. Are you wavering?

GORKY. Yes, I'm not sure if your article is right – certainly not if it purports to represent my views.

SUKHANOV (*offended*). All right, I'll publish it over my signature. (*Exit.*)

GORKY (*after a pause*). What's the latest news, Stroyev?

STROYEV (*joyfully*). It's all falling apart! The Germans are advancing on Pskov! Any day now they'll turn and attack Petrograd!

GORKY (*almost shouts*). How dare you be so pleased! How can you? Have you stopped to imagine for one second what'll happen if they break through and take the city? So you think the Kaiser's better than Lenin? If so, then you're no socialist! And if that's so – what are we doing working together? (*Overcome by a fit of coughing, sits down.*)

In the amphitheatre, a **WORKER** *stands up and the spotlight moves to pick him out.*

WORKER (*reads a telegram*). 'To Lenin, Smolny, Petrograd. The workers of the Konovalov District, after discussing the situation from every point of view, have reluctantly voted as follows: for immediate signature of a peace treaty – 44; against – 31.'

Scene Twenty-One

LENIN's *office.* LENIN *and* SVERDLOV *are bent over a map on the big table.*

SVERDLOV. They're still advancing. Our detachments put up a heroic resistance at Narva and Pskov, but . . .

LENIN. They're the prototype of our future army. They'll astound the world one day, but now they're just a drop in the ocean.

SVERDLOV. There is a real and increasing threat to Petrograd. We have printed a leaflet proclaiming 'The Socialist Fatherland is in Danger!', and it's being distributed at this moment.

LENIN. Unless we can make a desperate effort and turn this jelly into something solid, we're done for. You must issue a decree declaring martial law in Petrograd. Release all the tsarist generals under arrest in the St. Peter and St. Paul fortress and bring them to Smolny. Offer them the job of defending Petrograd. By this evening we must have mobilised all the workers and soldiers in the city.

SVERDLOV. Today Gorky's newspaper published an article with an open appeal to overthrow the Soviet government.

LENIN. What a moment to choose. Did he sign it?

SVERDLOV. No. It's signed by Sukhanov.

LENIN. Well, Sukhanov's article is the logical conclusion of the line Gorky has been taking. God, how embarrassed he'll be in years to come when he's reminded of it . . . Close down the newspaper and arrest Sukhanov! Ask Lunacharsky to write an article about Gorky, saying he's a proletarian writer in spirit and by origin, and can only exist as a proletarian writer. He mustn't be soft on him, but he mustn't slam the door on him either . . . When can we expect the German's reply?

SVERDLOV (*looking at his watch*). It should have come by now.

LENIN. They'll take their time.

SVERDLOV. You haven't slept for three days.

LENIN. I'm going out for some fresh air in a minute, that should perk me up.

Exit SVERDLOV. LENIN *goes over to the teletype machine at stage right, which is constantly working, and reads the latest news on the tape.*

Interlude Twelve

Red lights flash over the amphitheatre. The 'tick-tock' tune strikes up. The MAN IN WHITE TIE AND TAILS *appears, together with the huge clock-face and the* DANCERS *curled up on it to form the figures 12, 3, 6 and 9.*

MAN IN WHITE TIE. Life goes on, ladies and gentlemen! Let's be optimists and brush up our German we learned in school. Time is on our side!

As the music gets louder and faster, the DANCERS *come to life and sing the following song as they dance.*

'Who's now drinking coffee?
Why, Trotsky and Joffé!
Pawnbroker and tailor – both Jews!
They've sold poor old Russia
To the *junkers* of Prussia –
A *güte gesheft* – what good news!

At Brest-Litovsk in Poland
Our Russia was stolen
And sold by the Yids to the Hun.
Revolt of the peasants –
My goodness, how pleasant!
And Germans to rule us – what fun!

Ding-dong, ding-dong, bing-bong, bing-bong,
Tick-tock, tick-tock, tick-tock.
For oh! disaster – the Reds are master:
The times have changed – tick-tock!'

Enter a patrol of revolutionary SAILORS.

SAILOR. The socialist fatherland is in danger!

DANCERS *and* SPECTATORS *run off in all directions.*

LENIN *(to* TELEGRAPHISTS*)*. I'll be in my office. *(Crosses the stage to his office and sits down at the desk.)*

Scene Twenty-Two

LENIN*'s office. Enter* SIDORENKO.

LENIN. Come in. This is what I've written . . . *(Picks up a sheet of paper and reads from it.)* 'To Dzierzinski. The bearer, Sidorenko, was my personal secretary for a few days. I found his work entirely satisfactory. He was dismissed for a single incident when, in a state of insobriety, he shouted – as I'm told – that he was "Lenin's secretary". Sidorenko tells me that he profoundly regrets this, and I'm inclined to believe him. He's a good lad, and one should make allowances for youth. On the basis of these facts you should judge for yourself, bearing in mind the nature of the job you intend to offer him. Signed: Lenin.' Will that suit you?

SIDORENKO. Vladimir Ilyich, I . . . *(Struggles to say something, but cannot; takes the proffered reference and exits.)*

Enter BUKHARIN.

BUKHARIN. I'm ready.

LENIN. No, I'm too tired for our usual walk. Let's just sit here awhile instead.

BUKHARIN. All right, let's.

LENIN (*after a pause*). Hard times, eh, Nikolai Ivanych?

BUKHARIN. I've brought you today's *Pravda* with your article in it . . . So you've decided to publicise our disagreements . . .

LENIN. Yes, the time has come to oppose your ideas with another point of view. Then let the public choose.

BUKHARIN. You signed it 'Karpov', a pseudonym you used before the revolution.

LENIN. Yes. (*Pause.*) The Allied agents have been to see me – Robins, Sadoul and Bruce-Lockhart. They are offering us arms if we have to fight.

BUKHARIN. You won't accept, will you?

LENIN. We will – provided there are no political strings attached.

BUKHARIN (*bitterly*). What *are* we doing? We're turning the Party into a heap of shit. Their offer is *filth*.

LENIN. Oh – a prim young miss as editor of *Pravda*! That's all we need! Perhaps you also believe in immaculate conception?

BUKHARIN. Someone has to believe in immaculate conception, otherwise you can justify anything.

LENIN. No need to take offence. If we all took offence, I would have countless reasons to do so. We must keep working, not waste time being offended. You keep talking about a revolutionary war, but what concrete steps have you taken to prepare for it? Now if, for instance, you had organised the medical services, that would have helped. But all you do is write resolutions . . .

BUKHARIN *bursts into cheerful laughter.* LENIN *looks at him in amazement.*

LENIN. What's funny?

BUKHARIN. So you *are* thinking about a war, aren't you . . . That's the main thing. The Left S-Rs were saying the same to us this morning.

LENIN. What were they saying?

BUKHARIN. Proshyan came to see me today. 'Instead of writing resolutions,' he said, 'you'd do better to arrest Lenin for one night, declare war on the Germans, then re-elect him unanimously as head of the government, because no one can wage war better than he can.'

LENIN. You know, Nikolai, that's not quite as funny as it might seem . . . when people say such things, you must first of all wonder why they're talking to *you*, of all people . . . That's firstly. Secondly, please don't ever repeat that conversation to anyone else. It's enough that I know.

From near and far come the sounds of factory hooters and whistles.

LENIN (*listening*). The factories are mobilising.

BUKHARIN. It's music to my ears. When you hear that, and you remember the compromises you've been urging on us, I want to weep.

LENIN. Don't you weep rather too often, Nikolai?

BUKHARIN. Why are you so hard? How does one get through to you? . . . Today, when you said quite calmly that we should abandon Finland, my heart literally went cold. I couldn't say anything – there was such a lump in my throat . . .

LENIN. Don't claim a monopoly of suffering, please. That's ridiculous. You like hunting, don't you? You've waded through a swamp, haven't you? So you must know that if you walk straight ahead through a swamp you're likely to go in up to your ears, or worse. You have to move from tussock to tussock. Well, sometimes the next tussock is off to one side. And you may think that if you go there you'll never find your way again, so you must go back. Nonsense. That's only because you haven't got a compass. But *with* a compass you can go back or sideways, and you'll always find your way. But of course, if you will insist on repeating what Radek says . . .

BUKHARIN. I'm not repeating Radek, I've enough reasons of my own . . .

LENIN. Where fantastic ideas are concerned, you and he are well matched, and both of you together are only rivalled by Ryazanov! . . . But seriously, your reasoning goes something like this: by its nature, a revolutionary party excludes compromise; our Party has made a compromise, ergo it's no longer a revolutionary party.

BUKHARIN. It soon won't be . . .

LENIN. There was a hero in a novel who tried to persuade his little son, who had taken a lump of sugar without asking, that a person capable of such an act was undoubtedly capable of robbing a house, murdering his parents and assassinating the Tsar!

BUKHARIN. But he *did* take a lump of sugar, didn't he?

LENIN. Ten lumps!

BUKHARIN. Even so, Vladimir Ilyich, compromise always exacts a moral price . . . it corrodes the soul. Whatever you may say, it's immoral to leave the Ukrainians, the Estonians, the Latvians and the Finns in the lurch. It's immoral to buy your own safety at the cost of their misfortune.

LENIN. You're right: on one side of the scales are the misfortunes of the Ukrainians, Finns and Latvians. But what's on the other side? . . . Answer, Mr Guardian of Morality! . . . Bloody slaughter! Death for hundreds of thousands of Russian workers and peasants, who are powerless to withstand the efficient German war machine. Are you aware of such a moral category as responsibility for the lives of millions? Do you know what is meant by the burden of power? It means always being a political realist . . . It means always rejecting any play on one's emotions, even though at times the pressure on them becomes intolerable . . . It means for ever weighing up and calculating – because the fate of millions is in your hands . . .

BUKHARIN. But I can't vote to send my comrades to the gallows!

LENIN. Can I? Can I?

BUKHARIN. But there must be some other way . . . without trampling on one's principles? Surely we can do it without wading through filth? (*Bursts into tears.*)

LENIN. Oh come, Nikolai . . . don't. Calm down. I assure you it's just as hard for me. But you and I have got to save the revolution.

BUKHARIN. All right, but what if we were strong? Wouldn't you go to war then?

LENIN. I would still seek peace, only the price of that peace would not be what it is today.

Exit BUKHARIN. *As* LENIN *sits watching him go, enter* KRUPSKAYA.

KRUPSKAYA. What's the matter? What's happened?

LENIN. Oh, nothing . . . What's the news?

KRUPSKAYA. There's a complete change of mood among local people. They realise there's no alternative. Everybody's guessed that *you* wrote the *Pravda* article.

LENIN. Nadya, if those leftist hotheads get a majority again, I shall resign from the Central Committee.

KRUPSKAYA. What are you saying, Volodya?!

LENIN. I won't be the gravedigger of the revolution. I've given my whole life to it . . . All that leftist hot air, high-minded incantations – it's all a requiem for the revolution. But don't ask me to attend the funeral. I'm only human.

KRUPSKAYA. Have you tried every possibility?

LENIN. Yes. All I can do now is appeal to the public. They'll support me. They're fast coming to their senses, while the leftists keep harping on the same old tune. I told you and Inessa that this would happen, but you wouldn't believe me . . . I've made up my mind.

KRUPSKAYA. But that means a split.

LENIN. Obviously. But there are moments when it's a good thing to draw the line. Everything said, all paths explored. Either *with* the left and into the dark, dangerous whirlpool, or *without* them and into clear water. *(Suddenly, unexpectedly.)* Dammit, how we need a revolution in Germany now. Suppose . . . just suppose their revolution *was* breaking out?

KRUPSKAYA. Volodya – really!

LENIN. Who knows? Let's go!

Exeunt quickly.

Interlude Thirteen

A spotlight falls on the GERMAN GENERAL, *who stands up.*

GENERAL. This morning we sent our new ultimatum to the Bolsheviks. It must be said that the Foreign Ministry and the High Command have done good work. The ultimatum contains every demand that we could possibly have made. Under these new terms, Russia will lose forty-six million people, which is twenty-six per cent of her total population; seventy-five per cent of her coal; seventy-three per cent of her iron; thirty-seven per cent of her grain; twenty-six per cent of her railway mileage – and so on. The Bolsheviks will have to summon their leadership to discuss the ultimatum. I very much doubt if they will accept it, because it has been drawn up in such a way as to infuriate the Bolsheviks and make them reject it. And that is exactly what we want: we shall then advance on Petersburg and stamp out this infection that is threatening the whole civilized world.

Scene Twenty-Three

LENIN's *office. Several members of the Central Committee are leaning over the table to read the text of the German ultimatum.*

STALIN. What's in it?

BUKHARIN. The terms are a thousand times worse than before. They demand a reply by seven o'clock tomorrow morning.

Enter LENIN.

SVERDLOV. The ultimatum.

LENIN. Any news from Germany?

SVERDLOV. As before. No change.

One by one the Central Committee members enter the office and take their seats around the table.

SVERDLOV. Comrades, we must now, in effect, decide on the fate of our revolution. I consider it my duty to remind you of that. So – do we accept their terms or not?

BUKHARIN. You mean – do we give them half of Russia or not? The very question is absurd. Wouldn't it be better for all of us to go out on to the square in front of Smolny and commit suicide in public? At least it would be more honest!

SVERDLOV. What way out can there be?

BUKHARIN. Gather all our forces together and strike! The revolutionaries' answer to imperialist arrogance.

LENIN (*in an outburst of unbelievable force*). Enough! That will do! I will not tolerate this for a second longer! Stop playing games! For a revolutionary war we need an army – there is none. For a revolution we need peace – and we can have it! The politics of hot air are finished! Finished, comrade Bukharin! If any more hot air is produced I shall resign from the government and from the Central Committee and appeal straight to the public. But I will tolerate no more of this revolutionary phrase-mongering! That is all. I request you kindly to accept my resignation!

Long silence. Everyone is dumbfounded.

TROTSKY. Comrades, we have heard comrade Lenin's announcement. What can one say? I find comrade Lenin's arguments quite unconvincing. If we were unanimous, we could deal with the situation perfectly well. I could raise further objections to comrade Lenin's views. But that is not important at this moment. We need total unanimity. We don't have it, and therefore I will not assume the responsibility of voting for war.

STALIN. I suggest we don't sign the treaty but simply resume peace negotiations.

LENIN *shrugs his shoulders in exasperation, but* STALIN *does not see him.*

STALIN. These terms are purposely meant to provoke us and make us reject them. Since we don't have the means to stop the German advance by armed force, we must use other means. Either a breathing-space or see the revolution destroyed – there's no other way.

DZIERZINSKI. There will be no breathing-space, that is utopia. On the other hand, if we sign the treaty, it will strengthen German imperialism. Let us face the facts. Signing on these terms is no guarantee against being faced with further, new ultimatums. If we sign this treaty, we save nothing. But I agree with Trotsky: if the Party were strong enough to withstand the resignation of Lenin, we might be able to vote for war. But we are not.

LENIN. I see that some people are reproaching me for my ultimatum to resign. I would only offer it in an extreme situation. And that situation has come. Stalin is quite wrong when he says we need not sign the treaty. These conditions must be signed as they stand. If you don't sign them, you will be signing the death sentence of Soviet rule in three weeks' time. These conditions do not affect the status of the Soviet government – will you finally get that into your heads?! . . . *(Pause.)* I shall not hesitate for a moment. You may reject my ultimatum, but I didn't make it simply to withdraw it again.

LOMOV. Lenin's proposed response to the Germans would destroy the revolution, and therefore I will not go along that road. Everyone is talking about panic in the army, but in fact there is no panic. People are frightened of shadows. If only we want to, there is plenty we can do. Don't be frightened by Lenin's threat to resign. We must take power without him! We must go to the front and do everything possible. Enough of this cowardice – start tackling the tasks the proletariat has laid upon us!

SVERDLOV. Anyone else?

Silence. LENIN *paces up and down in his corner of the room – three paces forward, three paces back.*

SVERDLOV. Then we must come to a decision . . . Would anyone else like to speak?

Silence.

We shall therefore vote on one motion only: Immediate acceptance of the new German terms – or not.

DZIERZINSKI *(bursts out)*. Comrades! Before we vote, we must call a short recess! We all need to calm down. We are too tense. We're not listening to each other. We might well bring irreparable disaster upon the Party, upon our entire movement! We are on the brink of a split! I demand a short break!

SVERDLOV. Who else would like a break? . . . No one. We shall therefore take a vote. Those in favour of accepting the new terms? . . . Lenin, Sverdlov, Stasova, Stalin, Zinoviev, Smilga, Sokolnikov. Those against? . . . Bukharin, Lomov, Uritsky, Bubnov. Who abstains? . . . Trotsky, Dzierzinski, Joffe, Krestinsky. Therefore seven members vote for acceptance of the German terms, and four against it, with four abstentions.

BUKHARIN. That's no majority, when the four abstainers also oppose the motion! They were simply frightened off by the threat of resignation!

URITSKY. I request the floor in order to make the following statement on my own behalf and on behalf of C.C. members Bukharin, Lomov, Bubnov, Pyatakov, Smirnov and probationary member Yakovleva: not wishing to bear responsiblity for the motion adopted today, which we consider profoundly mistaken and destructive of both the Russian and the world revolution, especially since the motion was carried by a minority of the Central Committee and the four abstainers in fact support our position, we announce our resignation from all Party and governmental posts, while retaining the right to canvas and conduct propaganda within the Party in support of the position which we consider to be the only correct one.

STALIN. This is a split, a faction.

Silence. No one can find words to say.

TROTSKY. I think I should explain my motives for abstaining. I am sceptical of the possibility of achieving peace, even at the price of capitulation. But I did not want to hinder the formation of a majority.

LOMOV. Comrade Lenin, will you allow open opposition to signature of the peace treaty?

LENIN. Yes, I will.

STALIN. I would like to ask this question: does these comrades' resignation from their posts mean their effective resignation from the Party? After all, the resolution on policy for Brest-Litovsk – no peace, no war – was also passed by a majority of one vote, and yet we all accepted it.

LENIN. Resignation from the C.C. does not mean leaving the Party.

URITSKY. Although Stalin is inviting us to leave the Party, we will not do so. We are resigning from our jobs, but not from the Party. And the next Congress will decide which of us represents the opinion of the Party at large.

STALIN. Comrades, I blame no one and I think you have the right to do whatever you think best. I only want to express the sense of pain that I feel at the departure of these comrades. Lomov, Smirnov and Pyatakov are quite irreplaceable. Do these comrades realise that their action will lead to a split in the Party? If we want unity and not a split, I would ask you to postpone the announcement of your resignation till tomorrow, or better still, till the Party Congress.

THE PEACE OF BREST-LITOVSK

LOMOV. No! You won't postpone sending our answer to the Germans, and we won't postpone our announcement!

SVERDLOV. Comrades, it is premature for the supporters of peace to rejoice. Our answer to the Germans must not come from the C.C. of our Party but from the sovereign body of the state – the All-Russian Central Executive Committee of the Soviets, which we must persuade to accept our decision, and that will be far from easy. Given the presence of opposition parties, and the likelihood that the Left S-Rs will probably vote against us, I must tell you that every vote will be worth its weight in gold. If there is not absolute unity in the Bolshevik ranks, then our decision will *not* gain a majority in the C.E.C.

BUKHARIN. Are you going to deprive us of our freedom to vote?

SVERDLOV. Yes, comrades, there will be no free voting. All the Bolsheviks must vote as one, in accordance with C.C. rules. Comrades, I'm asking all members of the C.E.C. to be at the session. Postpone any other engagements. I repeat: every vote counts. Who can't come? . . . No absentees? Excellent. If we are united, we may even entice a few Left S-Rs to vote with us. I declare this meeting of the Central Committee closed. Please go over to the Tauride Palace for the C.E.C. Session at once. There is not too much time left before 7 a.m.

Exeunt all but LENIN *and* SVERDLOV.

LENIN. D'you think there'll be any backsliders among us when it comes to the C.E.C. vote?

SVERDLOV. There may be.

LENIN. Well, I'll make use of my last chance . . . I'll go to the rostrum and shout, demand, persuade . . . with my eyes. I will stare at every one of our Party and prick his conscience.

DZIERZINSKI *returns*.

DZIERZINSKI (*very agitated*). Comrades . . . you know me well enough . . . the revolution has been my whole life . . . hellish struggle . . . but I'm human . . . my heart bleeds when I see injustice . . . I still can't reconcile myself to the Brest treaty . . . but I see now that if we don't sign it, others will have to start all over again from the beginning. (*Exit*.)

SVERDLOV. I quite forgot. (*Pulls from his pocket a sheet from a notepad.*) Robins asked me to give this to you.

LENIN. Is it the American government's reply?

SVERDLOV. It's in English . . . I'm afraid I never progressed beyond German.

LENIN (*takes the paper, reads and translates the contents*). 'The support of honourable people all over the globe . . .' (*Smiles.*) That's important, very important, Colonel Robins. And one day it will be a decisive factor. (*To* SVERDLOV.) Time for us to go, too. What's the matter, Yakov Mikhailovich? Are you unwell?

SVERDLOV. Tired. Hellishly. (*Sits down.*) A total split . . . I don't know . . . whether we can survive it . . .

LENIN (*after a long pause, gathering his thoughts*). Yes, it is our worst crisis so far . . . But public opinion will be on our side. The facts themselves will make people realise that our 'breathing-space' policy was right, and the split will be healed . . . (*Pause.*) An order of knighthood, eh? Well, well . . .

SVERDLOV (*stands up*). Ready. Let's go.

Scene Twenty-Four

The amphitheatre and the front acting-space now merge to represent the Plenary Session of the Central Executive Committee of the Soviets, the members of the CHORUS *now being the members of the C.E.C. Much noise and loud argument. As* LENIN *and* SVERDLOV *enter, the noise quickly dies down.* LENIN *takes his seat in the front row among the Bolsheviks,* SVERDLOV – *as chairman* – *goes to the rostrum.*

SVERDLOV. Comrade members of the All-Russian Central Executive Committee! There is today only one motion before you: whether or not to accept the Germans' new peace terms. In view of the importance of this issue for the fate of the Russian and world revolution, and wishing to stress the responsibility borne by each member of the C.E.C., I shall use the procedure of individual voting by name. I request each member, as their name is called, to come up to the rostrum and announce his or her vote loudly and clearly. Let us begin.

Absolute silence. LENIN *stands up and goes to the rostrum, standing in such a position that every member will meet his gaze as they vote.*

SVERDLOV. Avdeyev!

AVDEYEV. Against the treaty!

SVERDLOV. Absolute silence, please. Akulov?

AKULOV. For the treaty.

SVERDLOV. Karakhan?

KARAKHAN. For the treaty!

SVERDLOV. Kakhovskaya?

KAKHOVSKAYA. Against.

SVERDLOV. Steinberg?

STEINBERG. Against!

SVERDLOV. Martov?

MARTOV. Against!

SVERDLOV. Spiridonova?

SPIRIDONOVA. Against the treaty.

SVERDLOV. Yenukidze?

YENUKIDZE. For the treaty.

SVERDLOV. Dan?

DAN. Against!

SVERDLOV. Lunacharsky?

LUNACHARSKY. For the treaty!

SVERDLOV. Kollontai?

KOLLONTAI. I agree to signature of the treaty.

SVERDLOV. Dzierzinski?

DZIERZINSKI. Yes. Sign.

SVERDLOV. Lomov?

LOMOV. For the treaty.

SVERDLOV. Uritsky?

URITSKY. Sign.

SVERDLOV. Bukharin?

BUKHARIN (*goes up to the rostrum: to* LENIN *alone*). You would cease to respect me if you knew that I, Nikolai Bukharin, your

ACT TWO 79

disciple, raised my hand in support of a decision, against my Party conscience and against my profound conviction that it is fatal to our revolution.

LENIN *says nothing, but only looks at* BUKHARIN.

BUKHARIN. Vladimir Ilyich . . .

LENIN *remains silent.*

SVERDLOV. Bukharin?

BUKHARIN. What am I to do, Vladimir Ilyich?

SVERDLOV. Bukharin!

BUKHARIN. Against the treaty.

The members in the amphitheatre break out in cries of 'Bravo!', 'Shame!', 'Quiet!', 'Traitor!'

SVERDLOV. Quiet, please! I shall continue. Gorbov?

GORBOV. I abstain.

SVERDLOV. Stalin?

STALIN. For the treaty.

SVERDLOV. Sokolnikov?

SOKOLNIKOV. For the treaty!

SVERDLOV. Joffe?

JOFFE. For the treaty.

SVERDLOV. Fabricius?

FABRICIUS. I abstain.

SVERDLOV. Trotsky?

Silence. No answer. Everybody looks round for TROTSKY.

SVERDLOV. Trotsky?

VOICE. Not present!

SVERDLOV. Zinoviev?

ZINOVIEV. I'm for the treaty.

SVERDLOV. Ryazanov?

RYAZANOV. Definitely against!

SVERDLOV. Lenin?

LENIN. For the peace!

SVERDLOV. Sverdlov – for the treaty. Kamkov?

KAMKOV. Against!

The lights go out and come on again. The voting is finished.

SVERDLOV. The voting is therefore complete, comrades. With your permission, I shall announce the results of the vote: for signature of the peace treaty – 116; against – 85; abstentions – 26. I therefore declare the motion, introduced by the Bolsheviks, to be passed!

SVERDLOV's *last words are drowned in howls and shouts: 'Traitors!' 'You've betrayed Russia!' 'Shame!' The Bolsheviks stand up and, grouped around* LENIN, *they advance to the forestage.*

LENIN (*to his comrades and to the auditorium, in a conversational, confiding tone of voice*). We were forced to sign it . . . One must have the courage to look unblinkingly at the unvarnished truth. The more clearly we realise that, the firmer will be our unwavering determination to ensure that Soviet Russia should fulfil its chief international duty – to build a new society, to give a shining example to the peoples of the world, to oppose the war, filth and meanness of capitalism with the peace, purity and honourable ideals of socialism. What do we need to achieve this? Peace or war? We do not acknowledge these as alternatives. We need to build, to create, and therefore our thirst for peace is not a tactical device in moments of weakness – it is the aim of all our policies, all our life. Every hour of peace gives socialism a thousand times more than every hour of war, even of a victorious war. Learn from the hard but valuable lessons of the revolution, comrades . . . Learn, in order to win.

Curtain.

THE BOLSHEVIKS

Author's Note

The Bolsheviks is not a documentary drama, although it is based on documentary sources. In a number of passages in this play, the author has taken the liberty of departing from strict chronology in a few instances of secondary importance (e.g. some of the telegrams despatched by Lenin; the rebellion at Livny), with the aim of creating on stage a more complete picture of the time.

M. Shatrov.

Characters

SVERDLOV, Deputy Chairman, *Sovnarkom* (Council of People's Commissars)

LUNACHARSKY \
ZAGORSKY \
KRESTINSKY \
PETROVSKY \
CHICHERIN \
NOGIN \
TSURUPA } People's Commissars \
STUCHKA \
YENUKIDZE \
VINOKUROV \
KRUPSKY \
POKROVSKY

STEKLOV, editor of *Izvestiya* \
BONCH-BRUYEVICH, Executive Secretary, *Sovnarkom* \
PROF. MINTZ, physician \
PROF. WEISBROD, surgeon \
PROF. OBUKH, surgeon \
GILL, LENIN's chauffeur \
TELEGRAPHIST \
BATULIN, soldier \
KOLLONTAI, People's Commissar \
KRUPSKAYA, LENIN's wife \
ULYANOVA, LENIN's sister \
KIZAS, Assistant Secretary, *Sovnarkom* \
DR VELICHKINA, physician \
GIRL TELEGRAPHIST \
GIRL

Translator's note

Throughout the greater part of this play the dialogue is frequently punctuated by the GIRL TELEGRAPHIST dictating LENIN's outgoing telegrams to her male colleague. The author uses this device for a number of purposes: one aim is, by carefully selecting the contents of the messages, to provide an indirect commentary on the subject-matter of the dialogue in progress between the main characters at a given moment; another, achieved by the detail, breadth and variety of the topics in the messages, is to stress the extraordinary degree of LENIN's direct involvement in every conceivable aspect of running this vast country in the grip of civil war, and hence his indispensibility to the struggling Soviet regime; a third purpose is to keep reminding us of how, although LENIN is on the brink of death, the power of his personality continues to be emitted in the form of this seemingly endless stream of telegrams, conveying as it does a sense of LENIN as the chief source of unity, dynamism and continuity in the Russian Revolution.

PART ONE

Moscow; 30 August 1918. The Kremlin. The set is divided into two unequal halves: stage right, the larger half is taken up by the 'cabinet room' – the room in which the Council of People's Commissars (Sovnarkom) holds its meetings; stage left is the hallway of the apartment occupied by **LENIN** *and* **KRUPSKAYA**; *the two areas are joined by a corridor. The Sovnarkom room is furnished with two large tables and one smaller table, placed together to form three sides of a rectangle; the combined tables are covered with a cloth of heavy green baize. Placed down the longer sides are two inward-facing rows of elegant, white-and-gold 'Empire'-style chairs with arms, their seats upholstered in red velvet; these are for the People's Commissars. In the middle of the short side of the open rectangle, facing towards the auditorium, is the Chairman's seat – a plain chair with bare, unpadded arms and a cane back. Stage right and slightly behind the Chairman's place are two tables for secretaries, on one of which is a telephone. Chairs for visitors are ranged along two of the walls. The room is empty.*

In the hallway of the apartment stand a small table and a few chairs in dust-covers; the hallway, too, is empty.

In the linking corridor is a Hughes teletype machine, manned by a **TELEGRAPHIST**. *Beside him sits a* **GIRL TELEGRAPHIST**, *dictating messages. A clock strikes: it is 7.30 p.m. Two women enter the Sovnarkom room; one is an Assistant Secretary, a woman in her late thirties –* **ANNA PETROVNA KIZAS**; *the other is a young* **GIRL**. *They set out papers and pencils on the table.*

GIRL TELEGRAPHIST. (*dictates to the teletype operator*). 'TO ALL STATIONS: THIS MORNING, FRIDAY 30TH AUGUST 1918, URITSKY, CHAIRMAN OF THE PETROGRAD CHEKA, WAS SHOT DEAD IN PETROGRAD. THE MURDERER HAS BEEN ARRESTED AND IS BEING QUESTIONED. PRELIMINARY EVIDENCE SUGGESTS THE COMPLICITY OF THE RIGHT S-R PARTY. COMRADE FELIX DZERZHINSKY HAS BEEN DELEGATED TO GO TO PETROGRAD TO SUPERVISE THE INVESTIGATION. SIGNED: SVERDLOV, CHAIRMAN, ALL-RUSSIAN CENTRAL EXECUTIVE COMMITTEE OF THE SOVIETS.'

KIZAS (*to* GIRL). Put this small notepad in comrade Lenin's place.

GIRL. Very good.

KIZAS. And one on the window-ledge, too.

GIRL. On the window-ledge?

Telephone rings.

GIRL TELEGRAPHIST (*dictates*). 'TO ZINOVIEV, SMOLNY, PETROGRAD . . .'

KIZAS (*picks up telephone receiver*). Kizas speaking.

GIRL TEL. 'MY TALK WITH RAVICH AND KALININ . . .'

KIZAS. The Council of People's Commissars meets at eight, as usual.

GIRL TEL. '. . . AND SHADURSKAYA'S TELEGRAM . . .'

KIZAS. No, comrade Lenin's not here yet. He'll be coming soon . . .

GIRL TEL. '. . . INCLINES ME TO THINK . . .'

KIZAS. No, Dzerzhinsky won't be at the meeting. He's been called to Petrograd. Urgently.

GIRL TEL. '. . . THAT NINE-TENTHS OF SENIOR GOVERNMENT OFFICIALS IN PETROGRAD . . .'

KIZAS. What – you don't know?

GIRL TEL. '. . . SIT ON THEIR BOTTOMS AND DO NOTHING . . .'

KIZAS. Moisei Solomonovich Uritsky was shot dead in Petrograd this morning.

GIRL TEL. '. . . ADVISE YOU TRANSFER DOZENS . . .'

KIZAS. He had just arrived and was walking towards the lift – and there were several shots . . .

GIRL TEL. '. . . IF NOT HUNDREDS OF THE BEST OF THEM . . .'

KIZAS. Yes, he's been arrested.

GIRL TEL. '. . . TO CARRY OUT A PHYSICAL CHECK OF ALL PUBLIC TRANSPORT . . .'

KIZAS. I don't know, I don't know.

GIRL TEL. '. . . OTHERWISE WE ARE LOST.'

KIZAS. Very good, I will . . .

GIRL TEL. '. . . SIGNED: LENIN.'

GIRL (to KIZAS). Why on the window-ledge?

KIZAS. By the end of a meeting the tobacco-smoke's so thick, you can cut it with a knife. So comrade Lenin goes over to the window-ledge and chairs the meeting from there. Put these ashtrays over there, in front of Yenukidze and Petrovsky – they're the heaviest smokers.

GIRL. But suppose they don't sit there?

KIZAS. They will. Everyone has their place. Yenukidze and Petrovsky moved over here not long ago. They changed places with Chicherin and Krestinsky, because they were always talking during meetings and got a ticking-off from comrade Lenin – so they moved further away from him. Stalin sits here, he smokes like a chimney too, but you needn't put an ashtray in front of his place: he's at Tsaritsyn, and Pokrovsky doesn't smoke. Give some more paper to Tsurupa – here. Trotsky's away at the front, and Sklyansky always brings his own notepad. Bukharin and Rykov won't be here either; they've gone to a meeting at Serpukhov. Put out three pencils for Lunacharsky. That's it.

GIRL. I've brought a pot of glue, too.

KIZAS. That's for comrade Lenin. He calls it 'the gum-arabic with a spout', so if he asks for it, don't make a mistake.

GIRL. Oh, I made an awful mistake on Monday. He came out of his office at about midnight and said: 'Get me the board members of the Commissariat of Food'. I started ringing round and getting them all out of bed. Ten minutes later he came out again, terribly angry: 'Where's that list of the members of the board?' I realised what he'd meant and explained that I'd misunderstood him . . .

KIZAS. What did he say?

GIRL. He was embarrassed at first and he apologised for not expressing himself clearly. Then he and I sat down at the telephone together, rang them all up again and told them not to come . . .

KIZAS. Did you manage to catch them in time?

GIRL. Five of them came. Comrade Lenin didn't go to bed but

waited for all of them and apologised . . . Here comes Chicherin.

Enter CHICHERIN.

CHICHERIN. Good evening, comrades.

KIZAS. Good evening, Georgy Vasilych.

GIRL. Good evening.

CHICHERIN *sits down in his place and is immediately absorbed in studying his papers.*

KIZAS. Right . . . I think that's everything . . . Now there's another job for you: take this folder, go to the teletype, relieve the girl who's there and dictate comrade Lenin's telegrams. If I need you, I'll call you.

GIRL. Very good. (*Takes folder of telegrams and exits.*)

CHICHERIN (*to* KIZAS). Anna Petrovna, is Vladimir Ilyich in his office?

KIZAS. No, he's out at a meeting . . .

CHICHERIN (*recollecting*). Oh yes, of course – today's Friday . . .

GIRL TEL (*dictates*). 'TO ZINOVIEV, SMOLNY, PETROGRAD. JUST HEARD THAT DISTRICT SOVIET HAS EVICTED VERA IVANOVNA ZASULICH AND OTHER LEADING REVOLUTIONARIES FROM HOUSE OF WRITERS. THIS IS DISGRACEFUL. CAN IT BE TRUE? SIGNED: LENIN.'

GIRL *appears at the telegraph machine.*

Exit GIRL TELEGRAPHIST.

GIRL (*to* TELEGRAPHIST). Good evening. Let's start.

TELEGRAPHIST. Is there much?

GIRL (*shows him contents of folder*). Yes, a lot.

TELEGRAPHIST. Couple of hours'-worth. Off you go . . .

YENUKIDZE *enters the council-room, followed by* STEKLOV.

YENUKIDZE. Good evening, Georgy Vasilych!

CHICHERIN (*to* YENUKIDZE). Ah, so you're still in the land of the living! (*To* STEKLOV.) Good evening, Yury Mikhailych. You managed to get back here all right?

STEKLOV. With difficulty. What's on the agenda today? (*Reads.*) Yes, I see . . .

KIZAS. Your question is number eighteen – about the bourgeois press in Petrograd . . .

YENUKIDZE (*reads*). 'Report by comrade Steklov, editor of *Izvestiya*.'

STEKLOV. Yes, so I see . . .

YENUKIDZE (*to* CHICHERIN). Georgy Vasilych, what's been going on here this past week? I met Shlyapnikov and Semashko this morning – they were walking arm in arm!

CHICHERIN (*smiling*). Of course!

YENUKIDZE. But last week they were at daggers drawn! Talk about civil war!

CHICHERIN. They fought it out in the Sovnarkom the day before yesterday. Shlyapnikov has the medical insurance scheme, but Semashko wanted to have it in *his* department. As soon as they'd read the agenda, up got Semashko: supplementary item, please! Then Shlyapnikov asked for a rider to the supplementary. Semashko again: protest against that rider! So Vladimir Ilyich lost his temper and proposed a motion: the pair should be locked in his office and not let out on any pretext until they'd settled their differences. Passed unanimously, with two abstentions: comrade Semashko and comrade Shlyapnikov. They were solemnly led out, and an hour later they started hammering on the door – a *de facto* agreement had been reached.

YENUKIDZE (*laughs*). That's the way to do it! I wonder why they can't do the same thing to our two military strategists – Trotsky and Stalin?

CHICHERIN. Hopeless. Those two both suffer from the same defect – you'd never get them to sit down together and make peace. And supposing this local war between them threatens to turn into a national disaster?

YENUKIDZE. Sverdlov bears the brunt of it. He spends his whole time trying to keep the peace between them.

CHICHERIN. There was a clever American who wasn't so far wrong when he said 'Vanity is a bottomless pit, you can pour all the Great Lakes into it – but it will never be filled.'

Enter PETROVSKY, KRESTINSKY, NOGIN *and* STUCHKA, *followed a few moments later by* TSURUPA, POKROVSKY *and* LUNACHARSKY. *Noisy greetings all round.*

POKROVSKY (*to* STEKLOV). How are things in Petrograd?

STEKLOV. More or less calm.

NOGIN. Have you heard about Uritsky?

STEKLOV. Yes, I have . . .

GIRL (*dictates*). 'TO ANISIMOV, ASTRAKHAN. AM STILL NOT CLEAR ABOUT SITUATION IN BAKU. WHO IS IN POWER? . . .'

STEKLOV. I was with him only yesterday . . .

GIRL. '. . . WHERE IS SHAUMYAN? ASK STALIN AND THEN ACT AS CIRCUMSTANCES DICTATE . . .'

STEKLOV. He was so excited, full of plans . . .

GIRL. '. . . I TRUST SHAUMYAN COMPLETELY. IMPOSSIBLE SORT OUT SITUATION FROM HERE AND RAPID HELP IMPRACTICABLE. SIGNED: LENIN.'

STEKLOV. Still, on the whole they're coping with the situation there.

YENUKIDZE. Can anyone explain to me why the hell Zinoviev isn't sending us workers from Petrograd? We needed eight thousand to go to the front – and he sent us two thousand. We asked for fifteen hundred for food-requisitioning squads – he sent a thousand. It's sheer sabotage! And he's not the only one – almost the whole Petrograd Soviet is the same. And Uritsky agreed with me . . .

PETROVSKY. The old man sent them a furious telegram. He told them straight out: by delaying the mobilisation of Petrograd workers, *you* will be responsible if our entire cause is defeated.

STEKLOV. I talked to them about it. It's not just obstinacy on their part. It's the general situation.

KRESTINSKY. What situation?

STEKLOV. They're afraid of dispersing the Petrograd proletariat piecemeal and so destroying it.

NOGIN. So what's new?

LUNACHARSKY. It's one of the tragic contradictions of all revolutions, not only ours. Who prepared the revolution under the conditions of Tsarist rule? Who brought millions of people to the point of rebellion? A comparatively thin stratum of progressive, politically educated workers plus the revolutionary intelligentsia. Who are the first to go and defend that revolution once it is threatened? The same people. Who are the first to be killed? They are. Uritsky, for example . . .

STEKLOV. But who will take their place? That's the real question.

PETROVSKY. All right, but what does Petrograd propose to do?

POKROVSKY. They want to keep their best people there in case something happens tomorrow – it's quite simple.

PETROVSKY. Forgive me, Mikhail Nikolayich, but the fate of the revolution is being decided *today*. If the worst happens, because the Petrograd workers weren't at the front when they were needed, what use will they be to anyone *tomorrow*? There won't *be* a workers' state any more. It's a stupidly short-sighted policy.

LUNACHARSKY. But look, Grigory Ivanych, you can't argue in that sort of language either: 'victory at any price.' What price?

PETROVSKY. But I'm not arguing in those terms. I'm just as interested as you are in what will happen tomorrow. But I do know one thing: when the Czechoslovaks who've joined the Whites start to advance and we don't have the two divisions needed to stop them, while the Petrograd workers are sitting there and dying of hunger . . .

STUCHKA. But Grigory Ivanych – have you thought of who'll take their place if they go?

PETROVSKY. But for each day of fighting, ten more will appear in place of each one who went . . .

YENUKIDZE. And each day will carry off another ten – by starvation.

LUNACHARSKY. Don't you see that all the vermin we chased out of the door yesterday are going to crawl back in through the window today, either with Party membership cards in their pockets, or at the very least with red rosettes in their buttonholes? Don't you realise that in an overwhelmingly peasant country like Russia, the danger of our being swamped by the petty bourgeoisie is a very real one?

PETROVSKY. Yes, I do realise it. But do you agree with the people in Petrograd?

LUNACHARSKY. No. I simply appreciate their anxiety.

TSURUPA. We all do, but even so . . .

PETROVSKY. Of course, it's a very complex problem . . .

GIRL (*dictates*). 'TO AVERIN, COPY TO BUBNOV, YEKATERINOSLAVL. YOU MUST PRESS YOUR HARDEST FOR MOBILISATION OF WORKERS IN YEKATERINOSLAVL. YOU HAVE NOT BEEN SUFFICIENTLY ENERGETIC SO FAR. WIRE ME URGENTLY DESCRIBING WHAT MEASURES YOU HAVE TAKEN. NOTIFY ME ACTUAL RESULTS. SIGNED: LENIN.'

PETROVSKY (*continues*). I've been driving round several districts in Moscow and having a good look. It's amazing how being given an official position spoils some people. Make someone head of a sub-section and he thinks he's God Almighty. He only needs to take a five-minute walk round the corner – but no, it's beneath his dignity: he has to take a cab. He's rude and arrogant to members of the public. *We* learned what's what in prison, in Siberia, from being whipped by Cossaks . . . But *these* people . . . Take Tsurupa – he's People's Commissar for Food. Last week he fainted from hunger. Uritsky was going to write an article about it.

STEKLOV. Yes, Uritsky . . . I simply can't get it into my head that he's dead.

TSURUPA. At a meeting last Friday, I think it was, someone asked Lenin not to give Communist Party members any special privileges in the way of food and so on, otherwise crooks and black-marketeers would start worming their way into the party.

STUCHKA. Right now Party members only have one privilege – the right to be the first to die.

YENUKIDZE (*to* PETROVSKY). All right, but who are we going to get to do all that essential, routine office-work? Party members? Workers? Where will we find them? And who will let me have them if I do find them? We can't take all the best men out of the front line. The jobs can't be done by illiterates. So inevitably petty-bourgeois riff-raff get them. What else can we do?

KRESTINSKY. But don't you see the danger of that? Our new 'People's Commissariats' are still staffed by the same idle pen-pushers left over from the old days. They ring each other up, tell each other where the cushy jobs are, recommend their chums . . . And so it goes on, a self-perpetuating network . . .

YENUKIDZE. Let me tell you, my dear Krestinsky . . .

PETROVSKY. Krestinsky's right.

STUCHKA. The Party needs ways to defend itself against these people. One way is Lenin's suggestion of only electing delegates to the Party conference from people who were in the Party before the revolution.

KRESTINSKY (*to* KIZAS). By the way, Anna Petrovna, where is he?

KIZAS. At a meeting. He promised to be here by eight. There's half an hour yet.

GIRL. 'TO CHEKA HEADQUARTERS, KURSK. COPY TO PROVINCIAL EXECUTIVE COMMITTEE. ARREST KOGAN . . .'

Telephone rings.

GIRL. '. . . MEMBER OF KURSK CENTRAL PURCHASING AGENCY BECAUSE HE WOULDN'T HELP 120 STARVING WORKERS FROM MOSCOW AND SENT THEM AWAY EMPTY-HANDED . . .'

KIZAS. Comrade Nogin, it's for you.

NOGIN. Thank you.

YENUKIDZE (*to* TSURUPA). By the way, Tsurupa, who was that creep of a pen-pusher we sent to Kursk?

TSURUPA (*reluctantly*). Kogan.

YENUKIDZE. D'you know what he did there? There was an awful scene when Vladimir Ilyich found out. I haven't seen him like that for a long time. I wouldn't be surprised if he raises the matter in the Sovnarkom.

TSURUPA. I've prepared a report on the case.

YENUKIDZE. You don't think he'll be satisfied with a report, do you? Don't you believe it. What will you say to him when he goes for you?

TSURUPA. I'll say that Kogan is a blockhead and he should be expelled from the Party for stupidity.

YENUKIDZE. But my dear fellow – they don't expel people for *that*! Unfortunately!

STEKLOV. Oh yes they do! Marx wrote somewhere that a man called Baecker was expelled from the First International, on the grounds that he was 'a hopeless idiot'.

YENUKIDZE. Vladimir Ilyich won't be satisfied with that either.

It was Tsurupa and I who sent that idiot to Kursk. Ah well, we shall have to take what's coming to us . . .

STUCHKA (*to* KRESTINSKY). By the way, Krestinsky, talking of idiots – tell me, what happened about the case of Persikova?

KRESTINSKY. What case was that?

PETROVSKY. Oh, you remember – a girl from Tsaritsyn, Valya Persikova, found a picture of Lenin in some brochure and she took a pen, made his beard bigger and drew a moustache and a pair of glasses on his face.

KRESTINSKY. Yes, now I remember.

LUNACHARSKY. And what happened?

PETROVSKY. The Tsaritsyn Cheka saw this as a counter-revolutionary plot and put the girl in prison, but some Red Army soldier sent us a telegram asking for her to be released.

KRESTINSKY. Vladimir Ilyich laughed – said it was ridiculous.

GIRL (*dictates*). 'TO HEAD OF CHEKA, TSARITSYN. NO ONE SHOULD BE ARRESTED FOR DEFACING A PICTURE. RELEASE VALENTINA PERSIKOVA IMMEDIATELY. SIGNED: LENIN, CHAIRMAN, SOVNARKOM.'

POKROVSKY (*to* STEKLOV). By the way, I quite forgot to ask you: what news of Gorky? Did you have any success in making peace with him?

STEKLOV. No. Gorky's in a strange mood. He's restless, swings from one extreme to another . . . One moment he defends us and shouts: 'Let no one dare touch Lenin' – his Bolshevik past still shows through, you see – then at the next moment he's accusing him of every sin in the book . . . One moment he's cursing bourgeois culture, the next he's howling at us to save it . . . one moment he's stirring up discord in the Party, the next he's calling on it to show unity, and so on . . . It's a sad sight, I'm afraid . . .

CHICHERIN. He hasn't changed . . . He's been like this for the past eighteen months. A pity.

YENUKIDZE. But what does this 'Stormy Petrel' of ours actually *want*?

POKROVSKY. He wants to prove that Russia lacks the necessary pre-conditions for the creation of socialism and that we are nothing but a gang of usurping crooks.

YENUKIDZE (*explodes*). I see – we're uncivilised, we're illiterate, yet we have the effrontery to want socialism! We're obviously getting ideas above our station. (*To* LUNACHARSKY.) Tell me, Anatoly Vasilych, you always defend him – why can't we first take power, as Vladimir Ilyich said, and *then* use it to give the people culture? Why not, I ask you?

LUNACHARSKY. Ask Gorky.

YENUKIDZE. Our people in Petrograd offered to have a public debate with him about this, but he wouldn't condescend to go.

STUCHKA. Abel, you really can't talk about Gorky in that tone of voice. It's a tragedy, but he is a great writer, who is – or was – fundamentally on our side, on the side of the working class.

LUNACHARSKY (*to* YENUKIDZE). Vladimir Ilyich was closer to him than any of us, and he would express his feelings rather differently, despite the pain that the break with Gorky caused him.

YENUKIDZE. When Ilyich breaks with someone politically, he breaks with them personally!

LUNACHARSKY. But he never descends to vulgar abuse.

YENUKIDZE. I don't know what you call abuse. I agree with the people who say about Gorky that the revolution can neither forget nor bury its dead. It's time he was consigned to the archives.

POKROVSKY. You know, Abel, it's worth fighting to bring Gorky back into the fold, otherwise, I'm sorry, but we may throw overboard most of the great values that he represents.

YENUKIDZE. Who do you propose fighting?

LUNACHARSKY. Gorky himself, chiefly.

POKROVSKY. And the people around him – the very worst elements of the bourgeois intelligentsia.

CHICHERIN. The same sort of people, Abel, who were furious at the persecution of Tolstoy and the banning of Korolenko yet were completely indifferent to the fact that the government behaved in such a shifty, hole-and-corner way when they allowed Russia to be dragged into the war.

LUNACHARSKY. And what was so disgusting about their so-called 'humanitarianism' was that any limitation of the freedom of the individual produced a howl of protest, but the persecution and destruction of *millions* of human beings evoked nothing but their tacit complicity.

STUCHKA. No, you're wrong, you know – in all fairness it must be said that Gorky is sickened by the company of people like that poisonous Menshevik Sukhanov, but *they* hang on to *him* like limpets . . . It's like the old joke – the soldier shouts: 'I've caught a Turk and I'm holding him prisoner!' – 'Bring him here, then!' – 'But he won't go!' – 'Then come here yourself!' – 'He won't let me!'

YENUKIDZE. To be honest, of course, it's a terrible pity about Gorky . . .

STUCHKA. I'm sure he'll come back, but it'll need something to make that happen . . . Time, perhaps?

Pause.

Enter KOLLONTAI.

KOLLONTAI. Good evening, everyone. I'm not late, am I?

KRESTINSKY. Vladimir Ilyich isn't here yet.

LUNACHARSKY. Were you out speaking today?

KOLLONTAI. Yes, at the Corn Exchange. With Vladimir Ilyich. Then he went on to another meeting.

TSURUPA. Was it heavy going, Alexandra Mikhailovna?

KOLLONTAI. Very. There was only one question – bread. Ilyich didn't promise anything; he told them the truth.

Enter VINOKUROV.

YENUKIDZE. Ah, here's Vinokurov.

VINOKUROV. Good evening. I've just been on the line to Petrograd. Uritsky's funeral is tomorrow. The mood in the factories is nervous and volatile. The workers are angry and want revenge. The Communist Party is trying to persuade them not to come out on to the streets, but the possibility of a riot can't be ruled out. Dzerzhinsky has already started to interrogate the murderer.

PETROVSKY. They shouldn't allow demonstrations, but there must be a thorough investigation and a show-trial.

KRESTINSKY. It's so awful about Uritsky . . . Do you remember his favourite lines from Goethe's *'Über allen Gipfeln'*:

'. . . The birds sing no more;
Wait awhile; soon
Shalt thou also find peace.'

GIRL (*dictates*). 'TO ZINOVIEV, SMOLNY, PETROGRAD . . .'

STUCHKA (*to* KIZAS). Anna Petrovna, please ring that factory and ask them if the meeting has finished.

KIZAS. Yes, of course.

GIRL. '. . . A FEMALE RELATIVE OF A FORMER CENTRAL COMMITTEE MEMBER OF THE CONSTITUTIONAL DEMOCRATS' PARTY . . .'

KIZAS (*into telephone receiver*). 60-212, please . . .

GIRL. '. . . AND FORMER BARRISTER VIKTOR IVANOVICH DOBROVOLSKY . . .'

KIZAS. Hello. Give me the factory committee of the Bolshevik Party, please . . .

GIRL. '. . . HER HUSBAND WORKS FOR THE SOVIET GOVERNMENT . . .'

KIZAS. . . . Tell me, comrade, has the meeting ended yet?

GIRL. '. . . HAS APPROACHED ME ASKING FOR HIS RELEASE . . .'

KIZAS. Thank you very much. (*Replaces receiver; to* STUCHKA.) The meeting has just finished, so Vladimir Ilyich will be here shortly.

GIRL. '. . . ON THE FOLLOWING GROUNDS: "HE GAVE UP POLITICAL ACTIVITY IN 1907. HE IS OLD AND ILL AND NOT LONG BEFORE HIS ARREST HE SUFFERED A BAD ATTACK OF PNEUMONIA . . .'

Enter ZAGORSKY.

ZAGORSKY. Good evening, comrade commissars!

GIRL. '. . . AND A ONCE HEALTHY FIFTY-YEAR-OLD HAS BECOME A MISERABLE, SICKLY OLD MAN. HIS FAMILY, WHICH WAS SUPPORTED ENTIRELY BY HIS EARNINGS, IS POVERTY-STRICKEN . . ."

ZAGORSKY (*noticing how gloomy and depressed everyone is, to* KOLLONTAI). Why are you all looking so miserable?

KOLLONTAI. Uritsky . . .

GIRL. '. . . PLEASE CONSIDER POSSIBILITY OF RELEASING HIM ON BAIL. GIVE ME YOUR ANSWER AND REACTION OF CHEKA. GREETINGS! LENIN.'

KOLLONTAI (*to* ZAGORSKY). Tell us one of your funny stories. We must cheer them up a bit!

ZAGORSKY. I'm afraid I'm not really on top form either . . . Well, all right – I'll try . . . (*Loudly.*) Comrades, tell me – what's the matter with Lunacharsky and Pokrovsky today? They look miserable . . .

LUNACHARSKY (*to* POKROVSKY). Here we go!

POKROVSKY. The only thing we can do is to play along . . .

ZAGORSKY. But then I know what the trouble is. Imagine, comrades, what a burden we've thrown on the shoulders of the Commissariat of Education and Culture – monumental propaganda! Just think: it's their job to beautify Moscow and Petrograd with statues and busts. Where will they get the materials? And the talent? Well, let's suppose they can manage that. But how to tell the difference between the head of Sophia Perovskaya and the pyramid of Cheops – now *that* is much more difficult.

KOLLONTAI. That isn't a monument, comrades, it's a monstrosity! A disgrace! It should be removed at once!

LUNACHARSKY. The fact is that the monument was executed in the Cubist manner, and that assumes . . .

ZAGORSKY. What does it assume?

Realising that he has risen to the bait, LUNACHARSKY *merely gestures dismissively.*

ZAGORSKY. I was driving along the Tverskaya just now, and I saw an enormous pile of wood. I'm told it's a monument to Emelyan Pugachov . . .

VINOKUROV. It's next winter's supply of firewood for the Commissariat of Health . . .

ZAGORSKY. You don't say?! I must say it damn well looks like it! You shouldn't laugh, comrades! It's very unkind to put all this responsibility on Pokrovsky and Lunacharsky – and then laugh at them. You're laughing now, comrade Tsurupa, but what are your problems with the grain supply compared with the problem of a bust of Radishchev? Just imagine – the comrades have carved a bust and they've actually achieved a likeness of the great man. D'you realise? A likeness! They put him on his pedestal, they come along next morning – and he's gone! Someone's pinched him! Who, one wonders? According to unconfirmed information, it was the girls from a hat factory, who thought he was just what they needed as a dummy for testing hats for size. Of course, they could always have another bust made, but the People's Commissar and his deputy are afraid the sculptor may not produce a good likeness the second time. It was pure luck the first time . . . No, you shouldn't laugh, comrades . . . Futurism is an important artistic phenomenon, and we should study it. As for the fact that they make Karl Marx in his old age look like Friedrich Engels as a young man . . .

LUNACHARSKY (*growing agitated*). You don't understand anything at all about Futurism! It's a serious matter, which needs careful attention . . .

POKROVSKY (*to* LUNACHARSKY). Calm down, calm down . . .

ZAGORSKY. I confess my sin, comrades. I *don't* understand it. If I did, I'd know what to do about this note I received from comrade Lenin . . . (*Produces a note from his pocket, reads.*) 'Vladimir Mikhailych! Today I heard Vinogradov's report on busts and monuments, and I was extremely disturbed: for months nothing has been done; not a single bust has been put up; the disappearance of the best of Radishchev is a farce. There is no bust of Marx for the streets yet, and nothing is being done about the propaganda inscriptions needed for various buildings. The Moscow City Soviet and the People's Commissariat of Education are obviously sabotaging these projects, each trying to push the responsibility on to the other while doing their best to wriggle out of it themselves. Draft an article for *Pravda* which will nail the saboteurs and idlers, and I suggest the men in charge of those two organisations, Kamenev and Lunacharsky, should be strung up – and you can put that into the article too!'

LUNACHARSKY. After Vladimir Ilyich had written that note, he and I went to the exhibition of designs for those busts and statues, and the question was settled.

ZAGORSKY. Was it really? Don't keep us in suspense, Anatoly Vasilych – tell us what happened.

LUNACHARSKY (*enthusiastically*). As you know, we took down the statue of Alexander III that stood in front of the church of Christ the Saviour, so the question arose of what to put in its place. We organised an exhibition of designs. Quite a lot of artists, of various persuasions, submitted entries. Vladimir Ilyich and I went to look at the exhibition, on the day before he . . .

ZAGORSKY. Yes, yes, I know . . .

LUNACHARSKY (*looks at* ZAGORSKY, *laughs*). No – you tell it, I won't spoil your fun!

ALL. Tell it, Vladimir Mikhailych! . . . Go on, tell it! . . . Please! . . . Tell it!

ZAGORSKY. No, it has to be performed. Where's Tsurupa? Alexander Dmitrych – you play Lenin. He only spoke two sentences. (*Whispers to* TSURUPA.) Got it? And I'll play Lunacharsky. (*To* LUNACHARSKY.) Or perhaps you'd like to play yourself, Anatoly Vasilych?

LUNACHARSKY. No, no, you can do it better!

ZAGORSKY. Thank you for your confidence . . . So, comrades, we arrived at the exhibition. There were forty entries – yes, that many! Just watch the expression on Tsurupa's face and you'll understand everything. We started our tour of inspection with a monument to the World Proletariat, represented by something in the shape of a triangle . . . Alexander Dmitrych, there should be a look in your eyes of profound despair . . . That's it – like that . . .

ZAGORSKY *and* TSURUPA *'inspect' an imaginary exhibition. Each one of the others adopts an attitude representing an 'exhibit'.* TSURUPA *acts the part of* LENIN *with great tact and affection. The 'exhibits', which he examines with care, reduce him to a state of horror.*

ZAGORSKY. Did you like *this* monument, Vladimir Ilyich?

TSURUPA (*playing* 'LENIN', *with a deep sigh*). I'm afraid I don't understand anything about modern art. Ask Lunacharsky . . .

ZAGORSKY. But, comrades, I must say that to Lunacharsky's credit he didn't like any of this junk either. (*Playing* 'LUNACHARSKY'.) None of this is good enough, Vladimir Ilyich.

TSURUPA (*playing* 'LENIN', *delighted*). I'm so glad you think so. What a relief! Otherwise, I must admit, I thought you were going to put up some Futurist thing that looked like a scarecrow. Then what would happen? We'd simply have to take it down again.

ZAGORSKY. Thus ended Ilyich's disastrous introduction to Futurism.

LUNACHARSKY. Unlike some people, however – naming no names – Vladimir Ilyich does not make his personal aesthetic likes and dislikes into laws to which *everyone* has to conform!

From the street comes the screech of a car braking sharply.

PETROVSKY. He's arrived. Judging by the speed the car must have been going, he knew he was late.

NOGIN. As far as I know, this is the first time in history that Vladimir Ilyich has ever been late for a meeting of the Sovnarkom.

KOLLONTAI. So why not apply his own rule to *him*? He must pay his fine for being late!

ALL. Quite right! . . . Hear, hear! . . . Yes, he should! . . .

TSURUPA. He'll say: 'Comrades, I'm fifteen minutes late, do please forgive me. The fact is . . .

ALL. No, we won't forgive you! . . . No exceptions to the rule! . . . Pay your fine, Ilyich! . . . Fine him!

TSURUPA (*continues to play* 'LENIN', *laughs*). Oh, all right! . . . There you are! (*Takes out money and puts it on the table.*)

The door is flung open. ULYANOVA, LENIN's *sister, is standing on the threshold.*

ULYANOVA. Comrades! Vladimir Ilyich is . . . Someone shot at him . . . They've just brought him back . . . Quick! Get a doctor! (*Exit*).

All freeze in horror.

TELEGRAPHIST (*to* GIRL). Carry on dictating!

GIRL (*in tears*). I can't go on . . .

VINOKUROV (*rushes out after* ULYANOVA). I'm a doctor, I still remember something about gunshot wounds from my army days . . .

All the COMMISSARS *crowd out of the room and across the corridor to* LENIN's *room.*

TELEGRAPHIST. Go on, I tell you! Dictate!

GIRL (*pulling herself together, dictates*). 'TO PROVINCIAL EXECUTIVE COMMITTEE, TAMBOV. COPY TO DISTRICT COMMITTEE, BORISOGLEBSK. RECEIVED COMPLAINT FROM IVAN BOGDANOV ABOUT ARREST OF HIS SON VLADIMIR, AGED SEVENTEEN . . .'

102 THE BOLSHEVIKS

> GILL, LENIN's *personal driver, runs out of the room where* LENIN *is lying and runs to the telephone which is on a small table in the corridor. The* COMMISSARS *mill about in the corridor; some go into* LENIN's *room, others stay outside.*

GILL (*into the telephone*). Get me Bonch-Bruyevich – emergency . . . Vladimir Dmitrych? Quick! Something terrible's happened! Vladimir Ilyich is wounded! . . . On the bed, in his flat . . .

VINOKUROV *runs out of* LENIN's *room.*

VINOKUROV. We need bandages and iodine . . . (*Returns to* LENIN's *room.*)

GILL (*into the telephone*). Exchange, get me a chemist's shop.

ULYANOVA. We haven't any bandages.

GILL (*into the telephone*). A chemist's shop! Any chemist!

ULYANOVA. We haven't any bandages!!

Enter KIZAS.

GILL. We could tear up a shirt for bandages, or use a sheet . . . (*Into the telephone.*) Is that the chemist's?

ULYANOVA. Yes, of course . . . Here's one of Volodya's shirts . . . Please, comrade Gill, tear it up into bandages, you obviously know how.

GILL tears the shirt into strips.

GIRL (*continues to dictate*). '. . . WHO IS ILL WITH BRONCHITIS . . .'

ULYANOVA (*to* KIZAS). Ring Velichkina and Krestinsky's wife – they're both doctors, they'll have bandages . . .

KIZAS. Right. (*Runs to the telephone.*)

GIRL. '. . . CHECK THE PRISONER'S ILLNESS, YOUTH, INEXPERIENCE. INVESTIGATE WHETHER THE REAL SABOTEURS WERE THE THIRTY EMPLOYEES OF THE LOCAL AUTHORITY WHO REFUSED TO DO THE WORK AND BLAMED IT ON BOGDANOV. WIRE RESULTS OF YOUR INVESTIGATION. SIGNED: LENIN, CHAIRMAN, SOVNARKOM.'

VINOKUROV (*in the doorway*). There's a bullet somewhere around the heart . . . Hurry those doctors up, I've done what I can but I've got nothing to hand. Boil some water. And tell those doctors to hurry!

NOGIN *goes up to the door into* LENIN's *room.*

VINOKUROV (*to* NOGIN). No, don't go in there, he's unconscious . . . He asked me to take off his collar and tie, then he lost consciousness . . .

ULYANOVA. What does it mean? What can we do?

BONCH-BRUYEVICH *runs in, carrying bandages and bottles of iodine. He gives them all to* GILL, *who goes into* LENIN's *room and shuts the door behind him.*

KRESTINSKY (*to* BONCH-BRUYEVICH). Vladimir Dmitrych, my dear fellow, in here – quickly.

BONCH-B. (*to* ULYANOVA). Be brave, Maria Ilinichna! Above all, we must keep calm. We must give all our attention to him. (*To* KIZAS.) Don't cry, it only upsets people more. (*Goes into* LENIN's *room.*)

KIZAS. I'll try not to . . . (*Sobs.*)

GIRL (*dictates*). 'TO CHAIRMAN, PETROGRAD SOVIET, SMOLNY, PETROGRAD. IS IT TRUE YOU HAVE ARRESTED ROPP, CATHOLIC ARCHBISHOP OF MOGILEV? PLEASE NOTIFY ME ON WHAT CONDITIONS HE MAY BE RELEASED. THE POPE HAS APPEALED TO ME. SIGNED: LENIN.'

ZAGORSKY. Sverdlov is addressing a meeting, someone's been sent to fetch him . . .

ULYANOVA (*weeping*). I sensed it . . . I knew it would happen . . . I purposely didn't go to work. Zagorsky rang up and asked him not to go. I asked Bukharin to have lunch with us and persuade him not to make that speech at the factory. Bukharin came, we all had lunch together, he spent a whole hour trying to persuade him not to go. Volodya kept joking about it and laughing, but in the end he gave his word that he wouldn't go . . . Bukharin was completely calm when he left and I stopped feeling nervous – but then at six o'clock Volodya came into the room wearing his overcoat, laughing, and said he was going after all. I begged to be allowed to go with him, but he wouldn't take me . . . It was some woman . . . she fired three shots.

VINOKUROV (*appearing in the doorway*). Where are those doctors? For God's sake hurry them up! (*Exit.*)

Enter BONCH-BRUYEVICH, *who runs to the telephone.*

BONCH-B. (*snatches the receiver*). One four, please . . . Lyolya, where's Mama? . . . She's on her way here? . . . Good . . . My wife will be here soon. (*Depresses the receiver-rest and releases it. Into the telephone.*) Two eight, please . . . Comrade Malkov? . . . Bonch-Bruyevich speaking. Put all the Kremlin sentries and all other Red Army personnel on a state of full alert. Double the men in every guard-post. Keep a round-the-clock watch on all gates, on the wall, and at the entrances to the Sovnarkom and the Central Executive Committee building. Vladimir Ilyich has been shot and wounded.

GILL *comes out of* LENIN's *room.*

GILL (*to the group of People's Commissars*). When we brought him here, we wanted to carry him upstairs, but he wouldn't have it . . . He walked up all three flights, and blood was seeping from his wounds all the time . . . He got as far as here, then he collapsed in that chair.

ULYANOVA. He saw me and started joking about it: 'It's nothing special, they just grazed my arm – luckily it was the left one. They must have known I was one of the scribbling tribe . . .' (*Weeps.*)

Enter VELICHKINA, *carrying her doctor's bag.*

STEKLOV. Velichkina!

VINOKUROV (*appearing in the doorway*). He's unconscious.

VELICHKINA. Has he been unconscious for long?

VINOKUROV. Yes.

VELICHKINA *and* VINOKUROV *go into* LENIN's *room.*

GIRL (*dictates*). 'TO DISTRICT EXECUTIVE COMMITTEE, YELETS. INVESTIGATE IMMEDIATELY INCIDENT ON YELETS STATION WHEN SACKS OF RYE WERE TAKEN AWAY FROM GORYACHOV AND HIS COMRADES . . .'

Telephone rings.

BONCH-B. (*picks up the receiver*). Yes . . . Comrade Sverdlov? . . . The situation's serious, Yakov Mikhailych. He only regains consciousness for literally seconds at a time. He's been asking for you . . . Yes, I've sent for them . . . right, I'll do it . . .

VELICHKINA *comes out of* LENIN's *room.*

GIRL (*dictates*). '. . . WERE THEY GIVEN RECEIPTS, WAS IT TAKEN LEGALLY, SHOULDN'T THEY GIVE BACK SOME OR ALL OF IT? WIRE REPLY. SIGNED: LENIN, CHAIRMAN, SOVNARKOM.'

VELICHKINA. I'm afraid of a collapse. I've given him morphine. Have the surgeons been sent for?

PETROVSKY. Mintz.

VELICHKINA. Mintz – that's good. We won't do anything more until the surgeons arrive. We'll just keep him going as best we can and undress him as far as possible.

In LENIN's room a bottle falls and breaks; everyone jumps at the noise.

VELICHKINA. Don't worry, it's only a bottle of ammonia. We'll need a cloth to mop it up.

Exit LUNACHARSKY, to find a cloth.

GIRL (*dictates*). 'TO BOLDYRYOV, EXECUTIVE COMMITTEE, ZADONSK. TAKE FIRM ACTION AGAINST THE KULAKS AND THE LEFT-S.R. SWINE WHO ARE IN CAHOOTS WITH THEM.'

ZAGORSKY. I rang him and tried to dissuade him from going . . . and look what happened . . .

Silence, except for the voice of the GIRL dictating the telegram.

GIRL. '. . . MAKE AN APPEAL TO THE POORER PEASANTS AND ORGANISE THEM . . .'

LUNACHARSKY *enters with a cloth and goes into* LENIN's *room.* ULYANOVA *comes out of the room carrying shoes, jacket, overcoat and shirt, which she takes off to the kitchen.*

VINOKUROV (*appears in the doorway, hands the blood-soaked bandages to* KIZAS). Wash these. (*Exit.*)

KIZAS. Right. (*Exit to kitchen.*)

GIRL (*dictates*). '. . . REQUEST HELP FROM YELETS. THOSE BLOOD-SUCKING KULAKS MUST BE RUTHLESSLY SUPPRESSED. WIRE REPLY. SIGNED: LENIN, CHAIRMAN, SOVNARKOM.'

LUNACHARSKY, *carrying a wet cloth, comes out of* LENIN's *room and exit to kitchen.*

VINOKUROV (*appearing in the doorway*). Comrades, please hurry those doctors up!

GILL. They've arrived! Mintz and Weisbrod!

MINTZ *and* WEISBROD *rush into the apartment. All look at them with hope. Without stopping to greet anyone, they throw off their coats as they go and quickly enter* LENIN's *room.* MINTZ *is already wearing a white coat.* WEISBROD *rolls up his shirtsleeves.*

VINOKUROV. Gunshot wounds from the rear. Severe loss of blood.

MINTZ. Morphine.

VELICHKINA. I've already done that.

MINTZ. Good.

VINOKUROV. The heart appears to be affected.

MINTZ. We shall need camphor.

VINOKUROV. We have no camphor.

MINTZ. Where's my bag? You'll find some in there.

VINOKUROV. He's still unconscious. We broke a bottle of ammonia just now, and he regained consciousness for a short while.

The two surgeons go into LENIN's *room, from whence their voices can be heard.*

VINOKUROV's *voice*. Vladimir Ilyich . . . Vladimir Ilyich . . . can you hear me?

WEISBROD's *voice*. Vladimir Ilyich! It's me, Weisbrod. Doctor Weisbrod. He's not coming round.

MINTZ's *voice*. Let's start the examination . . . I see . . . One in the arm. Where's the other? Here? . . . No . . . This is bad, very bad . . .

WEISBROD's *voice*. Where's the other one?

MINTZ's *voice*. The major vessels are intact . . . Where is it? Can you see the entry wound? Where does the wound-channel run? . . . Where is it? Where is it? Here?

WEISBROD's *voice (anxiously)*. It can't be! . . . What about the oesophagus?

MINTZ's *voice*. Yes, yes – it's here. There! Can you feel it?

WEISBROD's *voice*. Yes, here . . .

MINTZ's *voice*. Shut the door.

All move away from the door of LENIN's *room, which is closed from inside.*

GIRL (*dictates*). 'TO KNYAGININO, COPY TO ICHALKI. ANY MEASURES OF COMPULSION AIMED AT FORCING PEASANTS TO UNDERTAKE

COMMUNAL TILLING OF FIELDS ARE IMPERMISSIBLE. VIOLATION OF THIS INSTRUCTION WILL BE PUNISHED WITH FULL SEVERITY OF REVOLUTIONARY LAW. SIGNED: LENIN, CHAIRMAN, SOVNARKOM.'

VELICHKINA *comes out of* LENIN's *room.*

VELICHKINA (*distractedly*). I must have some cardboard. We need to put his arm in a splint.

LUNACHARSKY. Where's the bullet?

VELICHKINA *silently points to her throat.* BONCH-BRUYEVICH *tears the cardboard bindings off a ledger and gives it to* VELICHKINA, *who goes back into* LENIN's *room, followed by* LUNACHARSKY.

VINOKUROV *comes out of the room, the members of the Sovnarkom surround him.*

VINOKUROV. He regained consciousness and he said: 'Why did they have to torture me, why didn't they kill me at once?' and passed out again . . . Lemons. We need lemons . . . He's racked with thirst, but he can't drink. They fear the oesophagus is pierced.

VELICHKINA *comes out of the room.*

PETROVSKY. Well?

VELICHKINA (*feverishly buttoning and unbuttoning her white coat. Anxiously*). The wound is extremely dangerous . . . I would even say mortal, but there are some hopeful signs . . . The next two or three hours will be decisive . . . He found the bandaging extremely painful. (*Goes back into* LENIN's *room.*)

SVERDLOV *strides briskly into the apartment.* ULYANOVA *rushes up to him; he embraces her, silently strokes her hand, but is unable to say anything to her.*

ULYANOVA. Yakov Mikhailych, he's been asking for you.

SVERDLOV. What's the situation?

WEISBROD (*appearing in the doorway*). He's unconscious.

MINTZ (*appearing in the doorway*). I have just dressed the wounds with fresh bandages.

SVERDLOV. What's your assessment of the situation?

MINTZ. It's extremely serious. There is a deep wound in the thoracic cavity.

SVERDLOV. What can be done?

MINTZ. We need a specialist. I'm very worried about his lung. A bullet went right through it.

SVERDLOV. Dr Obukh will be here soon. He's speaking at a meeting, we're trying to find out where it is . . .

WEISBROD. Obukh – that's good. He knows Lenin's medical history better than anyone.

MINTZ. Has he treated him before?

WEISBROD. Yes.

SVERDLOV. Think, comrades – what else can be done? Whatever's possible – and impossible – will be done.

VELICHKINA (*in the doorway*). He's conscious. He heard your voice, Yakov Mikhailych, and wants you to come in . . .

SVERDLOV, MINTZ, WEISBROD *and* VELICHKINA *go into* LENIN's *room. A moment later,* MINTZ, WEISBROD *and* VELICHKINA *come out again, closing the door behind them.*

VELICHKINA. He asked us to leave them alone for a few minutes.

Silence. All stare at the white door.

GIRL (*dictates*). 'TO PROVINCIAL EXECUTIVE COMMITTEE, ASTRAKHAN. IS IT TRUE THAT PEOPLE IN ASTRAKHAN ARE ALREADY TALKING ABOUT EVACUATING THE TOWN? IF SO, YOU MUST ACT RUTHLESSLY AGAINST ANY SUCH COWARDS AND IMMEDIATELY APPOINT YOUR MOST RELIABLE MEN TO ORGANISE DEFENCE OF ASTRAKHAN AND CARRY OUT FIRM POLICY OF RESISTANCE IN CASE BRITISH FORCES ADVANCE. WIRE REPLY WITH FULL DETAILS. SIGNED: LENIN, CHAIRMAN, SOVNARKOM.'

The door into LENIN's *room is suddenly flung open.* SVERDLOV *is standing in the doorway.*

SVERDLOV. Comrades! . . . It looks bad . . .

The three DOCTORS *rush into* LENIN's *room.*

MINTZ's *voice.* Morphine! Repeat injection! At once!

VELICHKINA's *voice.* Pulse very weak.

WEISBROD's *voice.* Haemorrhage from the throat.

MINTZ's *voice.* The left pleura is full of blood. Keep him absolutely still. Cover him with a sheet.

ULYANOVA. Oh, not a sheet – that's terrible!

BONCH-B.. The windows are open – he may catch a chill. A blanket's too heavy, a sheet is light . . .

KRUPSKAYA enters the corridor from the front door. She stops and looks at GILL in silence.

KRUPSKAYA *(speaking with difficulty)*. No, no . . . Don't say anything, only tell me . . . is he alive or dead?

GILL. He's only slightly wounded! Honestly!

KRUPSKAYA, head lowered, stands in silence. SVERDLOV comes up to her.

KRUPSKAYA. What's going to happen now?

SVERDLOV. Ilyich and I have agreed on everything . . .

KRUPSKAYA *(to herself)*. Agreed on everything . . . That means it's the end . . .

ULYANOVA *(to KRUPSKAYA)*. Nadya, he's come round . . . Go in and see him . . .

KRUPSKAYA. It'll only excite him, but . . . *(Goes into LENIN's room.)*

General gloom and silence.

GIRL *(dictates)*. 'TO IVANOV-KAVKAZSKY, DETACHMENT COMMANDER, BIRYULEVO. A COMPLAINT HAS BEEN MADE AGAINST YOU THAT YOU REQUISITIONED DESK AND WRITING MATERIALS BELONGING TO THE STATIONMASTER. RETURN THEM AT ONCE AND WIRE YOUR EXPLANATIONS. COMPLY IMMEDIATELY. I DEMAND THAT ALL RAILWAY PERSONNEL BE TREATED CORRECTLY AND LOYALLY. SIGNED: LENIN, CHAIRMAN, SOVNARKOM.'

KRUPSKAYA comes out of LENIN's room.

ULYANOVA. What did he say?

KRUPSKAYA. He said: 'Is that you, Nadya? You must be tired. Better go and lie down . . .' He didn't really mean to say that – his eyes were trying to tell me something quite different . . . I'll sit down out here . . . I'll be able to see his face, but he can't see me . . . *(Picks up a chair and places it opposite the open door into LENIN's room.)* Who are those people with him?

ULYANOVA. Doctor Mintz and Doctor Weisbrod.

KRUPSKAYA. And who's that with his back to us?

ULYANOVA. Lunacharsky. He just keeps standing there and watching. I tried to make him leave the room, but he won't.

ZAGORSKY (*to* KRUPSKAYA). I spoke to him by telephone this morning and tried to persuade him not to go, but he wouldn't listen. I couldn't bring myself to insist. And now . . .

GIRL (*dictates*). 'TO BOKII, SPECIAL DEPARTMENT, SAMARA. NOTIFY ME WHETHER EVIDENCE AGAINST LEONID SERGEYEVICH VIVIEN IS SERIOUS AND WHETHER IT IS ABSOLUTELY NECESSARY TO SEND HIM TO SAMARA. AM TOLD THERE HAS BEEN A MISUNDERSTANDING. MEANWHILE AM KEEPING HIM IN MOSCOW. LUNACHARSKY HAS SPOKEN TO ME ON HIS BEHALF. SIGNED: LENIN, CHAIRMAN, SOVNARKOM.'

Shaking with grief, and seeing nothing around him, LUNACHARSKY *stumbles out of* LENIN's *room.* KOLLONTAI *puts an arm around his shoulders and helps him to sit down.*

LUNACHARSKY. 'What is there to see here, Anatoly Vasilych?' he said. 'Go and rest . . .' His eyes were trying to smile, but his forehead was quite yellow, like wax . . .

MINTZ's *voice.* Syringe!

The DOCTORS *suddenly leap into activity.*

ULYANOVA (*to* KRUPSKAYA). Nadya . . .

KRUPSKAYA. No, I'm not leaving this spot . . . Don't worry about me.

WEISBROD (*appearing in the doorway. To* SVERDLOV). Yakov Mikhailych, we need Obukh urgently.

SVERDLOV. He'll be here soon . . . two cars were sent to find him . . . they'll arrive any minute now . . .

WEISBROD (*pointing to the crowd in the corridor*). Get all these people out of here.

SVERDLOV. I understand . . . I'll be in the council-room if anything . . .

WEISBROD. All right . . . (*Goes into* LENIN's *room and shuts the door.*)

SVERDLOV. Come along, comrades . . .

The COMMISSARS *follow* SVERDLOV *into the council-room.*

GIRL (*dictates*). 'TO THE PRAESIDIUM OF THE MOSCOW SOVIET OF WORKERS AND RED ARMY DEPUTIES. DEAR COMRADES! RECEIVED YOUR DOCUMENT NO. 24,962 CONTAINING EXCERPT FROM RESOLUTION OF THE PRAESIDIUM. HONESTY OBLIGES ME TO SAY THAT THIS RESOLUTION IS SO POLITICALLY ILLITERATE AND SO STUPID THAT IT MAKES ME FEEL SICK . . .'

TELEGRAPHIST. Go on.

GIRL (*through tears*). I can't . . . I was going to the theatre the other day. I saw Chaliapin arrive, but he was immediately surrounded by a crowd of hooligans, so I crossed the street and ran for it. Next morning I told comrade Lenin about it and he scolded me: 'Why didn't you take steps to have the hooligans arrested? You have to stand up and fight for what's right – after all, you're a Party member. Ring up Chaliapin's home and find out if he's all right.' And he wouldn't calm down until I'd made enquiries. Today he heard there were some former women political prisoners lying ill in St. Catherine's Hospital, so he and Nadezhda Konstantinovna put together a parcel of food for them and I took it to the hospital. He said he'd be sending me there regularly . . .

Slowly and silently the COMMISSARS, *crushed with grief and anxiety, file back into the council-room and take their places at the table. To avoid sitting in* LENIN's *seat,* SVERDLOV, *the Deputy Chairman of the Sovnarkom, takes one of the chairs that are ranged along the wall, puts it alongside* LENIN's *place and sits down on it. No one speaks. The silence becomes unbearable.*

SVERDLOV. Comrades . . . There is no one capable of replacing Vladimir Ilyich . . . We shall not even attempt to do so . . . We will only try to do one thing: to make up, in some degree, for his absence . . . That means showing three times more calmness than usual . . . being three times more systematic and efficient . . . We have an obligation . . . to maintain the continuity of leadership. I ask you all to collect your thoughts . . . to concentrate . . . Everybody has been given a copy of the Sovnarkom's agenda for today. Any comments? Supplementaries?

Long pause.

SVERDLOV. I'm sorry, comrades . . . Right now I can't go through with it.

GIRL (*dictates*). '. . . YOU WRITE: ". . . THE PRAESIDIUM REFUSES TO ACCEPT RESPONSIBILITY . . ." THAT IS HOW CAPRICIOUS YOUNG

LADIES BEHAVE BUT NOT ADULT POLITICIANS . . . "REFUSES TO ACCEPT RESPONSIBILITY" IS BEHAVIOUR TYPICAL OF GIRLS AND IRRESPONSIBLE RUSSIAN INTELLECTUALS. FORGIVE MY FRANKNESS AND ACCEPT COMMUNIST GREETINGS FROM SOMEONE WHO HOPES THAT A SPELL IN PRISON MAY TEACH YOU THAT NO GOVERNMENT BODY MAY EVER ABDICATE ITS RESPONSIBILITIES. YOURS INDIGNANTLY, LENIN.'

NOGIN. Let's postpone the session till tomorrow. Same time, same agenda.

SVERDLOV. Yes, of course. We'll postpone it till tomorrow. But I believe there are some urgent matters that can't be put off. This shouldn't be an excuse to evade them.

TSURUPA. Yes, there is one such point. It concerns the grain supply. I realise this isn't a good moment, but you must understand the position of the Commissariat of Food. We are responsible for bread, the staple foodstuff. You have also passed a resolution making us responsible for combatting the activities of the massive illegal trade in grain by peasants from the provinces. We didn't object, and we are starting to get results. But a decree by the Moscow City Soviet has produced total disorganisation. The entire bread supply is threatened with catastrophe. We cannot allow a second's delay in dealing with it.

STEKLOV. What's the problem?

TSURUPA. The Moscow City Soviet has given permission for every inhabitant to bring half a hundredweight of foodstuffs into the city. This has led to an influx of black-marketeers and 'bagmen'. All our work has been thrown into chaos. Kamenev, as head of the Moscow Soviet, has acted arbitrarily and high-handedly. We demand that he be called to order and the decree of the Moscow Soviet be rescinded. When the right hand does one thing and the left hand does something else, it means total anarchy. Otherwise I must ask you to accept the resignation of myself and the entire Board of the Commissariat of Food.

ZAGORSKY. But how are we going to feed Moscow? You are fighting the black-marketeers? Fine! But you must give us bread too! And you're not doing it! What is the Moscow Soviet to do? People are asking it for bread – because they have long since given up hope of getting any from your Commissariat! Under the circumstances, the Moscow Soviet's decision was absolutely correct. If their 'half-a-hundredweight' policy saves Moscow from starvation but interferes with the anti-black-market campaign, then long live the black market and down with the Commissariat of Food, which is incapable of feeding the city!

TSURUPA (*restraining himself*). That is a disgraceful attitude! When the Sovnarkom reviewed the decree on bread rationing on the 26th of this month, the Moscow Soviet's action went unchallenged, thanks to the demagogic behaviour of certain of its officials – who, it now turns out, were following the example of their leader, Kamenev. Nevertheless I propose that the decision of the Moscow Soviet be annulled – not at once, but on something like the following lines: the Sovnarkom's resolution to that effect should be passed *now* and published. The resolution will indicate the date at which 'half-hundredweighting' will cease to be legal – let us say the fifteenth of September.

KRESTINSKY. But will there be any bread by the fifteenth?

TSURUPA. There should be.

YENUKIDZE. The Petrograd Soviet issued an order similar to the Moscow Soviet's decision. The guard detachments, whose job is to arrest black-marketeers, are totally confused and don't know what they are supposed to do.

ZAGORSKY. Tsurupa's remarks about demagogy carry about as much weight as his promises to feed the whole country.

TSURUPA (*explodes*). There's only one word to describe what you and Kamenev have done – sabotage!

SVERDLOV (*shouts*). Comrades!

GIRL (*dictates*). 'TO PROVINCIAL EXECUTIVE COMMITTEE, PENZA. COPY TO PROVINCIAL COMMITTEE OF COMMUNIST PARTY. INTERNAL CONFLICTS BETWEEN COMMUNISTS UTTERLY DEPLORABLE. IT WILL BE DISGRACEFUL IF THEY ARE NOT SETTLED. SET UP AN ARBITRATION COMMISSION IMMEDIATELY AND SETTLE THE DISPUTE IN TWO DAYS. SUGGEST YOU DIVIDE UP DISTRICTS BETWEEN LEADING PARTY OFFICIALS IN ORDER TO SEPARATE THOSE WHO ARE QUARRELLING. WIRE ME THE COMMISSION'S DECISION. SIGNED: LENIN.'

Long pause. TSURUPA *and* ZAGORSKY *calm themselves.*

ZAGORSKY. I apologise, Alexander Dmitrych . . . but . . . we need bread. We must find some way of getting it . . .

TSURUPA. Yes, yes, I understand, Vladimir Mikhailych . . . Forgive me for flying off the handle.

SVERDLOV *(to* TSURUPA*)*. What does Lenin think about this problem? Does he support your viewpoint?

TSURUPA. On the 26th he still had no firm opinion, the question remained open. I spoke to him this morning by telephone . . . but he still didn't have anything definite to say. He promised to think it over . . .

PETROVSKY. Do you think there is a realistic chance of ensuring grain supplies for Moscow?

TSURUPA. Today – no; tomorrow – yes.

SVERDLOV. Anyone else? Questions, proposals . . .

CHICHERIN. The trouble is, both of them are right . . .

STUCHKA. The solution proposed by comrade Tsurupa is the only feasible one.

NOGIN. Everything depends on whether or not adequate supplies of grain can be physically brought into the city.

SVERDLOV. Yes, we can only make a decision when there is a realistic chance of supplies, as Petrovsky says.

TSURUPA. It will be literally in a few days' time.

SVERDLOV *(to* TSURUPA*)*. Alexander Dmitrych, literally in a few days' time we shall have to make a firm decision. People must be able to count on the definite prospect of bread supplies. It's no good saying 'they should be here', I'm afraid. So I propose that when you can say 'the grain is coming on such-and-such a day', we will take a vote. Any objections? Zagorsky?

ZAGORSKY. No.

SVERDLOV. Tsurupa?

TSURUPA. No.

SVERDLOV. Very good. Motion carried.

GIRL *(dictates)*. 'TO TURLO, PROVINCIAL COMMITTEE, PENZA. COPY TO MINKIN. I DON'T UNDERSTAND HOW MINKIN CAN HAVE REFUSED TO CARRY OUT A RESOLUTION PASSED BY A MAJORITY OF YOUR COMMITTEE . . .'

SVERDLOV *(to* KOLLONTAI*)*. Alexandra Mikhailovna, would you please go and find out what's happening in the sickroom? And please ask Gill to come in here.

Exit KOLLONTAI. *The others remain silent.*

GIRL. '. . . I HOPE THIS IS ONLY A MISUNDERSTANDING. I INSIST THAT AT A TIME OF CIVIL WAR EVERYONE SHOULD WORK TOGETHER IN HARMONY WITH MAXIMUM RESOLUTENESS, SUBMITTING TO THE MAJORITY AND REFERRING ANY CONFLICTS TO THE CENTRAL COMMITTEE WITHOUT INTERRUPTING THEIR WORK. SIGNED: LENIN.'

Enter GILL.

SVERDLOV. Comrade Gill – come in and tell us exactly what happened.

GILL (*visibly nervous, sits down in an empty seat at the table*). Well, after the Corn Exchange we went to Mikhelson's factory. There was a lot of people in the yard as I drove in. We had no bodyguard with us in the car and there was none in the yard neither. Nobody came to meet comrade Lenin, not the local Party secretary, nor anybody else . . . Well, he gets out, completely alone, and goes into one of the workshops. I turned the car round so it was facing the way out of the yard, like that . . . a dozen or so paces away from the door into the workshops. About ten minutes later a woman comes up to me . . . Ordinary-looking woman, except she was carrying a briefcase. And she says: 'Was that comrade Lenin who just arrived?' I says to her I didn't know who it was. She laughs and says: 'You're a fine chauffeur if you don't know who you're driving . . .' So I says to her: 'How should I know? Some speaker from the Party. I drive all sorts, can't remember 'em all.' And away she went, into the workshop. No one else came up or spoke to me after that. About an hour later, it must have been, a crowd comes pouring out of the workshop – this meant the meeting was over, so I started the car up. Comrade Lenin comes out. There's a crowd of people all round him and I could hear him answering questions as he walks towards me. And just when he'd turned round to get into the car – there was a shot from behind him. At that moment I happened to be looking at him, so I turns my head – there's that woman taking aim at him and all at once she fires two more shots. I ran towards her, drawing my own revolver. She throws down her gun at my feet and starts running towards the factory gates. I runs after her, meaning to shoot, but I didn't dare: the crowd was all terrified and they were rushing for the gates too, so I didn't fire for fear of hitting someone. Then I suddenly remembered comrade Lenin was left alone so I ran back. People all round shouting: 'They've shot him! They've shot him!' and there's a regular stampede for the gates – so many, they were struggling to get out. Comrade Lenin was lying on the ground, no one near him. The Party secretary was still inside the factory.

Enter KOLLONTAI. *She shakes her head negatively and resumes her place at the table.*

LUNACHARSKY. Well? What news? What's happening?

KOLLONTAI. As before. No change.

TSURUPA. Please go on, comrade Gill.

GILL. So I bends down to him, like this . . . He's lying face-down on the ground, and this cheek (*Points to his left cheek.*) was all dirty with sand. I says to him: 'Vladimir Ilyich!' And he opens his eyes and asks me: 'Did they catch him?' He thought it was a man who shot him, you see. And his voice was funny – sort of hoarse. I told him not to talk, 'cos he was finding it hard to speak. I starts to lift him up and suddenly I see a sailor running towards us from the workshop, with his right hand in his pocket. I dropped comrade Lenin and fell on top of him to cover him. Must have crushed him a bit, I'm afraid. I points my revolver at the sailor and shouts: 'Stop!' – but he keeps on running. Then I shouts: 'Stop or I'll shoot!' and the sailor turns aside. All of a sudden a woman throws herself at me, grabs my arm, she's crying and shouting: 'Don't shoot! That's Lenin! Don't shoot!' Seems she thought *I'd* shot Vladimir Ilyich. Just then the Party secretary comes up and I told him what'd happened. I got up and helped Vladimir Ilyich on to his feet. He wouldn't let me pick him up and carry him. Walked to the car himself, white as a sheet. Someone told me to drive him to a hospital, but I said I'll only take him to the Kremlin and nowhere else. That's all. And that woman was caught.

PETROVSKY. Thank you very much, comrade Gill. Now please drive to the Lubyanka and repeat your testimony to Peters.

Exit GILL. *Enter* KURSKY.

KURSKY. We've interrogated her twice. I've brought both her statements.

SVERDLOV. Go ahead, Kursky. Read them out, please.

KURSKY (*reads*). First statement: 'I am Fanya Yefimovna Kaplan. I have used that name since 1906, and under that name I was imprisoned by the Tsarist authorities in Akatui for illegal political activity. I shot at Lenin today. I shot at him on my own initiative. I don't remember how many times I fired. I will not tell you the type of revolver I used. I do not intend to go into such details. I didn't know the women who were talking to Lenin in the factory yard. I made up my mind to shoot Lenin long ago. I have never previously lived in either Moscow or Petrograd. The woman who was, it seems, wounded at the same time, is a complete stranger to me. I shot at Lenin because I consider he has betrayed the revolution and his continued existence would undermine the people's faith in socialism. I do not wish to explain what I mean by "undermining faith in socialism". I regard myself as a socialist, but at present I belong to no political party. I was arrested in 1906 as an Anarchist. I think it unnecessary to explain to what social group or class I now belong. I was exiled to Akatui for taking part in a bomb explosion in Kiev.' Interrogator: Kursky, People's Commissar of Justice.

Pause.

KURSKY (*continues*). Second interrogation: 'I am twenty-eight years old, of no fixed abode. I was born in the province of Volhynia. I served a term of hard labour in Akatui as an Anarchist. I was arrested at the factory gates. I belong to no political party. I shot at Lenin because I consider that the longer he lives he is preventing the attainment of socialism by ten years for every further year of his life. I did it on my personal initiative. Fanya Kaplan refused to sign her statement. Witnessed by Dyakonov, chairman of the Moscow Revolutionary Tribunal.' Postscript: 'Kaplan requested it should be made clear that she is not an Anarchist, but was only imprisoned in Akatui on suspicion of being an Anarchist.' That is all for the present. Interrogations are continuing.

YENUKIDZE. But she's insane!

KRESTINSKY. At the very least a psychologically inadequate personality.

SVERDLOV. I'm not so sure. I have a feeling she's not telling the whole truth . . .

KURSKY. The impression she makes is of an extremely limited, colourless but neurotic person, almost hysterical I would say . . . She seems confused, talks incoherently. One moment she's so worked up that she's shouting, the next she's reduced to a state of depression. She denies any connection with the Social Revolutionary party. We are far from having unravelled the wider ramifications of this business yet. It is just possible that some connection may exist between what this woman did and this morning's assassination of Uritsky. At the same time, we can't rule out the version that it's the act of a mentally unbalanced loner. We do have certain information that Vladimir Ilyich was the victim of an organised hunt, and that gunmen from Savinkov's organisation were waiting for him at today's meetings all over Moscow, but we still haven't been able to check the information. So far we can't confirm that Kaplan belonged to that organisation. In about two hours' time there will be further statements obtained from her continuing interrogation.

CHICHERIN. What was that explosion she was talking about?

KURSKY. It was a plot to assassinate the Governor-General of Kiev. Kaplan was a schoolgirl at the time, and she was chosen to carry it out. She was supposed to finish him off if he was still alive after the bomb exploded. She was arrested in her flat, in possession of a loaded revolver. Are there any more questions? . . . Then I must get back to the Lubyanka . . .

SVERDLOV. Very well, you'd better go.

Exit KURSKY.

GIRL (*dictates*). 'TO BADAYEV, SMOLNY INSTITUTE, PETROGRAD. COMRADE BADEYEV! STOP BEING CHILDISH! YOU WERE NOT ASKED WHETHER YOU REGARDED "ALL YOUR ACTIONS" AS "ABSOLUTELY CORRECT". THAT IS RIDICULOUS. YOU WERE ASKED WHETHER YOU HAD CARRIED OUT ALL YOUR INSTRUCTIONS FROM THE CENTRE. AND YOU SAY NOTHING ABOUT THAT! . . .'

LUNACHARSKY. It can't be . . . it can't be . . .

GIRL (*continues*). '. . . KEEP WORKING. WE DO NOT ACCEPT YOUR RESIGNATION. HENCEFORTH CARRY OUT ALL INSTRUCTIONS FROM THE CENTRE AND STOP TALKING PERNICIOUS NONSENSE ABOUT "MACHINATIONS" AND "INTRIGUES" AGAINST YOU. GREETINGS! LENIN.'

LUNACHARSKY. Our whole cause will be lost . . .

SVERDLOV (*explodes, to* LUNACHARSKY). Anatoly Vasilych – pull yourself together. You must not talk like that! He said to me just now: 'There's to be no moaning and snivelling! Our cause is right and just, but if you weaken or start splitting up it will mean disaster!' Pull yourself together. The fate of the revolution cannot . . . *must* not depend on a single individual. That would be a tragedy. Without a Sverdlov, a Lunacharsky, a Nogin, a

Krestinsky – without all of us, even Lenin – the revolution goes on. To think otherwise is the worst thing of all. I beg you, Anatoly Vasilych – calm down. Right now we . . .

Enter KIZAS.

KIZAS (*to* SVERDLOV). Yakov Mikhailych, the doctors are asking for you.

KRESTINSKY. How is he?

KIZAS. The same . . . no better . . .

SVERDLOV *hurriedly buttons up his jacket and goes out of the council-room. He walks down the corridor to* LENIN's *quarters, where* ULYANOVA *is seated at a small table and* KRUPSKAYA *is sitting on a chair by the door.* SVERDLOV *goes into* LENIN's *room and shuts the door behind him.*

GIRL (*dictates*). 'TO DISTRICT EXECUTIVE COMMITTEE, TULA. PLEASE SEND ME ANSWERS SOONEST TO THE FOLLOWING QUESTIONS. FIRSTLY: WAS A REGIONAL CONGRESS OF PEASANTS HELD IN TULA? SECONDLY: WAS THERE A PROPOSAL (WHOSE?) TO SEND GREETINGS TO LENIN? THIRDLY: DID ALL DELEGATES VOTE TO SEND IT BUT VOTED AGAINST SENDING IT IN THE NAME OF COMMUNIST PARTY MEMBERS ONLY? FOURTHLY: WAS THE CONGRESS STOPPED AND DISPERSED BECAUSE OF THIS? . . .'

KOLLONTAI. Someone or some group is organising an operation to murder Lenin and we haven't lifted a finger to prevent it . . .

GIRL (*continues*). '. . . I REQUIRE AN IMMEDIATE ANSWER. I INSIST ON AN ANSWER WITH MAXIMUM SPEED AND I MAKE THE DISTRICT EXECUTIVE COMMITTEE RESPONSIBLE FOR THIS. SIGNED: LENIN, CHAIRMAN, SOVNARKOM.'

SVERDLOV *comes out of* LENIN's *room, goes over to* KRUPSKAYA.

SVERDLOV. Nadezhda Konstantinova.

KRUPSKAYA. Don't say anything, Yakov Mikhailych. I understand . . . Let's sit here awhile together . . .

SVERDLOV *sits down. In the council-room* ZAGORSKY *breaks the heavy silence.*

ZAGORSKY. I rang him at two o'clock this afternoon: 'Vladimir Ilyich, the Bureau of the Moscow Party Committee has just passed a resolution that you should not go out to speak in public today.' Answer – laughter. 'What am I, a capitalist minister? You want to keep me hidden from view.' Then I read him an extract from the Bureau's resolution. 'I disagree with that resolution in principle, and what's more it was passed in my absence.' – 'We're quite prepared to repeat it in your presence.' – 'Very well, I'll come to the Party Committee after the meeting. I can't cancel the engagement to speak there, firstly because I've promised to go, and secondly because I regard it as right in principle and absolutely essential to speak to the workers, *now* of all times.' Then came his usual fusillade of ironic remarks . . .

All are silent.

SVERDLOV (*after a pause*). You know, Zagorsky and I were not yet fourteen when we brought our first revolutionary proclamation into school . . . (*Catches* KRUPSKAYA's *enquiring glance.*) We were at school together, you see. We were inseparable. Only in those days his name was Volodya Lubotsky. Then we got a gun from somewhere and hid it in the loft. We went on demonstrations, held secret meetings. Our first arrest – two days in clink. We were happy but stupid. Then we read Vladimir Ilyich's pamphlet 'What is to be Done?' and we started acting seriously, in an organised way. Zagorsky was arrested and tried in 1902, and he and Zalomov got fifteen years. Gorky described it in his novel *The Mother.* He was then exiled for life to Siberia, because he beat up a policeman during a demonstration. Soon after that I was sent to prison too. I'd always wanted to meet Vladimir Ilyich, but never once managed to. I met him in April last year for the first time. I've only known him for sixteen months . . .

KRUPSKAYA *says nothing.* BONCH-BRUYEVICH *goes into the council-room.*

BONCH-B. (*to* ZAGORSKY). Here's a note for you from the Moscow City Soviet. (*Hands him a note.*) His condition is still dangerous. They've found Dr Obukh and are bringing him here. Vladimir Ilyich keeps asking for something to drink. We need lemons. There aren't any to be found in Moscow, we've asked the comrades in Petrograd to go round the embassies – they may have some.

CHICHERIN. A good idea.

Exit BONCH-BRUYEVICH.

SVERDLOV. (*explodes to* KRUPSKAYA). So now I have to go around telling everyone the revolution doesn't depend on a single individual, even on an individual such as Vladimir Ilyich

– although I know perfectly well that it *does*! The others look at me and I can read the same question in all their faces: 'What if . . .?' And I can't even bring myself to think about it! He *must* live . . . now of all times! I say all this and at the same time I can hear what he would say in reply: 'Comrade Sverdlov, don't you remember what Marx used to say on this subject? "Great men only seem great to us because we are on our knees." Come on, Yakov Mikhailych – let's get up off our knees . . .' That's the whole problem – *can* we?

KRUPSKAYA *says nothing.*

YENUKIDZE. Comrades, I think that Vladimir Ilyich has no right to take such risks in future. We must pass a special resolution.

LUNACHARSKY. What resolution?

CHICHERIN. About what?

YENUKIDZE. About comrade Lenin's lack of discipline and the measures needed to guard him.

STUCHKA. It wouldn't do any good – he'd always be dodging his bodyguards anyway. Any one of us would do the same. Don't you see that?

YENUKIDZE. We must reprimand him. Discipline has to be the same for everybody. If *I* had disobeyed that resolution of the Party's Moscow Committee, for instance – just imagine the ticking-off he'd have given me. (*To* ZAGORSKY.) If you don't protest to him tomorrow, I shall cease to respect you!

NOGIN. It's not a question of being disciplined or not. He loathes the idea of a guard in principle. How many times has he said: 'How can I face the workers if I'm surrounded by bodyguards? We are a workers' government. What will we become if we cut ourselves off from the workers by hiding behind a screen of guards?' So that's the position. It's up to us to think of reasonable measures to eliminate the contradiction between his attitude and the demands of the time.

YENUKIDZE. But what will become of us if any lunatic, any psychopath, any agent of the Entente can take a pot-shot at Lenin without the slightest difficulty? Isn't it enough for you that Uritsky and Volodarsky were murdered?!

KRESTINSKY. Get off your soap-box, Abel. What do you suggest? Stop the Old Man from ever meeting the people?

YENUKIDZE. That's your suggestion, not mine!

POKROVSKY. Assassination attempts are the occupational hazard of being a politician.

YENUKIDZE. Well – so what? Do we just *accept* that? Come on then! Let's all go out into the streets and put the whole Central Committee and the Sovnarkom in the firing-line. There are enough gunmen out there, it seems! (*With heavy sarcasm.*) Ah, those brave Bolsheviks! They're afraid of nothing!

PETROVSKY. And you, I suppose, wouldn't go out into the streets?

YENUKIDZE. I would, but that's not the point!

LUNACHARSKY. What are you talking about, Abel? If we all did that today, there'd be no need of guards tomorrow because we'd all be dead.

ZAGORSKY. Comrades! The Moscow Party Committee and the Moscow Soviet appeal to you . . . Right now spontaneous meetings are springing up all over Moscow . . .

KOLLONTAI. Where must we go?

ZAGORSKY. We'll divide up the city by districts. Krestinsky – will you go to Sokolniki?

KRESTINSKY. Right.

ZAGORSKY (*to* TSURUPA). Presnya?

TSURUPA *nods agreement.*

ZAGORSKY (*continues*). Lefortovo? Lefortovo – Kollontai. Central – Milyutin. We must phone him at the City Soviet and tell him.

PETROVSKY. I'll see to that.

ZAGORSKY. Khamovniki – Chicherin and Semashko. The Mikhelson factory?

LUNACHARSKY. May I go there?

ZAGORSKY. Of course. Taganka? Pokrovsky and Podbielsky. Khodynka? Yenukidze and Avanesov. Simonovsky?

PETROVSKY. I'll go.

ZAGORSKY. Agreed. Zamoskvorechye? Nogin and Yelizarov. Basmanny district? Stuchka and Rudzutak. Trubnaya Square? Steklov – and take Osinsky with you. Cars are waiting downstairs, by the main entrance. Has anyone not got a personal weapon?

LUNACHARSKY. I haven't.

ZAGORSKY. Take this one. (*Takes an automatic out of his pocket and hands it to* LUNACHARSKY.)

LUNACHARSKY. Perhaps . . .

ZAGORSKY (*firmly*). No, no – you *must* take it. Let's go, comrades . . .

One by one the COMMISSARS *file out of the council-chamber.* LUNACHARSKY *stands holding the automatic, not knowing what to do with it. Finally he puts it in his brief-case and exits.*

SVERDLOV *enters the council-room. He sits down at the table and bursts into tears.* KRUPSKAYA, *still seated in the corridor, starts to darn the bullet-hole in* LENIN'*s overcoat.*

Off-stage can be heard a rising hum of voices of people at crowded open-air meetings, while the voices of two speakers are heard rising above the noise.

FIRST SPEAKER (*a woman*). Our banners have been dyed with too much crimson blood of the fighters for the people's cause! The time to spare the murderers and their paymasters is past! We must strike down our enemies by tens and by hundreds, without mercy and without compassion! Let them die by the thousand! Let them choke in their own blood! Let us follow the example of the French Revolution! In revenge for the blood of comrade Lenin, for the death of comrade Uritsky, for the attempt on the life of comrade Podvoisky, for the unavenged blood of Volodarsky and Nakhimson, for the blood of thousands of soldiers, workers and sailors – let the blood of the bourgeoisie and its hirelings flow in torrents! Long live the red terror!

SECOND SPEAKER (*a man*). Comrades! We need no words, no tears! Do not weep, comrades – we must *act*! Comrades, we demand that for each one of us killed by treachery and for our mortally wounded leader the bourgeoisie and the social traitors of the so-called left must pay with a thousand lives! I propose we adopt the following resolution: firstly, we demand that comrade Lenin be saved and stays alive. Secondly, in reply to the gunman's treacherous shots from around corners and from doorways we demand that the Soviet government declare the start of a red terror. We demand the blood of the bourgeoisie!

Curtain.

PART TWO

GIRL (*dictates*). 'THREE ADDRESSEES: TO SYTIN, KOZLOV: TO TROTSKY, TSARITSYN: TO VOROSHILOV, TSARITSYN. WE ARE RECEIVING DESPERATE TELEGRAMS FROM VOROSHILOV ABOUT NON-ARRIVAL OF AMMUNITION DESPITE HIS REPEATED AND INSISTENT REQUESTS. SUGGEST YOU CHECK THIS IMMEDIATELY AND TAKE DRASTIC MEASURES TO ENSURE SUPPLIES. INFORM US OF YOUR ACTIONS. SIGNED: LENIN, CHAIRMAN, SOVNARKOM AND SVERDLOV, CHAIRMAN, ALL-RUSSIAN CENTRAL EXECUTIVE COMMITTEE.'

SVERDLOV *is seated in the council-room, speaking on the telephone.* KIZAS *stands beside him.*

SVERDLOV. Good. That's agreed. If the British advance in force, the railway bridges will have to be blown up . . . Yes, I understand . . . But if the British join up with the White Czechoslovaks, then the whole Revolutionary Military Council, and you and I into the bargain . . . All right. Get in touch with Kedrov, he's fully in the picture. I'm at the Sovnarkom in the Kremlin . . . Good. (*Replaces the receiver, hands two notes to* KIZAS.) These are urgent – to Chubar and Admiral Altvater.

Telephone rings.

SVERDLOV (*picks up receiver*). Sverdlov here . . . I haven't time to deal with that now, come and see me tomorrow. (*Listens impatiently.*) No, no . . . (*Explodes.*) Will you get it into your head once and for all and make it clear to all your staff on the newspaper: We don't want you to *believe* in us, we want you to *understand* us! Go to bed, you're tired. (*Slams down the receiver, to* KIZAS.) Where's Yenukidze?

KIZAS. He's coming.

Telephone rings.

KIZAS (*picks up receiver*). Kizas here . . . (*To* SVERDLOV.) Yakov Mikhailych, it's Petrograd. Dzerzhinsky.

CHICHERIN *and* LUNACHARSKY *enter the council-room.*

SVERDLOV *(takes receiver).* Hello . . . yes, it's me . . . It still looks bad . . . Obukh, Weisbrod and Mintz . . . Yes, Kursky and Peters . . . If his condition doesn't improve by tomorrow morning, we'll call all members of the Central Committee to Moscow . . . I've already sent out a call for him, and I'm just about to repeat it . . . We'll hold out. What's the situation in Petrograd? . . . Good. Get here as soon as you can. We're waiting for you. *(Replaces receiver.)*

KIZAS. Yakov Mikhailych, you're wanted at the teletype.

SVERDLOV goes over to the teletype machine. Telephone rings in the corridor of LENIN's flat. KRUPSKAYA picks up the receiver.

KRUPSKAYA. Hello . . . Yes, it's me . . . I know you have a meeting . . . It's already started? . . . No, I haven't forgotten . . . the fact is, comrades . . . my husband has been wounded . . . If you can, please postpone it till tomorrow. I'll be there tomorrow without fail . . . *(Replaces receiver.)*

POKROVSKY *enters the council-room, followed shortly afterwards by* STEKLOV.

POKROVSKY. What happened at your meeting?

LUNACHARSKY. I could barely restrain them from violence.

CHICHERIN. It was the same at Khamovniki.

SVERDLOV, standing by the telegraph apparatus, reads the ribbon of telegraph tape. YENUKIDZE *stands beside him.*

SVERDLOV *(to the* TELEGRAPHIST*).* Transmit: 'Sverdlov here.'

STEKLOV *(picking up telephone receiver).* This is Steklov. Get me the *Izvestiya* office, please.

SVERDLOV *(dictates).* 'An hour ago I sent you a telegram.'

POKROVSKY *(to* STEKLOV*).* What happened at your meeting?

STEKLOV. They're demanding the blood of the bourgeoisie.

SVERDLOV *(dictates).* 'Lenin wounded, not known as yet how seriously.'

STEKLOV *(into the telephone).* Take down the following for tomorrow's front page.

SVERDLOV *(dictates).* 'Come at once. Your request will be passed on to the addressee. Measures will be taken.' That's all.

TELEGRAPHIST. End of transmission.

STEKLOV (*into the telephone*). I dictate: 'Uritsky has been killed. Lenin has been wounded. Point.'

SVERDLOV (*handing a note to* YENUKIDZE). Abel, find Altvater at once, give him this, tell him it's urgent and give him any men he may need to help him.

Exit YENUKIDZE.

SVERDLOV *leaves the council-room and goes along the corridor to* LENIN's *flat.*

STEKLOV (*dictates*). 'Using their hirelings, Russian and foreign capitalists want to cut off the head of the workers' revolution. Point.'

WEISBROD *comes out of* LENIN's *room and takes* SVERDLOV *aside.*

WEISBROD (*anxiously*). Yakov Mikhailych . . .

STEKLOV (*continues dictating*). 'The proletariat will respond by mercilessly punishing the murderers and by redoubled efforts at the front. Point.'

WEISBROD. Just now Vladimir Ilyich regained consciousness and taking advantage of the fact that we were alone . . .

STEKLOV (*dictates*). 'Workers, remain calm and steadfast! Exclamation point.'

SVERDLOV. What's happened?

WEISBROD. We had a very painful conversation.

STEKLOV (*dictates*). 'There are to be no individual acts of reprisal. Point.'

SVERDLOV. I'm listening.

WEISBROD. He asked me: 'Will the end come soon?' I replied there was no need to think of any such thing. Then he asked: 'Are you a Bolshevik? In that case you must realise that you mustn't try to spare me the truth. Greater things are at stake. I must hang on long enough to talk to Sverdlov. He and I still have a few little things to discuss. You will warn me, won't you?'

SVERDLOV. What did you reply?

STEKLOV (*dictates*). 'We must close the ranks. Point.'

WEISBROD. I promised I would. Then he half-raised himself and asked: 'Is it too early yet?' I replied that it was much too early yet, and that I would be sure of warning him, but that, as you must realise, may be impossible to do . . . he could go very suddenly . . .

STEKLOV (*dictates*). 'A speedy recovery and long life to the leader of the proletariat! Exclamation point.'

SVERDLOV. He's right. We must warn him . . . we *must* warn him, if it's humanly possible.

STEKLOV. Got that? Good. I'm at the Sovnarkom. (*Replaces receiver.*)

SVERDLOV. All the same . . . it's a hideously cruel thing to have to do . . . You haven't lost hope, have you?

WEISBROD. Not yet, but . . .

SVERDLOV. I understand . . .

GIRL (*dictates*). 'TO PROVINCIAL EXECUTIVE COMMITTEE, RYAZAN. WHAT MEASURES HAVE YOU TAKEN TO DEAL WITH THE BLACK-MARKET RING UNCOVERED BY STATE CONTROL COMMISSION IN PUBLIC RESTAURANTS? SIGNED: LENIN, CHAIRMAN, SOVNARKOM.'

Enter PETROVSKY *in considerable agitation.*

Exit LUNACHARSKY.

PETROVSKY (*to* SVERDLOV). Yakov Mikhailych, I've come straight from the Commissariat. Both we and Dzerzhinsky's office are being overwhelmed by telegrams. There is great unrest in the provinces. People are demanding mass arrests and executions.

SVERDLOV (*harshly*). No such action will be approved without an appropriate decree of the Sovnarkom.

PETROVSKY. I'm only afraid people won't wait for that.

SVERDLOV. Send telegrams immediately to all chairmen of Executive Committees and to the Cheka: They will be held personally responsible if matters get out of hand in their area . . . Right-wing reactionaries have always exploited the blind fury of the masses – remember the pogroms? That is something we do *not* need.

GIRL (*dictates*). 'TO RED ARMY COMMANDER VLADIMIROV, KOZLOV. I HAVE RECEIVED A COMPLAINT THAT YOU HAVE REQUISITIONED NINE

FIRST CLASS RAILWAY COACHES, INCLUDING ONE RESTAURANT CAR, ONE KITCHEN CAR, TWO SALOON CARS. THIS IS HELD TO BE EXCESSIVE, CAUSING RESENTMENT AMONG THE WORKERS AND PROBLEMS FOR THE WORK OF THE RAILWAY. HOW MANY COACHES ARE YOU ALLOWED BY THE DECREE OF THE CENTRAL EXECUTIVE COMMITTEE? SIGNED: LENIN, CHAIRMAN, SOVNARKOM.'

ZAGORSKY *runs into the hallway of* LENIN's *flat.*

ZAGORSKY (*to* SVERDLOV). Yakov!

SVERDLOV. What's happening out there?

ZAGORSKY. The situation's serious. They want revenge. Red Square is full of workers' delegations. No violence so far. We've collected a group of veteran Party members. We want to send them round the factories to cool things down. What do you think?

SVERDLOV. Do it.

Exit ZAGORSKY.

SVERDLOV *goes to join* KRUPSKAYA, *who is sitting at a little table talking to* ULYANOVA *and* KOLLONTAI.

KRUPSKAYA (*continues*). . . . that always worried him very much. We must re-examine all our theories, he used to say, to bring them in line with the latest historical experience of war and peace, and of our own and other people's revolutions. He admitted he couldn't do all that work himself. He said that when one is in a permanent state of activity it is terribly difficult to theorise. To think clearly he needed to settle down quietly in the country. If only, he would say, there were scholars and thinkers outside Russia – in America, in England or in continental Europe – who could observe what we were doing, study it, reflect on it and tell us their conclusions. We need objective criticism! When there's a storm at sea the captain needs the advice of intelligent observers who are far away from the centre of the storm and therefore in safety. But we're not getting that sort of criticism from abroad. Instead, the reaction in the West is one of ignorant horror, induced by the appalling problems that we're facing. Ignorant onlookers can only see the huge waves, a disciplined crew, the occasional passenger falling overboard and that's all. We feel it all much more keenly than our critics. We need to know how to overcome these difficulties and reach our goal, which is the goal of everyone looking for the meaning of life. We have different ideas about how to get there, but we're fully agreed about the destination. I think those are his thoughts, but I may have left something out . . .

ULYANOVA. Before the October Revolution he used to say that making a revolution is much more enjoyable than writing about it.

SVERDLOV. That's quite understandable – there's nothing paradoxical in that feeling . . . (*To* KRUPSKAYA.) Nadezhda Konstantinovna, if the doctors want me I'm in the council-room. Come on, Alexandra Mikhailovna . . .

SVERDLOV *and* KOLLONTAI *go into the council-room.*

TELEGRAPHIST (*to* GIRL). Is there much more?

GIRL. Lots.

TELEGRAPHIST. I'll just have a couple of drags at a cigarette . . . (*Lights a cigarette.*) Who's going to take his place? We'll never find anyone like him.

GIRL. The other day I was delayed in the council-room, writing out the minutes of a meeting. Vladimir Ilyich was talking to some American, who asked him the same question: 'Who will be your successor?'

TELEGRAPHIST. And what did he say?

GIRL. He said he had realised years ago that he wasn't a jack-of-all-trades.

TELEGRAPHIST. Well – and then?

GIRL. Then he asked me for a blank sheet of paper and began drawing a diagram . . . When they'd gone, I looked at it. He had drawn a large circle, divided up by lines into unequal segments, like a cake cut into different-sized slices . . . (*Demonstrates on a piece of paper.*) Do you see?

TELEGRAPHIST. Yes, of course.

GIRL. As he was drawing it he said: 'I can take care of *this* sector here . . . and *this* sector . . . so I will shade in those segments of the circle . . . But I am not competent to look after *these* sectors or *these*. To begin with, I tried being responsible for all of them myself, then gradually other people joined me who had more specialised competence than I did, and together we comprise the Party's collective jack-of-all-trades. Only that composite personality can hope to embrace all the parts of a vast whole . . .'

130 THE BOLSHEVIKS

TELEGRAPHIST. Was that all he said?

GIRL. Yes, that was all.

TELEGRAPHIST. But what did he mean by that? What about his successor?

GIRL. I don't understand it either.

TELEGRAPHIST. You say he drew a circle?

GIRL. Yes . . .

CHICHERIN, LUNACHARSKY, KRESTINSKY *and* POKROVSKY *are in the council-room.*

Enter PETROVSKY *and* BATULIN. *A few moments later* SVERDLOV *and* KOLLONTAI *enter, followed one after another by the remaining* COMMISSARS.

PETROVSKY. This is comrade Batulin. He arrested the Kaplan woman. I suggest we all sit down and hear what comrade Batulin has to say. (*To* BATULIN.) Please tell us exactly what happened.

BATULIN. My name's Batulin . . . I'm second-in-command of a regiment . . . Our barracks are not far from that factory, so I went along to hear comrade Lenin speak . . . Well, it was like this . . . I was about the last person to come out of that workshop where he was speaking. I started walking towards his car when I suddenly heard a loud bang, then two more . . . I thought it was the noise of a car backfiring. And the crowd, which had been standing around quite calmly, scattered in all directions. Then I saw comrade Lenin by the car. He was lying – like this (*Demonstrates.*) – face down on the ground, quite still. I realised someone had shot him. I didn't see who had fired the shots, but I started shouting: 'Stop the murderer! They've shot comrade Lenin!' – and I ran with everyone else out on to Serpukhovskaya Street. They were all terrified by the shots and the confusion. Well, anyway, I ran on shouting and shouting, until suddenly I had a strange feeling which made me turn round. I saw a woman standing beside a tree. Funny-looking she was, with a briefcase, just standing there and looking at me. Her face was white, with a sort of hunted look. She was staring at me, so I went over to her.

POKROVSKY. Why did you do that?

BATULIN. I don't honestly know. There was something odd

about her. She was out of breath because she'd been running too, and then she had just stopped – not very far from the factory.

PETROVSKY. She stopped of her own accord? Not because she'd been caught?

BATULIN. I asked her what she was doing there, and she answered in a trembling sort of voice: 'Why do you want to know?' I asked her the same question again, and she gave me the same reply: 'Why do you want to know?' I leaped at her, searched her pockets, took away her briefcase and umbrella and asked her why she had shot at comrade Lenin. And she just repeated the same thing: 'Why do you want to know?' At that moment I was sure it was her. I took a firm grip of her, and at that moment some children came up and shouted: 'She's the one' . . .

NOGIN. Did you say, comrade, that she first ran away and then stopped at a point not far from the factory?

BATULIN. Yes, she stopped of her own accord.

NOGIN. Comrades! This convinces me that she's a Social-Revolutionary. A typical S-R terrorist. Their code of honour forbids them to run away from the place where they commit a deed of terrorism.

BATULIN. Why?

KOLLANTAI. To show that it's not a criminal but a political act.

POKROVSKY. The S-Rs have long since abandoned their high-minded principles.

NOGIN. The leaders have, but the rank-and-file members still observe them.

PETROVSKY. It's coming back to me now – I *do* remember her. When our batch of prisoners was taken to the Alexandrov prison, I met several of the S-R leaders there, including Spiridonova and Bitsenko. With them was a young, extremely short-sighted girl from Kiev. They were already old inhabitants of the place. They gave us food and drink, exchanged news with us – it was a very heart-warming encounter . . . Yes, it's her all right.

ZAGORSKY. It's an absurd paradox of history: we were tried side by side; we were shipped out to Siberia together; we shared a blanket between four of us; we served our time together; we escaped together – and all so that we could end up shooting at each other.

SVERDLOV. The S-Rs have had a wonderful opportunity to remain in opposition, to criticise us and appeal to the masses. They have their own newspaper, their own organisations – they've had everything an opposition party could dream of! But having lost mass support, they've turned to plotting and violence. Instead of acting as a loyal opposition they've become conspirators and, in effect, pawns in the hands of the White counter-revolutionaries and similar vermin. It's the suicide of a once-great party, for which we are not responsible.

NOGIN. Remember what we used to say before the revolution: 'We will destroy together; but we can never build together . . .'

Enter KURSKY.

KURSKY. Here are the latest statements from Kaplan.

ZAGORSKY. Is she an S-R?

KURSKY. You'll hear in a moment.

BATULIN. If it's possible . . . please tell comrade Lenin that the people are furious . . . we all hope . . . he'll soon be back with us again. (*Exit*.)

KURSKY. Third interrogation: 'I arrived at the meeting around seven o'clock. I will not say who gave me the revolver. I had no railway ticket. I wasn't in Tomilino. I have no trade-union membership-card. I haven't worked for a long time. I refuse to say where I got the money. I have already told you that my surname has been Kaplan for the past eleven years. I shot at Lenin from personal conviction. I never said to any woman that for us the revolution was "a failure" I have never heard of any terrorist organisation connected with Savinkov. I don't want to talk about it. I don't know if any of my acquaintances have been arrested by the Cheka. My attitude to the present government of the Ukraine is negative. I will not say what I think of the present governments at Samara and Archangel . . .' Interrogator: Kursky, People's Commissar of Justice. (*Slight pause*.)

Fourth interrogation: 'In 1906 I was arrested in Kiev in connection with the assassination of the governor-general. I was imprisoned as an Anarchist. The attack was carried out with a bomb, and I was wounded by the explosion. I was carrying the bomb for the purpose of an act of political terrorism. I was tried by court-martial in Kiev and sentenced to hard labour for life. I served part of my term in the Maltsevskaya prison, then in exile at Akatui, where my fellow-prisoners included Spiridonova, Bitsenko and Terentieva. My political views were formed there, and from having been an Anarchist I became a Social-Revolutionary.

The COMMISSARS *exchange glances.*

I changed my views because I was very young when I joined the Anarchists. When the Bolshevik revolution took place in October last year, I was in hospital in Kharkov. I did not approve of that revolution. I supported the Constituent Assembly, and I still do. Of the various tendencies within the S-R party, I support the section headed by Chernov. I fully accept the Samara government, and I am in favour of an alliance with France, Britain and America against Germany. I shot at Lenin.' Interrogator: Peters . . . And that, comrades, is all for the moment.

CHICHERIN. Yes, they must be celebrating in Paris and London today.

KURSKY. I believe that Sovnarkom should decide on what is to become of Kaplan.

STUCHKA *runs into the council-room.*

STUCHKA *(agitated).* An uprising against us in Livny! The peasants have seized the district Soviet, the telegraph office and the greater part of the town! The entire district is up in arms! Every Party activist has been torn to pieces by the mob. An international detachment which tried to resist has suffered two-thirds casualties. Today . . .

SVERDLOV *(grabbing the telephone).* Get me Sklyansky! It's urgent.

STUCHKA. Any Red Army troops they captured were tortured in the most horrible way. They flayed them alive, gouged out their eyes and then finished them off. The chairman of the local Cheka was literally hacked to pieces. It all happened suddenly . . .

SVERDLOV *(into the telephone).* Sverdlov speaking. What's happening at Livny? . . . I see . . . Yes, I see . . . Agreed . . . Good . . . No, move the Orlovsky Regiment there, and have them take the town by storm. The rebellion is to be ruthlessly suppressed. Declare a state of siege in the town and the surrounding district, then carry out a purge . . . We're all in the Sovnarkom . . . It's not clear yet . . . Obukh is with him now. (*Replaces the receiver.*) Well, we've done what we can. (*To* STUCHKA.) What happened at your meeting?

STUCHKA. They're howling for revenge. They expect us to take steps.

SVERDLOV. Well, comrades, it seems that warlike action is afoot in the rear areas as well as at the front. The Central Executive Committee will have to issue a decree putting the entire Soviet Republic under martial law, with all the consequences. Our reply to the assassinations and rebellions must be a sharp increase in aggressive action on all fronts. On the other hand, we are getting a flood of telegrams from all over the country demanding permission to carry out mass arrests and executions. In other words, the question of deploying a 'red terror' now faces us in all its complexity and urgency. In our decree we must lay down a plan of armed action, though not forgetting for a moment that our 'red terror' is not an act of revenge for the attacks on our leaders but a military operation in a civil war. I shall now try and draft a series of appropriate directives which will be approved tomorrow or the day after at a joint session of the Central Executive Committee and the Sovnarkom. It's likely to be complicated, so we must discuss it from every angle and without delay. I must ask you all to remain here and participate in this extremely important discussion. (*Sits down at the table, takes a sheet of paper and starts writing.*)

During the subsequent scene this sheet will be passed round to all members of the Sovnarkom in turn.

KRESTINSKY. We've brought it on ourselves. Vladimir Ilyich was right when he said: 'Our dictatorship? What dictatorship?! Show it to me! What we have isn't a dictatorship, it's a muddle. Nothing but hot air and muddle!'

STUCHKA. Don't overstate the situation – we've done a lot . . .

POKROVSKY. What have we done? What, I ask you? All we've ever done is turn the other cheek!

STUCHKA. Exaggeration is the prerogative of poets, not of politicians!

PETROVSKY. Exaggeration? Not at all. Immediately after the October Revolution we abolished the death penalty.

KOLLONTAI. And what was Lenin's reaction to that? He roared with laughter. Comrades – which of you was there at the time? It was on the morning of the 26th of October. I remember exactly what he said: 'How can you make a revolution without firing-squads? Do you really think you'll dispose of all our enemies if you consciously disarm yourself at the very outset? What other means of repression are left to you? Imprisonment? Who will give a damn for imprisonment in a civil war, when each side expects to win?' We all rounded on him, saying how necessary it was, but he was adamant: 'It's a mistake, a luxury we can't afford, a pacifist illusion.' But we couldn't make him change his mind and he couldn't change *our* minds.

PETROVSKY. And then what happened? General Krasnov gave his word of honour that he wouldn't attack us, and we let him go. How much workers' blood was shed because of that? On January 1st a group of counter-revolutionaries shot at Lenin, and all of them were arrested. Were they tried? They were not. From the first Lenin himself put every possible obstacle in the way of the investigation of that case. Dozens of times he asked us to check and re-check what had already been proved; next he asked us to give the prisoners more books to read; then when they asked to be sent to the front he wrote an order: 'Close the case. Release the prisoners. Send them to the front.'

NOGIN. But he realised that they were just a lot of confused boys.

PETROVSKY. There are plenty more examples. On January 7th a kangaroo-court of anarchistic sailors pronounced sentence on Kokoshkin and Shingaryov. We passed a resolution protesting against unofficial tribunals of that sort and expelled the remaining ministers and big capitalists. Then in March, at *Uritsky's* suggestion, we passed a resolution that executions, even for serious crimes, were absolutely impermissible. On May 1st we announced an amnesty and released people who were our declared enemies: soon afterwards Volodarsky was murdered.

POKROVSKY. The Petrograd workers wanted to respond to that murder with mass terror, but the Petrograd Soviet restrained them. Vladimir Ilyich wrote to Zinoviev: 'I must vigorously protest. We are compromising ourselves; on the one hand we openly threaten terror in sessions of the Soviet, but on the other hand, when the workers try and put those threats into practice we tie their hands'.

PETROVSKY. They didn't listen to the Old Man then and they restrained the Petrograd workers. And what have we come to today? Insurrection in Yaroslavl; Nakhimson executed; massacre of Party members; secretaries of Party cells murdered; assassination of Uritzky; Lenin badly wounded – and thousands of Red Army casualties at the front. So are we going to restrain our people *once again*?

GIRL (*dictates*). 'TO MONASTIRSKY, PERM. YOUR INSTRUCTIONS ARE TO ACT MORE ENERGETICALLY AND DECISIVELY AGAINST THE WHITE ARMY AND THE KULAKS. REPORT RESULTS MORE FREQUENTLY AND IN GREATER DETAIL. SIGNED: LENIN.'

KURSKY. It's strange: when we're dealing with the White army on the other side of the front line, no one has any doubts about using force. As soon as we're faced with those same White Guards here, but in another guise – as participants in a terrorist plot – then we start to have doubts . . .

POKROVSKY. Avoiding the use of terror because we want to bypass that phase of the revolution reminds me of a man who, let's say, decided to cross the sea on foot. Unfortunately one has to *sail* across the sea. Like it or not, we've got to get into a boat – the same kind of boat in which our enemies have already put out to sea.

LUNACHARSKY (*explodes*). Every one of us here knows and understands why we wanted to avoid the use of terror! And it is to our credit and honour, comrade Pokrovsky.

POKROVSKY. You've no cause to get so heated, Anatoly Vasilych. We'd all be happy if we could avoid using terror, but I'd like to remind you that a revolution is not just a change of government – it's the overthrow of one class by another and the suppression of any resistance by the class that's being overthrown. There is a logic of revolution and no one has yet succeeded in escaping from its iron grip.

SVERDLOV. We have not attempted either to bypass terror or to avoid it. It is simply a question of timing. Yesterday was too early; tomorrow, I fear, may be too late. Today it has become a matter of harsh necessity.

CHICHERIN. Our situation is exactly reflected in what Arthur

Arnoux said about the Paris Commune, which never completely believed in the vileness of its enemies.

YENUKIDZE. But now, perhaps, we do believe in the vileness of *our* enemies?

CHICHERIN (*smiling, ironically*). Historical experience exists in order to be ignored!

ZAGORSKY. But people who prefer to forget the lessons of the past are doomed, as a rule, to experience them all over again.

KURSKY (*to* CHICHERIN). Georgy Vasilych, you reminded us of the Communards, who were crushed as a result of being too trusting and too slow to act. But you should also remember the Jacobins, who knew what it meant to suppress counter-revolution with the utmost ruthlessness. We have something to learn from them . . . Surely you must all realise that for us at this moment delay means – literally – death.

STEKLOV. Delay is nowhere more useful than in anger. We are about to take a decision that is 'super-important', as Vladimir Ilyich would say . . .

PETROVSKY. Super-necessary, you mean . . .

STEKLOV. I don't dispute that. So it's all the more essential to examine all the pluses and minuses. The experience of the Jacobin dictatorship shows that . . .

POKROVSKY. In my opinion, talking about the excesses of the Jacobin terror is out of place at this moment. It'll make us lose our grip.

LUNACHARSKY. I categorically protest. To refuse to talk about the excesses of a reign of terror is absurd. How can we deprive ourselves of such a powerful and priceless weapon as the critical assessment of history? Don't you see? For faint hearts, all the minuses of the French Revolution are excuses for not making a revolution at all, whereas for us they are there to remind us that we must do it better.

YENUKIDZE. Quite right!

SVERDLOV. Anyhow, what does that remark mean? Does it mean that we can talk about some things and not about others? If so, we'll soon reach a point where we can only refer to things that favour us at the given moment. (*To* POKROVSKY.) By passing over certain facts in silence, my dear Mikhail

Nikolayich, we shall turn history into a prostitute who only gives herself to whomever pays her the most. It's a very dangerous line to follow . . .

STUCHKA. Cervantes proposed that falsifiers of history should be hung, like coiners of counterfeit money.

POKROVSKY. What I meant was that your Russian intellectual is too soft-hearted and is incapable of taking decisive measures of revolutionary terror. And talking about 'excesses' will simply reduce us to helpless despair.

KOLLONTAI. Why should it? Vladimir Ilyich never turned a blind eye to unpleasant facts. Paradoxical though it sounds, he actually used to love them, because one can only arrive at the correct decision by being fully aware of all the possible consequences.

YENUKIDZE. Why do you say he 'never *turned* a blind eye'? Why 'he *used to* love them'? Why the past tense? He *doesn't* turn a blind eye! He *loves* them!

DR OBUKH, *in a white coat, visibly anxious, comes out of* LENIN's *room.* KRUPSKAYA *and* ULYANOVA *stand up as he approaches them.*

OBUKH. I have decided to call in another opinion. We must send for Rozanov. He had a lot of experience of gunshot wounds when he was at the front during the war. The wound is extremely serious. Our only hope is the strength of his constitution. His heart is healthy, and fortunately his general health is good too.

KRUPSKAYA. Is there still hope?

OBUKH. I would very much like to reassure you. Personally I never lose hope.

ULYANOVA. How is he?

OBUKH. You know him . . . He comes to, and immediately he says: 'Why all this fuss? Why so many doctors?' I had to shout at him to make him be quiet. And he said: 'I'm keeping you away from your patients who really need you', and so on . . . He *must not* talk. At the moment, he's unconscious.

KRUPSKAYA. Vladimir Andreyich . . .

OBUKH. I understand, my dear . . . (*Exit.*)

ULYANOVA. Nadya, we absolutely must send for Anya and Mitya
. . . They'd never forgive us . . .

KRUPSKAYA. Yes, yes, of course we must . . . I've already asked
Kizas to send for them. (*Sits down.*)

In the council-room, **KRESTINSKY** *breaks the glum silence.*

KRESTINSKY. How is Nadezhda Konstantinovna?

NOGIN. She's darning the bullet-holes in his overcoat . . . More
with tears than with thread, I'm afraid.

SVERDLOV (*working on the draft document. To* CHICHERIN).
Georgy Vasilych, how will the proletariat in the West react to a
'red terror'?

CHICHERIN. You mean will they understand us or not? It all
depends on giving them absolutely precise information about
the state of affairs here.

STEKLOV. The Social Democrats as represented by Kautsky . . .

SVERDLOV. We all know what that rat Kautsky will say. But what
about Rosa Luxemburg?

CHICHERIN. That's likely to be more complicated. But again it's
a question of putting across the true facts.

SVERDLOV. Whose sympathies will we lose inside Russia?

LUNACHARSKY. The intelligentsia.

ZAGORSKY. Those of the intelligentsia who support us will
understand our motives, provided we don't allow any atrocities
or extreme brutality.

STUCHKA. I fear they still won't understand . . .

SVERDLOV. And what will Gorky and Sukhanov say in their
newspaper?

STEKLOV. They'll say that terror won't mitigate the civil war but
will only exacerbate it.

YENUKIDZE. Why?

LUNACHARSKY. Because bloodshed breeds more bloodshed. It
will start a chain reaction.

SVERDLOV. Clearly we must concentrate on the main issue –
saving the revolution. (*To* STUCHKA.) But how . . .

140   THE BOLSHEVIKS

TSURUPA *enters the council-room.*

TSURUPA (*waving a telegram*). Comrades, we must not allow this telegram to be published! It was sent to the editor of *Krasnaya Gazeta*. Just listen to this! (*Reads.*) 'The murder of Uritsky and the wounding of Lenin must not go unpunished. It is hard to fight when you know that in the rear your best comrades are dying at the hands of hirelings of the bourgeoisie. We appeal to the workers of Moscow and Petrograd: "Comrades! Smash the counter-revolutionaries without mercy or pity. We don't need courts, trials or lawyers! Let the workers' vengeance rage unchecked, let the blood of the bourgeoisie and the White terrorists flow in torrents. Destroy our enemies with ruthless fury." Signed: Smilga, Lashevich, Goloshchokin, Bela Kun' . . . Comrades, we *cannot* allow this sort of thing into print . . . Pseudo-revolutionary appeals of this kind will simply lead to wholesale slaughter. I'm afraid of excesses . . . After all, there is such a thing as justice and due process . . .

POKROVSKY. What sort of justice can we possibly expect at a time like this?

TSURUPA. What do you mean by that?

POKROVSKY. Normal legal processes are simply not adapted to putting down counter-revolutionary rebellion. There's a full-scale civil war in progress. Don't you realise that this is hardly the time to traipse off to Livny with judge, prosecutor, defence counsel and a jury?

TSURUPA. What's happening in Livny?

LUNACHARSKY. Rebellion!

KURSKY. Here's another example of what's happening. Last night, a secret store of weapons was found in Voronezh. It clearly meant that an uprising was being prepared. There were no clues, no specific culprits. From the standpoint of Roman law, the Cheka could not take action against anyone. But they knew how a plot of that sort had ended in Yaroslavl – hundreds of workers were drowned in the Volga. So our men acted on the promptings of their class instinct: they arrested all the town's leading bourgeois and the plot was discovered. But what if they had delayed, out of respect for due process of law? Today we'd not only be faced with trouble in Livny but in Voronezh too.

NOGIN. Isn't that exactly how Vladimir Ilyich replied to Gorky's moans and groans about our 'arbitrary' behaviour? If a dozen or even a few score pro-White intellectuals have to spend an extra week in prison as hostages and we thereby prevent the hatching of new conspiracies and the murder of thousands of workers and peasants, then *that* is what 'the dictatorship of the proletariat' means, that *is* the class struggle!

POKROVSKY. And talking of the Jacobin terror, which followed a tortuous path from the expedient to the absurd, its first and absolutely correct step was to adapt the processes of justice to the needs of the class struggle.

STUCHKA. But comrade Pokrovsky, revolutionary legality is not meant to be the total abandonment of *all* legality.

KURSKY. For us, revolutionary legality means the scrupulous observance of legal procedure when dealing with intra-class disputes – between workers, for instance, or between peasants. And no procedures whatsoever – except one – where counter-revolutionaries are concerned . . .

STUCHKA. Our position is not sufficiently clear, just as it isn't clear in that telegram either. 'Red terror' must be conducted along specific and strictly defined lines, otherwise we run the risk of repeating the lamentable experience of the Jacobins, whose law sanctioning 'preventive detention' was ultimately nothing but the ante-chamber of the guillotine.

POKROVSKY. That is all true. There were excesses under the Jacobins, but there was also something else – what Engels called 'the year of greatness', when people emerged who displayed the courage of lawlessness – do you hear, the courage of lawlessness – who shrank at nothing, people of relentless energy who succeeded in ensuring that not a single profiteer or black-marketeer – in a word, not a single bourgeois – dared to raise their head!

SVERDLOV. That's an elementary cliché. Whatever actually happened, Robespierre remains the model of a great revolutionary leader. But what interests us at this moment are the consequences of what they did: how did those excesses and atrocities come about under the Jacobins and what did it all lead to?

NOGIN. And we need to cool passions, not inflame them.

KOLLONTAI. Right. Now let's go back and begin at the very

beginning. What is terror? It is an atmosphere of fear, which threatens people with being found guilty even if their connection with some individual or event is so remote as to be effectively non-existent. Is that not so? It is. Counter-revolution in Russia today is not some handful of White officers, conspirators, spies and terrorists. The counter-revolutionary bourgeoisie draws support from much broader social strata, over which it retains its influence. None of those strata are notable for their civil courage, and they are not going to hurl themselves into a counter-revolutionary insurrection at the first call to arms put out by the bourgeoisie proper. Isn't that so? Being essentially counter-revolutionary, however, they will waver nervously and wait to see which way the cat jumps, but always hoping that the bourgeoisie will win in the end. The function of a 'red terror', in my view, is to paralyse those social strata – petty officials, small traders, domestic servants, shop assistants, clerks, but above all the *peasants* – in order to deprive the counter-revolution of its potentially formidable social base. In other words, if we deploy a policy of intimidation we shall achieve our aim without mass bloodshed.

LUNACHARSKY. How annoying therefore, Alexandra Mikhailovna, that while being thoroughly aware of that, the Jacobins nevertheless changed their policy of intimidation to one of extermination.

PETROVSKY. But Anatoly Vasilych – you can't have one without the other. A policy of extermination aimed at the open counter-revolutionaries, a policy of intimidation against the mass of the lower middle class. Neither one is a substitute for the other.

LUNACHARSKY. I'm not substituting them. It was the Jacobins who did, by pushing their policy of extermination too far. Think of Robespierre's last period. What would you call that?

TSURUPA. The terror reached its climax then, but the need for it had fallen away. The atmosphere of fear and horror which the Jacobins had initiated, ended by swallowing *them* too.

KRESTINSKY. The collapse of the Jacobin dictatorship was historically determined . . .

TSURUPA. That's true, it had exhausted itself. And Robespierre and his comrades would have perished anyway, but the whole question is – how? Did they perish at the hand of the king, the royalists or the foreign interventionists? No; the fact is they died at the hands of their fellow-revolutionaries, the very people who had taken the long and hard road of revolution alongside them. That's the paradox. The terror turned into an avalanche.

LUNACHARSKY. And why? Because what happened was a total degeneration of the machinery of government. Whereas at the beginning the terror was carried out by people who had been elected and were therefore answerable to the revolutionary populace, by the time Jacobin rule was coming to an end all that had changed. Firstly, the Committee of Public Safety had carefully centralised the punitive machinery, and the officials who originally were subject to popular election and supervision had been replaced by paid officials nominated by the government. The result was a merging of the organs of government and the organs of terror. And although the latter obeyed the government, the fact that they were now run entirely by salaried civil servants meant that they were no longer in any sense representatives of the people. Once this 'terrorist bureaucracy' had taken over all the jobs, there began the process of decay of a petty-bourgeois dictatorship. Abuses of power were widespread and enormous, but no one – neither Robespierre, nor St Just – could do anything about it. They could not take steps or even protest against this bureaucracy, because not only had *they* created it, it had become their only support. And in those conditions, even the expression of personal dislike by one member of the government for another could provide the spark which might flare up into an all-devouring flame.

CHICHERIN. Quite so, Anatoly Vasilych. St Just himself said that in the final period the terror had become unnecessary and even harmful. These were his last words before his death: 'The revolution has become ossified, all its principles have been fatally weakened; all that is left are red Phrygian caps covering up intrigue; the terror has blunted the perception of crime, just as strong drink blunts the palate.'

GIRL (*dictates*). 'TO CHAIRMAN PETROGRAD SOVIET, SMOLNY INSTITUTE, PETROGRAD. KRZHIZHANOVSKY INFORMS ME THAT CHAIRMAN OF HOUSE COMMITTEE OF NO. 15 ALEXANDROVSKY PROSPEKT ON PETROGRAD SIDE IS THREATENING TO CONFISCATE THE PROPERTY OF PROFESSOR HENRY OSIPOVICH GRAFTIO, OCCUPANT OF ONE OF THE FLATS. GRAFTIO IS A SENIOR PROFESSOR, SUPPORTER OF OUR CAUSE. HE MUST BE PROTECTED FROM ARBITRARY ACTION BY THE HOUSE COMMITTEE CHAIRMAN. PLEASE

NOTIFY ME YOUR ACTION IN THIS MATTER. SIGNED: LENIN, CHAIRMAN, SOVNARKOM.'

ZAGORSKY. Wait, wait a moment! What does it mean when you say that terror is unnecessary but it exists? You're taking an impossible example! When there are no objective conditions for terror – when there's no revolution, no civil war, when there's peace and prosperity – and suddenly a reign of terror begins, then, excuse me, that's not terror but butchery, and it no longer serves class interests but *personal* interests.

SVERDLOV. And whose interests does that person represent? I'm convinced that the blame for the reign of terror in the last period of Jacobinism belonged almost exclusively to the frightened bourgeoisie claiming to be patriots; to the bureaucrats; to the petty bourgeoisie who were shitting in their pants with fear; to a handful of scoundrels who had made their pile during the terror.

KRESTINSKY. That's right; and the result is that we are simply repeating the clichés of the liberal phrase-mongers who claimed that Robespierre only needed the terror in order to get rid of his dangerous rivals!

STEKLOV. That is *not* the result in our case, but you can't deny that in the final period of Jacobin ascendancy they had relegated the social function of terror to second place and terror became the leaders' means of self-preservation and of staying in power.

KRESTINSKY. But what was it that led to that situation? It was not Robespierre's personal ambition. It was the logic of the struggle. St Just said that evidently the power of events is leading us to results that never entered our heads. *That* is the key to the tragedy that occurred.

NOGIN. Don't forget that extreme swings of attitude and behaviour are typical of the petty bourgeoisie.

POKROVSKY. Apart from that, you mustn't lose sight of the rising threat of counter-revolution, which forced the scope of the terror to be spread wider and wider.

ZAGORSKY. He's right. The intensity of the terror depends on the intensity of the struggle – one is in direct proportion to the other.

LUNACHARSKY. With the Jacobins, they were in inverse proportion.

CHICHERIN. Whenever the correct balance between centralisation and democracy is disturbed, the possibility of a one-man military dictatorship appears. Napoleon came to power after the two Directorates had completed the extreme centralisation of power that was begun by the Jacobins, leaving nothing but the hollow forms of democracy that could only have deceived an infant.

STEKLOV. And don't forget that Napoleon, what's more, depended on the army, the police and the bureaucracy – in other words all the things that had come into being under the aegis of the Jacobins.

YENUKIDZE. Comrades, that's enough about the Jacobins, for heaven's sake! What they did is *not* something that threatens us!

KOLLONTAI. Why not?

YENUKIDZE. Because we are who we are ! Which one of us can't I trust? Which one of us must I suspect? You? You? Him? The very idea, applied to us, is blasphemous! You'll say I'm being emotional. All right, from one point of view that *is* an emotional attitude. On the other hand, there is a difference between a petty-bourgeois revolution and a proletarian revolution, just as there is a difference between eighteenth-century France and twentieth-century Russia. And there is Marx's remarkable comment to the effect that two sets of events may seem astoundingly similar but that if they occur in different historical contexts they can lead to completely different results.

KOLLONTAI. What are you talking about, Abel? Haven't we been hearing certain suggestions that it's time to turn terror into a weapon of our social policy, in other words to reduce all our methods of governing the country to terror pure and simple, as happened with the Jacobins?!

PETROVSKY. That is *not* what happened with the Jacobins.

LUNACHARSKY. Why do you say that? It is exactly what *did* happen. What's more, Marx said that the Jacobins and their methods were a classic example of crude, blinkered political thinking. Despite a maximum of political energy, they were incapable of finding any real or genuine means of curing social ills, because they saw the cause of those ills as lying exclusively in the counter-revolutionary attitudes of various enemies of the revolution, and the chief means of salvation as cutting off heads. In other words, the guillotine became the Jacobins' universal method of solving what were essentially economic problems.

KRESTINSKY. But you must admit it was pardonable for the French petty bourgeoisie to want to stamp out hoarders, black-marketeers and illegal traders by executing them!

LUNACHARSKY. True; but I fear that here in Russia our provincial Robespierres and our village Dantons may also turn the bullet into the chief means of solving all conflicts and problems.

SVERDLOV. You're right – they will, unless we forestall them and take the appropriate measures. Instead of going to the people and explaining, informing, persuading and organising, it will be all too easy to call on the Cheka for help.

LUNACHARSKY. I'm also afraid that certain comrades may blame all the contradictions and problems of the revolution on the efforts of counter-revolutionaries or agents of the Western Powers. Remember the rebellion of the Left S-Rs, which took place less than six weeks ago. The press immediately named the culprits – Anglo-French spies. And yet the inevitability of our split with the Left S-Rs was obvious to all of us, because it stemmed from the differences in class interests which divide the revolutionary forces.

STEKLOV. The press has nothing to do with it! You're picking on us deliberately, as you always do – the only bit of Achilles you can ever see is his heel!

STUCHKA. There's only one of us who's allowed to do that . . .

LUNACHARSKY. If, every time there's a crisis, I start shouting 'Treason! Spies! Foreign sabotage!' and never once cast a sober, appraising glance over what *I* am doing, then it is quite natural that I should appeal to the emotions and not to reason and, as a result, approve the concoction of false accusations and similar filth.

ZAGORSKY. By the way, Vladimir Ilyich proposed that we should deal much more severely with false accusations and execute people who fabricate them. We must take note of that.

YENUKIDZE. All right – but where is the line dividing necessity from pernicious absurdity? Who's going to draw that line?

ZAGORSKY (*flaring up*). You and I, Abel, you and I have got to draw it – that's what we're supposed to be sitting here for!

General noise and argument.

SVERDLOV (*shouts*). Comrades! Comrades! . . . Let's get this clear once and for all: no one here is either a supporter or an opponent of terror. We are all Marxists. What I want to say was brilliantly put by Goethe, and I will take the liberty of repeating what he said: 'People say that somewhere in between two opposing opinions lies the truth. Not so! What lies between them is the problem.' The problem, therefore, is the fact that terror is the deadliest but also the most necessary weapon of our revolution, and which is fraught with certain positive and certain negative consequences. Our task is to exploit the positive consequences to the full and to prevent the negative ones from developing. Our discussion can *only* be conducted on that level.

NOGIN. Quite right, Yakov Mikhailych. Passions on both sides must be cooled.

BONCH-BRUYEVICH *enters the council-room. All turn towards him.*

BONCH-B. (*to* SVERDLOV). Yakov Mikhailych, these are some papers that Vladimir Ilyich was intending to sign . . . He's not well enough at the moment . . . oxygen starvation. Dr Rozanov will be here at any moment.

SVERDLOV. Excuse me for a moment, please . . . (*Looks through the papers and signs them.*)

TSURUPA. Did you manage to find any lemons?

BONCH-B.. No. They've just telephoned from Petrograd. They drove round to all the embassies, but as soon as the foreign diplomats heard who the lemons were for, they all refused.

POKROVSKY. Swine!

BONCH-B.. We're now going to try sending private individuals whom they won't suspect. (*Exit.*)

LUNACHARSKY. Yakov Mikhailych, surely the worst isn't going to happen?

SVERDLOV. Calm yourself, Anatoly Vasilych . . .

LUNACHARSKY. How can we go on without him? How can we . . .

SVERDLOV. Anatoly Vasilych, don't . . . (*Puts his arm around* LUNACHARSKY's *heaving shoulders.*)

LUNACHARSKY (*whispers*). I couldn't go on living . . .

SVERDLOV. Now, Anatoly Vasilych, you mustn't . . . please . . .

LUNACHARSKY. I'd only tell this to you . . . the day before yesterday I met him in the courtyard, where he was taking a walk with Alexei . . . He saw me and smiled . . . and he said to Alexei: 'Our Anatoly Vasilych can do anything . . .' And he made a bet with Alexei that I could, there and then, give a frightfully 'scientific' lecture on the devil and the problems of diabolism . . . Well, I did . . . And how he laughed . . . how he laughed . . .

SVERDLOV. He was in an excellent mood this morning. I rang him up: to complain yet again about Vasiliev – how he was paying no regard to other people, how he was exceeding his powers, how he had no conception of a dialogue and could only ever conduct a monologue. Ilyich just burst out laughing: 'Neither you nor I, Yakov Mikhailych, can do anything about it. Oscar Wilde was right: self-love is a love affair that lasts a lifetime.'

Telephone rings in the council-room.

PETROVSKY (*picks up the receiver*). Petrovsky here . . . (*To the other* COMMISSARS.) There's fighting in Livny, using artillery. We've had heavy casualties. The uprising has been led by the S-Rs. Unrest in the whole district. (*Into the receiver.*) All right. Thanks. (*Replaces the receiver.*) Yakov Mikhailych, they're asking you to hurry up with that decree. The fact is that . . .

SVERDLOV. Don't try and hurry me, Grigory Ivanych. We will work on the decree exactly as much as is necessary . . . We are coming to the crux of the matter, comrades – the problem of the *degree* of terror to be applied. At first sight this is unconnected with the *principle* of terror, which in the circumstances is just and necessary. But we should always remember that the degree of force can significantly influence the principle itself, may in fact change it, just as the means often change the end. Broadly speaking, quantity can mutate into quality. I want to warn all of us against a loose interpretation of the limits of terror which could mean extending them too far, because that may lead to the terror starting to hit our own people. If that were to happen, the terror could change colour: the red terror would then begin, *objectively*, to perform the function of a White terror, regardless of the *subjective* aims and aspirations of those carrying it out. The same thing can happen if the principle of *timeliness* in the use of terror is disregarded.

TSURUPA. What are the guarantees against all those dangers?

SVERDLOV. On the one hand, in our being clearly aware of the dangers, and on the other – in a whole series of measures that must be taken: terror must be publicly declared.

STUCHKA. Openness about the actions of the punitive authorities.

NOGIN. Publication of the names of all those arrested, the names of all hostages and all those sentenced to death.

SVERDLOV. The selection of punitive bodies on a class basis.

ZAGORSKY. Firm observance of the basic principle of red terror: it is the terror of one class against another class, carried out by a particular class and in the name of that class.

SVERDLOV. Yes. I would stress: carried out by that class.

POKROVSKY. We don't need professional executants but workers from the shop floor, who will act from a class standpoint.

SVERDLOV. Any policy depends on who puts it into effect. Otherwise we may achieve results that are the exact opposite of those we intended. We must deploy our very best people, where possible those who belonged to the Party before the revolution.

STEKLOV. But comrades – that means making the very flower of the working-class movement do the dirtiest work. It's likely to be an absolutely suicidal job. Who will be able to endure it?

YENUKIDZE. But that's exactly the horror of it, my dear fellow – there is no other way. There's nothing for it but to wade through mud and blood, no matter how heartbreaking it will be . . .

NOGIN (*to* STEKLOV). Yury Mikhailych, when I've seen Dzerzhinsky doing his job, it's not work – it's torture to him. He'd find it easier to sentence himself to death than other people, but he signs the death sentences all the same . . .

TSURUPA. That's the kind of people we need, and not those who'd find it easy . . .

SVERDLOV. Comrades, to sum up our discussion, which has been of great value to all of us, I'd like to draw your attention to the following: Vladimir Ilyich has said to us more than once that there are no immutable dividing-lines between a bourgeois revolution and a proletarian revolution. Therefore the question of excesses and atrocities, which has occupied us so much today, is of enormous significance for us and is by no means a secondary issue. Atrocities resulting from a red terror are a sign of crass, petty-bourgeois 'revolutionism', and its potential emergence is, if you like, one of the chief dangers that lie in wait for us. Because if we don't keep a very tight rein on the petty-bourgeois element in the ranks of our revolution, we can slide backwards into something totally unwished-for, as happened in the French Revolution. That is the cardinal problem underlying today's discussion.

LUNACHARSKY. Atrocities! And what, pray, would you call what happened in Tsaritsyn – carried out by *our people* – when they filled a barge with prisoners, hundreds of whom were innocent, towed it out into the middle of the Volga and sank it? Or the senseless carnage proposed in that telegram that was read out to us just now?

PETROVSKY. I don't justify what happened in Tsaritsyn, but . . . Anatoly Vasilych, when these bastards are armed, you're not going to defeat them by putting up statues to Karl Marx. Every worker would simply spit on anybody who says you can induce a gendarme to drop his gun by making speeches at him.

KOLLONTAI. But a worker would also spit on anybody who says that terror must become a normal part of our life in the workers' state.

LUNACHARSKY. Yes, I agree that there are moments in history when violence is necessary. Even so, true socialism cannot be forced on the world with rifles and bayonets, but only by reason and a broad programme of educating the workers.

SVERDLOV. Comrades, the following basic directives are proposed as forming the content of the decree. (*Reads from his draft.*) 'The Council of People's Commissars finds that in the state of civil war that has arisen it has become urgently necessary to protect the civilian front by means of terror; that in order to strengthen and improve the work of the Cheka and to make it more systematic, a large number of senior Party colleagues must be drafted into that organisation; and that the

Soviet Republic must be secured against its class enemies by isolating them in concentration camps. All persons belonging to or connected with White Guard organisations, plots or rebellions are liable to execution by firing-squad; the names of all those so executed will be published, together with the grounds on which these measures have been taken against them.' Any questions or additions?

PETROVSKY. For my part, I would like to issue a decree from the People's Commissariat of Internal Affairs in which the Soviets, local and national, are required immediately to arrest all representatives of the upper bourgeoisie; all officers; all leaders of the Right Social-Revolutionary Party, and to hold them as hostages. Any attempt at concealment or escape or to raise anti-Soviet movements will be met with mass executions by firing-squad without right of appeal. Local Executive Committees and administrative bodies are to institute measures to investigate all persons living under a false name with the aim of avoiding arrest or punishment.

SVERDLOV. Any further additions? Any objections? I must know the views of all present, therefore I will allow myself to question you individually. Lunacharsky?

LUNACHARSKY. The hardest thing of all for a Communist is to be cruel. How many oaths of ruthless vengeance have we taken at the gravesides of our fallen comrades – and yet no one has yet raised a hand to carry them out. But now our cup is full and running over. I must raise my hand in approval.

SVERDLOV. Pokrovsky?

POKROVSKY. Yes, of course.

SVERDLOV. Stuchka?

STUCHKA. Yes.

SVERDLOV. Kollontai?

KOLLONTAI. No objections.

SVERDLOV. Kursky?

KURSKY. I approve.

SVERDLOV. Tsurupa?

TSURUPA. I agree to the draft.

SVERDLOV. Zagorsky?

ZAGORSKY. Yes.

SVERDLOV. Steklov?

STEKLOV. No objections.

SVERDLOV. Nogin?

NOGIN. I have no objections.

SVERDLOV. Krestinsky?

KRESTINSKY. No objections.

SVERDLOV. Chicherin?

CHICHERIN. Yes.

SVERDLOV. Yenukidze?

YENUKIDZE. I agree.

SVERDLOV. Petrovsky?

PETROVSKY. Yes.

SVERDLOV. And Sverdlov also votes in favour.

KOLLONTAI. Comrades, we have still not stated our position with regard to Fanya Kaplan, the would-be assassin.

SVERDLOV. Alexandra Mikhailovna is right. (*Looks round silently at all those present.*)

POKROVSKY. Shoot her.

KOLLONTAI. When the interrogation and investigation is completed – execution by firing-squad.

The verdicts pronounced by POKROVSKY *and* KOLLONTAI *are confirmed by their colleagues in the silence of assent.*

SVERDLOV. The Council's view on that question is clear enough.

LUNACHARSKY. What's the time?

STUCHKA. 3 a.m.

KIZAS (*appearing in the doorway, to* SVERDLOV). Yakov Mikhailych, the doctors would like a word with you.

SVERDLOV. Coming.

KOLLONTAI. How are things in there?

KIZAS. Much the same. (*Exit.*)

SVERDLOV *picks up his papers and exits.*

The COMMISSARS *sit in silence.*

GIRL *(dictates)*. 'TO PROVINCIAL EXECUTIVE COMMITTEE, NOVGOROD. COPY TO CHEKA. APPARENTLY BULATOV HAS BEEN ARRESTED FOR MAKING A COMPLAINT TO ME. I WARN YOU THAT FOR THIS I CAN HAVE THE CHAIRMAN AND MEMBERS OF THE EXECUTIVE COMMITTEE AND THE HEAD OF THE CHEKA ARRESTED AND SHOT. WHY DID YOU NOT REPLY IMMEDIATELY TO MY EARLIER ENQUIRY? SIGNED: LENIN, CHAIRMAN, SOVNARKOM.'

SVERDLOV *passes along the corridor to* LENIN'*s apartment, where* KRUPSKAYA *comes to meet him.*

KRUPSKAYA. When Rozanov began examining him, he kept trying to talk, then he passed out again.

Enter VELICHKINA *carrying oxygen bottles. She goes into* LENIN'*s room and shuts the door behind her.*

ULYANOVA *comes out of the kitchen.*

TELEGRAPHIST *(to* GIRL*)*. Take this down. It's from Petrograd. *(As the teletype tape creeps out of the machine, he dictates to the* GIRL.*)* 'To Lenin, Kremlin, Moscow. Terribly distressed, worried. Sincerely wish you rapid recovery. Keep your spirits up. Signed: Gorky, Maria Andreyeva.'

ULYANOVA. Yakov Mikhailych, look what I found in his pocket. *(Hands a note to* SVERDLOV.*)*

SVERDLOV *(reads the note, smiles faintly)*. Yes . . . I see . . .

ULYANOVA. Is it something important?

SVERDLOV. Yes, very. It's to Tsurupa about the 'half-a-hundredweight' question. We discussed the matter and it turns out that we resolved it in exactly the terms that Vladimir Ilyich is proposing in this note.

In the council-room the COMMISSARS *are settling down for the night. Some stretch out on chairs pushed together, some on the floor with newspapers for pillows, others sit on chairs or window-ledges. None sleep. The atmosphere is quiet, but tense. Occasionally a desultory remark is uttered, giving the impression of someone thinking aloud.*

KOLLONTAI *(continuing a conversation)*. . . . He and I had a rather odd encounter not so very long ago, in January. I went into his study and found it dark. Familiar silhouette by the window, hands in pockets, rocking back and forth from heel to toe, head lifted up high, looking out of the window at the stars. It was so unexpected, I stood stock-still. Everything was so quiet, I decided to creep out again unnoticed. He saw my reflection in the window-pane and without turning round he said: 'The stars. What a night for stars . . . Means it'll be even colder tomorrow . . .' Then he turned round and asked me: 'Have you ever looked at a starry sky?' I said I had, though only when I was at sea or in the country. 'At sea?' he said, surprised. 'Oh yes, of course – you've been to America. When I was a boy I knew all the constellations by name, but now I'm starting to forget them . . .' And he immediately started talking about business matters . . .

Doctors OBUKH, WEISBROD *and* VINOKUROV *come out of* LENIN's *room into the hallway.*

WEISBROD. Yakov Mikhailych, we've asked Dr Obukh to give you an objective account of the patient's condition.

OBUKH. The situation is grave. Very grave indeed. There has been a severe haemorrhage from the wound in the upper part of the left lung into the pleural cavity, which has caused the heart to move sharply to the right. The result has been a serious weakening of the pulse. Therefore our main concern at the moment is not his broken arm but that shock to the cardiac function. The second bullet pierced the neck from left to right and passed between the spine and the gullet. If that bullet had deviated by a fraction of a millimetre, Vladimir Ilyich would no longer be with us. Basing ourselves on our clinical experience, we have come to the following conclusion: if the patient can survive the cardiac shock, the immediate danger is past. The other remaining danger, however, is the possibility of infection from the bullet.

WEISBROD. We are also worried about the condition of the pleural region and the path of the bullet that runs through it.

OBUKH. We have prescribed the following measures: absolute rest; all attention to be concentrated on the cardiac function; the arm to be temporarily disregarded except for a light restraining dressing, so that the shattered fragments of bone, which may be disturbed by an involuntary movement, do not cause the patient unnecessary pain.

VINOKUROV. In order to have another opinion on the condition of the pleural region we've decided to call in the leading specialist, Nikolai Nikolayich Mamonov.

OBUKH. That is all, I think – at least in broad terms. Have you any questions?

KRUPSKAYA. Will he live?

VINOKUROV. We're doing everything possible, Nadezhda Konstantinovna.

SVERDLOV. In other words, everything now depends on whether his heart holds out?

OBUKH. Yes. Practically nothing depends on us for the moment.

SVERDLOV. I see. We must tell the bitter truth to the country and the world at large. For that we need a medical report. And as soon as possible. If I've understood you correctly, the outcome is still uncertain. But we must put it in such a way that people realise there is still hope.

WEISBROD. We've already drafted a report.

SVERDLOV. Please give it to Bonch-Bruyevich. Which of you will be on duty here for the rest of the night?

WEISBROD. Doctor Obukh and myself.

SVERDLOV. Do make use of us if necessary . . . The whole Sovnarkom is still next door, no one has gone home . . .

OBUKH. If we need you, we'll call for you.

Exeunt DOCTORS.

PETROVSKY (*to* ZAGORSKY). Do you remember when we were in exile in Siberia? A miserable little hut, the tundra, the insults from that police sergeant, the hunger . . . yet it was easier to bear than this . . .

ZAGORSKY. Yes, it most certainly was . . .

PETROVSKY. Tough business, revolution . . . Good, but hellish complicated . . . I wonder: if we eventually win, will we be the same afterwards?

ZAGORSKY. Yes, of course we will . . . But it'll file the rough edges off us. Like sandpaper.

PETROVSKY. True enough. And we've got to keep our eyes skinned.

ZAGORSKY. The Old Man was good at that. He was always the first to raise the alarm whenever there was any trouble brewing.

PETROVSKY. Yes, he knew how much our mistakes could cost us.

ZAGORSKY. When I think he might die, I have the feeling that all our lives are meaningless.

SVEDLOV (*to* KRUPSKAYA). Right now we all instinctively huddle together . . . like children . . . when there's danger . . .

BONCH-BRUYEVICH *goes up to the* TELEGRAPHIST.

BONCH-B.. Please transmit this document immediately to all stations.

TELEGRAPHIST. Right. Here's a telegram from Petrograd. How are things in there?

BONCH-B.. Not good. (*Returns to* LENIN's *apartment*.)

GIRL (*dictates*). 'OFFICIAL BULLETIN. TWO GUNSHOT WOUNDS HAVE BEEN LOCATED . . .'

BONCH-B. (*to* SVERDLOV). Telegram from Gorky.

SVERDLOV (*surprised; quietly*). From Gorky?

GIRL (*dictates*). '. . . ONE BULLET, ENTERING UNDER THE LEFT SHOULDER-BLADE, HAS DAMAGED THE UPPER PORTION OF THE LUNG, INDUCING HAEMORRHAGE INTO THE PLEURA, AND HAS LODGED IN THE RIGHT SIDE OF THE NECK ABOVE THE RIGHT COLLAR-BONE . . .'

SVERDLOV (*reads telegram*). H'mm . . . After eighteen months of fiercely attacking Vladimir Ilyich and all of us . . . Relations broken off . . . And now . . . It seems blood must flow before some people will stop and think . . .

GIRL (*dictates*). '. . . THE OTHER BULLET PENETRATED THE LEFT SHOULDER, SHATTERED THE BONE AND LODGED UNDER THE SKIN IN THE REGION OF THE LEFT SHOULDER . . .'

BONCH-B.. Vladimir Ilyich will be glad.

SVERDLOV. No, no, it'll excite him. He's very fond of Gorky. Don't show it to him for the time being.

GIRL (*dictates*). 'THERE ARE INDICATIONS OF INTERNAL HAEMORRHAGE. PULSE ONE HUNDRED AND FOUR. GENERAL CONDITION SERIOUS.'

SVERDLOV. When he gets better.

KRUPSKAYA. *Will* he get better?

SVERDLOV *says nothing.*

CHICHERIN. During the Brest-Litovsk crisis, he was almost alone against everyone . . . He was as steady as a rock. 'The mood of a class is one thing; its fundamental interests are another: the two may not coincide. I'm thinking of its interests. . .' He stuck it out – and he won.

KRESTINSKY. I remember it as if it were yesterday: at the decisive session of the Central Committee he came striding in like a lion . . . paced about the room as if it were a cage . . . He was ready to argue anyone into the ground . . . Bukharin was cowering in a corner, the rest of us were reduced to silence. He was angry, white in the face, his hands were shaking so much he couldn't even put them in his pockets when he tried to . . . We hadn't yet agreed on accepting the peace terms, and we kept on putting forward other proposals . . . Then he couldn't stand it any longer: 'I shall resign from the Central Committee! Enough of playing games! I will not tolerate it for a single second longer!' I can hear him saying it now: 'Not a single second longer' . . .

NOGIN. Yes, he has a raging temperament. Takes everything very much to heart. But usually keeps it bottled up. And he often suffered cruelly. Especially when there were splits in the Party. When he had to break with friends . . .

YENUKIDZE. How many scars there are on him . . .

PETROVSKY. And what about the Malinovsky affair, when we finally found out that he'd been a police spy all along? He shut himself up for a whole hour with the newspaper that had printed the extracts from the police records, and when he threw it away, his eyes were red . . .

ZAGORSKY. If one thinks about it seriously, we never took enough care of him.

LUNACHARSKY. What a row we had about the bombardment of the Kremlin . . . I didn't understand his attitude then, but he understood me . . . I said a lot of offensive things to him which I shouldn't have said . . . In fact, whenever he and I had a row we descended to bad language . . . I was told that when he was given my letter of resignation, it was as if something snapped inside him . . .

VELICHKINA *comes out of* LENIN's *room, carrying empty oxygen cylinders and collects new ones.*

SVERDLOV. Please let me go in and sit there for a while . . . I'll help you with these things . . .

SVERDLOV *picks up the oxygen cylinders and follows* VELICHKINA *into* LENIN's *room.*

KRESTINSKY. In 1912, when *Pravda* started up, he was in Cracow and bombarded us with articles. We corrected and rewrote his pieces shamelessly, and only published some of them. At the time we all thought we knew the state of affairs better than he did, because we were in Russia, so we thought we knew what sort of articles were needed and how they should be written . . . Then in one of his letters he burst out: 'I do not intend to talk about the main issue, but don't you realise that my sole source of income is what I earn from writing for newspapers? And if you keep on throwing all my contributions into the wastepaper-basket, I shall simply die of starvation in this hole . . .'

Silence. Suddenly SVERDLOV *bursts out of* LENIN's *room and runs towards the council-room.*

SVERDLOV. Comrades! Comrades!

All hastily get up from their places, and stare at the door in horror.
SVERDLOV *bursts into the council-room.*

SVERDLOV. The doctors say . . . the crisis is past . . . He said . . . he himself said: 'We're on our way again!'

Silence, then an explosion of joy. All rush towards SVERDLOV, *talking, shouting, in utter confusion. They embrace and congratulate each other.*
KOLLONTAI *laughs and weeps at the same time. Suddenly from the group surrounding* SVERDLOV *come several voices singing the opening bars of the 'Internationale':*

'Arise, ye starvelings, from your slumbers,
Arise, ye prisoners of want . . .'

Then, happy, transformed, all cluster together and sing the rest of the revolutionary anthem quietly, in a near-whisper . . .

Curtain.

ONWARD, ONWARD, ONWARD!

Translator's Introduction

The action of this play takes place on two planes, one realistic, one imaginary. The realistic action occurs on October 24th 1917, in Petrograd, the eve of the Bolsheviks' seizure of power by force from the Provisional Government; the imaginary action occurs in some timeless limbo of the indefinite future, when the erstwhile participants of the October Revolution meet and confront each other in the next world and argue about the revolution from their respective points of view. This device also provides the pretext for confrontations between the leading Bolsheviks on the course of events *after* the revolution, at the climax of which Lenin and Stalin argue passionately: Lenin accuses Stalin of having corrupted and betrayed the revolution; Stalin retorts that he was Lenin's faithful disciple and was merely completing what Lenin had begun. During the arguments between the protagonists, the author exploits the irony inherent in the fact that many of those who figure in the play – Trotsky, Ordzhonikidze, Zinoviev, Kamenev, Bukharin and Spiridonova – were done to death on Stalin's orders in the 'Great Purge' of 1936-38 and later. Where known, the dates of the characters' births and deaths are given in the cast-list.

Characters

Male

LENIN, V.I.	Russian; Bolshevik leader.	(1817–1924)
KORNILOV, L.G.	Half-Russian, half-Kirghiz; General.	(1870–1918)
SVERDLOV, Y.M.	Jewish; Bolshevik.	(1885–1919)
STRUVE, P.B.	Half-Russian, half-German; economist, liberal politician.	(1870–1944)
MARKOV, S.L.	Russian; general.	(1867–1918)
KERENSKY, A.F.	Russian, Socialist; Prime Minister, Provisional Government of Russia, April–October 1917.	(1881–1971)
TROTSKY, L.D.	Jewish; Bolshevik.	(1879–1940)
STALIN, J.V.	Georgian; Bolshevik.	(1879–1953)
PLEKHANOV, G.V.	Russian; Marxist Theorist; Menshevik.	(1857–1918)
ORDZHONIKIDZE, G.K.	Georgian; Bolshevik.	(1886–1937)
LUKOMSKY, A.S.	Russian; General.	(1863–1936)
DZIERZINSKI, F.E.	Polish Bolshevik; founder of CHEKA (political police).	(1877–1926)
ZINOVIEV, G.Y.	Jewish; Bolshevik.	(1883–1936)
KAMENEV, L.B.	Jewish; Bolshevik	(1883–1936)
MARTOV, Y.O.	Jewish; Menshevik leader.	(1871–1947)
DENIKIN, A.I.	Russian; General.	(1872–1947)
DAN, F.I.	Jewish; Menshevik leader.	(1871–1947)
BUKHARIN, N.I.	Russian; Bolshevik.	(1888–1938)

RAHIAA, EINO	Finnish; Bolshevik.	
POLKOVNIKOV, G.P.	Russian; Colonel.	

Female

SPIRIDONOVA, MARIA	Russian; Leader, Left Social-Revolutionary Party. (Left S-Rs)	(1884–1941)
KRUPSKAYA, N.K.	Russian; Bolshevik; Wife of LENIN	(1875–1939)
FOFANOVA, M.V.	Russian; Bolshevik sympathiser; owner of the apartment in which Lenin hid in October 1917 immediately prior to the Bolsheviks' seizure of power.	
LUXEMBURG, Rosa	Jewish; Leader of Polish and German Communist movements.	(1871–1919)

ACT ONE

Scene One

The curtain rises to reveal a part of the stage, brightly lit, on which 22 light armchairs are disposed in a semicircle. One by one the characters enter in the following order, introduce themselves and sit down.

KORNILOV. In this year of upheavals and national collapse, I, General Lavr Kornilov, summoned by the slobbering liberals of the Provisional Government, turned my troops against the capital, Petrograd, in order to drive the cattle back into their stalls, but I failed to do it thanks to the two-faced treachery of Kerensky. I hereby declare that I admit no regrets; I do not reproach myself for the attempt but for the half-hearted and irresolute way in which it was carried out. October 24th 1917 found me at Bykhov, in a girls' boarding school that had been turned into a prison for several senior generals of the Russian Army - my companions in the abortive march on Petrograd.

STRUVE. Pyotr Bernhardovich Struve, philosopher, economist, born in the same year - 1870 - as the younger Ulyanov, who came to be known as Lenin. As a young man I toyed with Marxism and collaborated with Lenin, with whom I had the pleasure, on more than one occasion, of sharing a meal. My stepmother, Kalmykova, was his fervent admirer, and he used to come and eat at our house. I even subscribed 5 roubles - perhaps more - to his illegal, underground newspaper *The Spark*. I came to my senses in 1905. To me, Bolshevism was a lethal mixture of Russian moonshine and the dregs of Karl Marx's hogwash. When the civil war started in 1918, I helped the White generals - Kornilov, Denikin, Wrangel - in their fight against the Reds. And later, as an émigré, I gave my services to anyone who shared my views. As for Kerensky and Milyukov, those two pinkos who led the Provisional Government, I hated them with equal intensity. I died in German-occupied Paris in 1944 - in despair. Stalin was battering the Germans, there seemed nothing left to hope for. Some of us Russian émigrés had been reconciled to Stalin: what does it matter, they said, whether the new Tsar of all the Russias calls himself 'General Secretary of the Communist Party' or anything else? He had enlarged the empire, he had recovered most of the territory we lost as a result of the revolution, he was winning the war, and Russia was becoming the second greatest power in the world ... But I don't trust Bolshevism, whatever disguise it puts on ...

On October 24th 1917, when everything could still have taken a different turning, I was in Petrograd, explaining, imploring, trying to convince people, but no one would listen. The bell was tolling for them, but they couldn't hear it.

SPIRIDONOVA. Maria Spiridonova, member of the Central Committee of the Left Social-Revolutionary Party, born into the Russian nobility. Having been a revolutionary since I was a young girl, in 1906, at the age of 22, I shot at a tsarist satrap, was arrested by the gendarmes and raped. I was moved from prison to prison, sentenced to hard labour in Siberia. Before and after the October Revolution I stood for collaboration with the Bolsheviks and sharing power with them in a coalition government. It was their signing of the peace of Brest-Litovsk with Germany that split us apart, although initially I had shared Lenin's position on the issue. On July 6th 1918, I led our party's armed rebellion against the Bolsheviks. I was arrested, given a year's suspended sentence, then amnestied. From 1921 to 1937 my life was an unbroken succession of arrests, imprisonment and exile, although I had given up politics and was working as a bookkeeper. My final arrest was in the city of Ufa, when I was accused of plotting a coup against the government of the Bashkir Republic. Admittedly, when a few days later all the members of that government landed up in the cells alongside mine, the charge was altered to one of plotting to assassinate Marshal Voroshilov – if he had suddenly taken it into his head to go to Ufa! As I watched and saw who was being put into the neighbouring cells, I realised that an anti-Soviet coup had taken place – which was, and remains, my interpretation of Stalin's so-called 'Great Purge'. When Bukharin was subjected to a farcical show-trial the following year, I was ordered to give false evidence at his trial to the effect that our revolt in July 1918 had been the result of secret collusion with him – and I refused. My former colleagues of the Left S-R Central Committee, Kamkov and Karelin, were equally firm in resisting Stalin's pressure to perjure themselves and also

refused to testify at the trial. In 1941, a few hours before the
German troops captured the city of Oryol, I was shot –
alongside a once-prominent Bolshevik, Christian Rakovsky . . .
On October 24th 1917, I was in Petrograd at the Smolny
Institute, helping in the work of the Military Revolutionary
Committee, which our party had formed jointly with the
Bolsheviks.

MARKOV. Sergei Leonidovich Markov, Lieutenant-General, chief
of staff of the South-Western Army Group. I was arrested and
held under guard at the girls' school in Bykhov. After the Jews
and Freemasons had seized power in Petrograd, I went south to
the Don, where I commanded a regiment made up of officers
and later a division of the White Army. I was killed fighting in
1918. I fully support everything that General Kornilov has said.

KERENSKY. I, Alexander Fyodorovich Kerensky, wish to address
you from the vantage-point of a life that lasted 89 years. Alas, I
celebrated that birthday quite alone: by 1970 none of the
participants in those disastrous excesses of 1917 were left alive,
except myself in New York and Molotov in Moscow.

I survived Lenin by half a century and saw with my own eyes
the disastrous consequences for Russia of his destruction of the
first revolution in 1917 – the February Revolution, a *democratic*
revolution – which I symbolised in the eyes of the people. Yes,
yes – I was the personification of the Russian people's hopes
and longings for a democracy. The February Revolution, you
might say, was only successful because I and not Lenin was in
Petrograd at the time, and it failed . . . (*Turns to* KORNILOV.) it
failed because Kornilov . . . that puppet in the hands of an
irresponsible clique of industrialists, that undistinguished
general whom I put in command of the army . . . somehow got
it into his swollen head that he was destined to be the saviour
of Russia. It was *he* who committed the crime that broke the
united front of government and army against the Bolsheviks . . .
I have to say this. I say it bitterly but sincerely . . .

KORNILOV (*interrupts*). As sincerely, I suppose, as you wrote on
September 17th 1917 (*Reads from an old newspaper.*) 'I have never
doubted Kornilov's patriotic love for his country. It was not ill-
will but ignorance and total inexperience of politics that caused
him to act in a way that threatened to undermine the state. He
should be executed for treason, but when that happens I will
bring flowers to his grave and bow the knee before the memory
of a great patriot.'

STRUVE. What do you expect from a senile 90-year-old? He knows practially nothing, and what he does know he gets hopelessly muddled.

SVERDLOV. This 'democrat' has a few things on his conscience . . .

KERENSKY (*hotly*). You're a fine one to talk about democracy! You began by dispersing the Constituent Assembly illegally and by force because you Bolsheviks didn't get a majority of seats in it – and how did you end? You ended by firing Alexander Tvardovsky – a man with all the instincts of a true democrat – from the editorship of *Novy Mir*! Another example of how democracy flourished under Bolshevik rule, I suppose?

SVERDLOV. I don't understand you. What does that prove?

KERENSKY. It proves that literally until my dying breath I was carefully following everything that was going on in Russia and I knew it all. So if you think I'm ignorant you're making a big mistake! I followed everything that happened! I'm not General Kornilov, who relied on his orderly to tell him what was in the newspapers, and then not every day. No! I sat in the Library of Congress and read and analysed everything, including the writings of Struve and his émigré friends, who explained in simple language exactly why Struve always foamed at the mouth at the very mention of Lenin: renegades, especially renegade Marxists, always fear and loathe their own past.

STRUVE. Once a windbag, always a windbag.

KERENSKY. On October 24th 1917, I, the prime minister and supreme commander-in-chief, was as usual at my post in the Winter Palace, in the room that had been the private study of Tsar Alexander III.

TROTSKY. I am Lev Davidovich Bronstein, Party code-name Trotsky, the son of probably the only Jewish landowner in Russia. In 1918 my father, who had lost everything he possessed thanks to our decree on land reform, came to see me in the Kremlin. To do that he had had to walk 125 miles from Kherson to take the train from Odessa to Moscow. He expressed all his feelings about me in one sentence: 'The fathers work their fingers to the bone to earn something for their old age, and then their sons go and make a revolution.' I was seventeen when I joined the revolutionary movement in 1896. I took part in the Second Party Congress, joined the Mensheviks and began my fifteen years of polemical arguments with Lenin . . . In 1905 I was one of the leaders of the first Russian Revolution, chairman of the Petersburg Soviet of Workers' Deputies; I was arrested, tried and condemned to exile for life in Siberia. I escaped and emigrated. I returned to Russia in 1917 after the February Revolution, thinking that I would have to learn from the revolution. But there were obviously not enough teachers who knew their business, so I realised it was up to *me* to teach people how to make a revolution. In August 1917 I joined the Bolshevik Party, and at the Sixth Party Congress I was elected to the Central Committee. In the autumn I again became chairman of the Petrograd Soviet; after the October Revolution I was in turn People's Commissar for Foreign Affairs, People's Commissar for War and chairman of the Military Revolutionary Committee of the Republic. There is no denying that I had profound disagreements with Lenin on fundamental questions of theory and practical politics, which he later expressed in his phrase about my 'non-bolshevism'. My even more profound disagreements with Stalin, which resulted in my being banished from the country, were equally real. My activities abroad in creating the Fourth International as a counterweight to the Third International were not an invention: it all happened as did much else of that kind. I am a soldier of the World Revolution, and I unhesitatingly submit my record to the judgment of posterity.

What did *not* happen – never could have happened and which I reject with contempt – were my alleged contacts with foreign intelligence services . . . (*Pause.*) On August 20th 1940, sitting in the study of my house in Mexico I was mortally wounded by a blow with an ice-axe on the back of my skull delivered by a certain Jackson, the pseudonym of a Spaniard called Ramón Mercader . . . Stalin's satanic thirst for revenge was satisfied.

STALIN. Retribution is not revenge. Retribution is always just. We Bolsheviks have always accepted that moral category. As for our Spanish comrade Ramón Mercader, his role was perfectly straightforward and understandable: he was merely carrying out the sentence of a proletarian court.

TROTSKY. You murdered me without the semblance of a trial, Stalin!

STALIN. We did not propose to tie our hands with formalities or with bourgeois moral concepts when it was a question of dealing with such ideological traitors as your gang of spies and murderers, a poisonous clique that had long since ceased to have any political significance for the working class. *(Turns to the audience.)* I have no need to introduce myself. The landmarks along my historic path have not yet been forgotten. The chief one was that I won the greatest war in human history. I preserved Lenin's heritage and I built socialism. I ask you to proceed from these facts.

KERENSKY. Generalissimo Stalin, on November 7th 1918, the first anniversary of the excesses of 1917, you wrote in *Pravda*: 'All the practical work of organising the uprising was carried out under the direct leadership of comrade Trotsky, to whom the Party is indebted more than to anyone else.' In 1924, however, you were saying that Trotsky played no particular role in the October uprising and could not have done. Then in 1938, in your *Short Course in the History of the Bolshevik Party*, you declared yourself to have been the effective leader of the insurrection. Which of these stories is the truth, Generalissimo?

STALIN. The sooner the proletariat forgets about certain services performed for them by this gentleman *(Points to* TROTSKY.), the better for them.

PLEKHANOV. Georgii Valentinovich Plekhanov . . . Until my very last breath I dedicated my life to the Russian working class and to the idea of socialism. October 24th . . . was the eve of the most tragic day of my life, when Lenin made the workers take a leap in the dark. For a man who had given his life to propagating Marxism in Russia, it was ruin, the end . . . I lived for less than a year after that . . . I was only 62 years old . . .

ORDZHONIKIDZE. Grigory Konstantinovich Ordzhonikidze, Party code-name 'Sergo'. Member of the Party since 1903. In 1926 I was elected a probationary member, then a full member of the Politburo. I was a friend of Stalin, my fellow-Georgian. In 1922, when we were in the process of forming the USSR and I was Moscow's representative in Georgia, I stupidly flared up and punched another Party comrade – an incident that became notorious as the 'Georgian affair'. Lenin proposed excluding me from the Party for two years as a lesson to anyone else who might be tempted to act the bully. Stalin saved me from that punishment. The question that worries me now is the problem of how far a Bolshevik should resist injustice committed in the name of the Party: how far can one go without ceasing to be a Bolshevik?

LUKOMSKY. Alexander Sergeyevich Lukomsky, born 1863, died in 1936, Lieutenant-General, brother-in-arms of General Kornilov, later an émigré. I fully support what General Kornilov has said.

DZIERZINSKI (*speaks with a marked Polish accent*). Felix Dzierzinski, son of a Polish nobleman. A Bolshevik. Active in the revolutionary movement from 1892 . . . The plenary session of the Central Committee of the Party on July 20th 1926, was my last. The doctors had categorically forbidden me to make any speeches . . . But Trotsky, Zinoviev and Kamenev so obviously wanted to stand the New Economic Policy on its head that I simply could not sit there in silence . . . When I stepped down from the rostrum, I was shaking all over . . . That was it . . . in three hours I was dead . . . I was only forty-nine . . . Fate did not let me live longer . . . But if I hadn't died in 1926, then it would have happened soon anyway, say in 1929, and if not then, no doubt I would have gone with the others during the purges of the late 'thirties . . . Why? Because I was incapable of undermining or betraying anything that Lenin had created. I have the most painful memory of my last conversation with Lenin on December 14th 1922, when I clumsily tried to make excuses for Ordzhonikidze and Stalin over the 'Georgian affair', and Lenin looked at me so sadly and with such understanding. You see, it was after that conversation that his condition got much worse and he never appeared in public again. I will always carry that terrible burden on my conscience.

ZINOVIEV. Grigory Yevseyevich Zinoviev.

KAMENEV. Lev Borisovich Kamenev.

ZINOVIEV. Personally, I would prefer to forget the days leading up to the October insurrection. Kamenev and I were against the armed uprising, thinking it was premature, and we leaked the planned date to the press. In spite of our stupid move, the insurrection went ahead successfully. But we made up for this lapse, because we later achieved a great deal that was to our credit . . . although there were also some things that are shameful to recall.

KAMENEV. Not only shameful but painful – such as the fact that in 1937 we, who had worked so closely alongside Lenin, gave in to Stalin's pressure to fabricate such bizarre confessions at the show-trials that he staged: confessions that we had maintained secret links with Hitler's Gestapo . . . that we had planned the murder of Kirov, when we knew it was the work of Stalin himself . . . that we had wanted to restore capitalism in Soviet Russia . . . In agreeing to admit to all these fantasies we not only destroyed ourselves – in the long run we discredited the Communist movement throughout the world . . .

ZINOVIEV. Of course, we could have taken one way out of it all before we were arrested, but . . . On December 1st 1934, after the murder of Kirov, the whole country was swept by a spontaneous wave of protest meetings . . . As a board member of the Union of Cooperatives I had to make a speech about it to the board, but I couldn't say anything, the words wouldn't come . . . I was so shaken, both because I had been a friend of Kirov's and because I realised perfectly well what was going to happen to us . . .

KAMENEV. But we lacked the strength to take the only honest decision . . . the only proper solution . . . suicide . . . as Tomsky and Ordzhonikidze and Gamarnik did . . .

ZINOVIEV. If we had done that, people would have seen it as an admission of our guilt.

KAMENEV. Yes. No doubt. But at least we wouldn't have humiliated and defiled ourselves . . . and would it have been any worse than being shot in the back of the neck? . . . *(Pause.)* On October 24th 1917, I was at the Smolny Institute, taking an active part in events. Our mistake in revealing the proposed date of the uprising had been forgotten.

ZINOVIEV. I was in hiding that day, writing for *Pravda*. Two of my articles appeared in the issue for October 25th – the leader and one other.

MARTOV. I am Julius Martov, the Menshevik leader. The Bolsheviks made me into some kind of bogeyman. Once I was one of Lenin's few close friends . . . Yes . . . October 24th . . . the day before it all happened . . . Well, of course I was in Petrograd and doing everything possible to prevent it happening, or if it had to happen, then not in the way that it did.

DENIKIN. Anton Ivanovich Denikin, Lieutenant-General. Yes, yes – I am *the* Denikin, the leader of the White Army for most of the four-year civil war that followed the revolution . . . In 1942, when German troops were besieging Stalingrad, I contemptuously rejected Hitler's proposal to leave France and move to Germany, where I was supposed to command a 'Russian Liberation Army' of ex-tsarist officers and renegade Soviet troops recruited from German prisoner-of-war camps. General Krasnov joined the Germans but I refused, because to the very end of my days, until my death in the United States in 1947, I never ceased to be a Russian patriot.

STALIN. I don't think the Soviet people will remember the Denikin who makes such play with his refusal to fight against his country; the Denikin *they* remember is the hangman-in-chief, who soaked the soil of Russia with the blood of Russian workers and Russian peasants during the civil war.

DENIKIN. I was fighting a war, Stalin – unlike you, who preferred to murder millions of your own subjects in what was supposed to be peacetime . . .

On October 24th 1917, I was at Bykhov with General Kornilov; as far as I remember, we were playing billiards.

DAN. Fyodor Ilyich Dan. Menshevik. By profession a physician. Until 1922 I was a deputy of the Moscow City Soviet, then was banished abroad, where I lived long enough to see Russia's victory in World War Two. Like Milyukov, I sent Stalin a telegram of congratulations. I realised that despite its profound defects Bolshevism had become a mighty factor in the realisation of the socialist idea . . .

On October 24th 1917, Martov and I (*Gestures towards* MARTOV.) were doing everything possible to ensure that the following day, the 25th, should *not* go down in history as the day of the Bolshevik revolution. Fortunately, we failed.

KRUPSKAYA. Nadezhda Konstantinovna Krupskaya. Lenin's wife. My work in the Party was concerned with education. On October 24th I was in the Party committee rooms of the Vyborg District of Petrograd when Fofanova brought me Lenin's letters, and I personally delivered them to the Smolny Institute.

BUKHARIN. Nikolai Ivanovich Bukharin, born in Moscow, 1888, son of a schoolteacher. In the revolutionary movement from the age of 17. At the Sixth Congress of the Bolshevik Party I was elected to the Central Committee, of which I remained a member until my arrest in 1937. Of the more significant stages of my political career, I should mention the weeks of dispute that preceded the signature of the treaty of Brest-Litovsk with the Germans in March 1918, in which I committed a major political error by obstinately opposing Lenin. He advocated signing the treaty at once, despite the harsh terms, because delay would only make the Germans increase their demands. He was right and I was wrong. But most of all I blame myself, as a Bolshevik and as a human being, for failing to prevent Stalin from implementing that 'great transformation', that 'revolution from above' that took place from 1929 to 1932 – the collectivisation of agriculture.

STALIN. I coined those expressions – 'great transformation' and 'revolution from above' – and I will not deny my authorship.

FOFANOVA. Margarita Vasilievna Fofanova, owner of the apartment that was Lenin's last illegal hiding-place. I could see it was agony for him – it was the moment when the success or failure of his life's work hung in the balance, and he was forced to sit there, unable to move and unable even to communicate with Party headquarters at the Smolny Institute. I know that some historians don't like me. I tell things as they really were and they correct me, because they think they know what *ought* to have happened.

RAHIAA. Eino Rahiaa, Finnish Bolshevik. In 1938, having reached the rank of Corps Commander in the Red Army, I was shot during Stalin's 'Great Purge'. In 1917 the Party appointed me to be Lenin's bodyguard. At the end of September I escorted Lenin from Vyborg to Petrograd. Stalin was furious: how had I dared to do that without the permission of the Central Committee? And on October 24th, again without Central Committee permission, I escorted Lenin to the Smolny Institute. I have no other 'sins' against the Party on my conscience.

LENIN. Vladimir Ulyanov, Party code-name Lenin. Making a revolution is much more interesting than talking or writing about it. Let us therefore get down to business.

A spotlight illuminates a raised acting-space which represents a room in FOFANOVA's *apartment.* LENIN *runs up the steps to the acting-space, followed by* KRUPSKAYA, FOFANOVA *and* RAHIAA.

LENIN *(examines the set carefully)*. Yes, it's a good likeness . . . *(Points to a vase of flowers.)* But *those* weren't there. Where would you get flowers like those in Petrograd in the late autumn? Did the designers check it out in the museum?

ACT ONE 173

KRUPSKAYA. That corner of the room was filled with stacks of newspapers. I was always nagging you about it . . .

LENIN. Yes, you called me an untidy brute!

FOFANOVA. The flowers are there because the apartment is used nowadays for the induction ceremony when children join the Young Pioneers.

LENIN. Children least of all need Potemkin villages. (*To the props-men, who are standing around the acting-space.*) And there wasn't a white linen tablecloth, only a piece of checkered oil-cloth . . .

A piece of oil-cloth is substituted for the white tablecloth.

Very good. That will do. We can begin.

A spotlight illuminates another raised acting-space, furnished as the former study of Tsar Alexander III in the Winter Palace.

KERENSKY *mounts the steps into the study.*

KERENSKY (*to props-men*). On my desk were the blotter, ink-wells and pen-holders that had belonged to Nicholas II. And over in this corner there was the Russian naval flag, the blue St Andrew's cross on a white background . . . No, wait a moment, that's not right. By October I was no longer Minister of the Navy . . . (*To the props-men.*) There should also be some revolutionary emblem . . . for instance . . . for instance . . . Lenin's study in the Kremlin looked like the manager's office of some small, third-rate bank . . . I was never there, but I know for certain . . . Lenin and I never actually met each other, although our paths were destined to cross more than once . . . We shared the same birthday, April 22nd, although I was eleven years younger than him . . . In Simbirsk, where we were born, our fathers were both senior officials of the Ministry of Education . . . I was six years old when Lenin's elder brother, Sasha Ulyanov, was executed for taking part in a revolutionary plot . . . My father was shattered. He was so shocked that the doctor had to put him to bed with a sedative. I remembered that day all my life. In fact, that execution was the basic psychological motivation for making me, later, go into revolutionary politics . . . Afterwards, my father more than once helped the Ulyanov family to survive the consequence of their son Sasha having been executed as a revolutionary . . . He awarded Vladimir the gold medal as the best student of his graduating class . . . gave him a character-reference so glowing that the university had to accept him . . . Unlike me, my father rated him very highly . . . Ah, yes! That's it! That's it! What I need is a rosette of red ribbon! Red ribbon!

A wardrobe assistant brings a red rosette, which she pins to **KERENSKY**'s *army-style khaki tunic, then brushes him down with a clothes brush.*

No! Don't do that! If my tunic is too clean, I won't look 'democratic' enough! Put some dust on it! . . . That's better . . .

A spotlight illuminates a third raised acting-space, representing part of the room in the Smolny Institute in which the Bolshevik Central Committee holds its meetings: a table, bentwood chairs, a few armchairs. The Bolsheviks mount the steps to the acting-space. At first their behaviour towards each other is somewhat stiff and awkward.

DZIERZINSKI. Yes, that is how it looked . . . It all began here . . .

TROTSKY (*to the props-men*). There was a large-scale map of Petrograd on the table . . . (*The map is brought.*)

BUKHARIN. Who sat where? I confess I've forgotten . . .

SVERDLOV. What does it matter?

STALIN. It matters a lot. I sat here, next to Lenin.

BUKHARIN. That's pure invention, Koba. You never sat there. You smoked all the time and Lenin didn't like tobacco-smoke, so you were always lurking by the window or in a corner.

STALIN. I sat here, next to Lenin. You can't accuse me of being forgetful. I always remember everything.

SVERDLOV. In any case, neither Lenin nor Zinoviev were ever here before October 25th – and they couldn't have been, because they had had to go underground and were in hiding, and after the 25th we moved over into Lenin's office.

BUKHARIN (*to* STALIN). All right, sit here if you like. But at least admit that you were usually lurking by the window.

STALIN (*obstinately*). I was always next to Lenin.

TROTSKY. Yes, we've all read that in your *Short Course*.

SVERDLOV. Stop it! None of these childish arguments divided us then. (*Takes a last look around the acting-space.*) We're ready.

A spotlight illuminates a fourth raised acting-space, representing the girls' high school in Bykhov where the generals are held prisoner: a classroom with a blackboard; desks piled in a corner; a few chairs, and a billiard-table in the centre. The generals mount the steps to the acting-space and inspect the set.

DENIKIN. What times those were . . .

LUKOMSKY. The designer is very talented. He has caught it exactly.

MARKOV *(to the props-man)*. A bottle of brandy – and make sure it's Shustov's. *(Bottle is brought.)*

KORNILOV. Now it's all ready – and so are we.

Scene Two

FOFANOVA's *apartment.*
00.10 hours, October 24th 1917

FOFANOVA *has just returned home after hours of queuing for a few essentials such as salt, sugar and bread. On a chair are her shopping-basket and her overcoat, hastily thrown over the chairback.* LENIN *sits at the table, looking through some papers that she has brought him.* FOFANOVA *enters with a tray of tea-things and pours out two glasses of weak tea.*

FOFANOVA. I was so worried all the time I was out, wondering how you were, sitting here all by yourself.

LENIN. I was waiting patiently. What's happening on the streets?

FOFANOVA. It's all quite calm. *(Hands him a glass of tea.)*

LENIN. Thank you. Let's mentally walk the route from here to Smolny.

FOFANOVA. What for?

LENIN. Just in case . . . I go out of your front door and I turn . . .

FOFANOVA. You're not going out of my front door without the permission of the Central Committee. And when they give their permission you won't be walking there on your own – they'll send a car for you.

LENIN. Of course. All sorts of unexpected circumstances may arise, though, don't you agree? So why not prepare oneself in advance?

FOFANOVA. But you won't go alone, will you?

LENIN. What – right across the city, where I may be arrested at any street corner?

FOFANOVA. All right, then . . . You turn right out of the front door . . .

LENIN. And I walk along Serdobolskaya Street until I come to Bolshoi Samsonievsky Avenue . . .

FOFANOVA. Where there's a grocer's shop on the corner . . .

LENIN. A grocer's shop on the corner . . . Was that where you spent all evening queuing?

FOFANOVA. I can't remember seeing such awful queues. And what did I manage to buy? Just a few scraps. (*Tips the contents of her shopping-basket on the table.*) Half a pound of sugar, a little packet of salt, a loaf of bread and a few other odds and ends. And for all that I paid exactly four times more than I paid four months ago, in June. You should have heard the things they were shouting in that queue . . .

LENIN. What were they shouting?

FOFANOVA. They were so bad-tempered, it was frightening. There was a man who'd come from Tver. It seems there's literally *nothing* in the shops there. You people don't know how lucky you are, he said . . . Look – we got rid of the Tsar because people had had it up to here. And now it's even worse. What *is* happening, Vladimir Ilyich?

LENIN. I think this is the most critical moment of the revolution.

FOFANOVA. There've been so many of these 'critical moments' . . .

LENIN. But none of them were like today. Roughly speaking, any revolution can be seen as being made up of three basic positions, three tendencies . . . (*Picks up the packet of salt.*) This is one position: back to the way things were. A complete or perhaps not quite complete, return to the past. Counter-revolution. Basically, hatred of the Russian people. (*Picks up the packet of sugar.*) The second position – to repaint the façade, without changing the essence of the old system. Marking time, in fact; fear of decisive action. Basically, they're afraid of the people. (*Picks up the loaf of bread.*) And here is the third position – forward, forward, nothing but a total break with the old system, staking everything on revolutionary initiative, spontaneous action by the masses, faith in the people. (*Stands up, walks round the table.*) Those are the three forces, the three tendencies. Six months ago the revolution proclaimed three slogans: peace, bread and freedom. What has actually been accomplished? Nothing. Because freedom without peace and without bread is nothing but the freedom to die of starvation or from a bullet, while being allowed to make all the speeches you like – which is, you must admit, not much comfort for ordinary people . . . In other words, not a single problem raised by the February Revolution has been solved – hence the collapse of society and the national crisis. We are told that the whole nation can be united and can solve these problems. This self-deception, this illusion is what the compromisers feed on, but just look around you – where on earth is the ground for this national unity? How are you going to bring those three positions together? How are you going to harness Kornilov, Kerensky and us to one cart? (*Pushes the salt and the sugar together.*) Now here is one possible way to form a bloc: these ones are pulling backwards, and these ones are marking time – but in a revolution marking time is the same as going three paces backwards . . . (*Looks sideways at the packets of salt and sugar that he has pushed together.*) But no, the generals won't forgive Kerensky, since he abandoned them during the Kornilov revolt . . . (*Moves the salt and the sugar apart.*) This is the gap we must push ourselves through, before they make up their past differences and come to terms again. Now is the very moment to seize power in the name of peace, bread and freedom, without bloodshed and with a minimum of losses. Tomorrow that chance will have gone. (*Smiling.*) That is why I must be at our headquarters in the Smolny Institute . . . So – I go along Bolshoi Samsonievsky Avenue until I come to Murinsky Avenue. Is that right?

FOFANOVA. That's right. Then you can take the tram to Botkin Street.

LENIN. No, I won't risk it . . . (*Looks at the packet of salt.*) I'll go along Liteiny Avenue and turn into Shpalernaya Street . . . (*Unable to restrain himself, he picks up the packet of salt.*) It's quite clear, of course, that the generals are cursing the day when they supported the February Revolution, and are undoubtedly preparing a second Kornilov revolt, a second military coup. And what about Kerensky? (*Picks up the packet of sugar.*) A coalition between them is clearly on the cards, although the formula for it hasn't been worked out yet.

FOFANOVA. Well – and what about Kerensky? What's become of him? Nobody has a good word for him any more.

LENIN. Repainting the façade isn't a revolution! Bureaucrats playing at reforms and not a single truly revolutionary move to smash the old tsarist bureaucratic machine! You can't arouse any heroism and enthusiasm in the masses without a decisive break with the past. Nothing will be achieved if you leave the old state apparatus intact, because if the executive arm is indifferent, hostile or obstructive it simply turns democracy into an empty talking-shop. Can you see that gigantic army of entrenched bureaucrats putting through reforms that are going to undermine their supremacy? How can anyone make a revolution by relying on the help of the very people who hate it so much? (*Rhetorically.*) Who do you think you're fooling, gentlemen?! . . . No, to try and carry out a revolutionary transformation of the country by using an apparatus like the Russian bureaucracy is the greatest possible delusion, self-deception, and deception of the people. And Kerensky has demonstrated this to the full! No – he's not such a fool as to publicly preach the policy of marking time. Wait, he's saying; the situation will improve, the right moment will come all in good time, so why start running ahead too fast, why stir things up to no effect – let's act carefully and thoughtfully . . . and so on and so forth. Under pressure from the right-wing camp he makes more and more little concessions to them, and meanwhile the revolutionary impetus of the people slowly but surely melts away and evaporates. And the right-wingers are not fools either: why should they go headlong, flat out for their objectives when day by day they are getting by degrees exactly what they want? The revolution is being squeezed out a bit here, curtailed a little more there, and even more somewhere else . . . And the short-sighted fools on our side shout 'Hurrah! We're winning!' They think they're winning simply because the right-wingers are not gobbling them all up at once.

FOFANOVA. So what are you going to do, Vladimir Ilyich?

LENIN. Go to Smolny. The situation now is this: either we fold our arms and wait for Kerensky and Co. to smother the revolution – or we make a dash forward.

FOFANOVA. Insurrection?

LENIN. Yes. Armed insurrection. Nothing and nobody is going to wait for us while we dither and argue: starvation won't wait;

economic breakdown won't wait; the peasants burning landowners' houses and seizing their land won't wait. The war won't wait. The generals out at Bykhov won't wait. But the people in our Central Committee want to wait! *That* is why I must go to Smolny. So – I go along Shpalernaya Street . . .

FOFANOVA. Look at the time, Vladimir Ilyich . . .

LENIN (*smiling*). Damn it, at this rate I'll never get to Smolny, someone is always getting in my way – if it isn't the generals, it's Kerensky, or it's our people . . . Good night, Margarita Vasilievna. I'll sit up a bit longer and do some more thinking.

Scene Three

BYKHOV
00.17 hours, October 24th 1917

An acting-space on the forestage represents a room in the former girls' boarding-school at Bykhov, where **KORNILOV** *and three other* **GENERALS** *have been temporarily imprisoned by* **KERENSKY** *for their attempted military coup against the Petrograd Soviet. The other characters in the play watch intently from their seats, prepared to intervene at any moment. The* **GENERALS'** *behaviour is relaxed: they walk on and off the acting-space, smoke, drink and so on.* **KORNILOV** *and* **MARKOV** *have taken off their tunics and are playing billiards in shirtsleeves and braces.* **LUKOMSKY** *is reading a newspaper.* **DENIKIN**, *a glass of brandy in his hand, is musing aloud.*

DENIKIN. I was made a company commander. And being a bright, progressive young officer, what did I do? I decided to show my men that discipline didn't have to be enforced by the stick. My company became so slack and inefficient that I was relieved of command. When that happened, Tsepura, my long-service company sergeant-major, paraded the men on the square, shook his fist meaningfully and said very plainly and clearly: 'You won't be having Captain Denikin any longer – you'll be having me. Got it?'

MARKOV. Cannon off two sides and into the middle. The trouble all started when they abolished serfdom.

LUKOMSKY. No, the trouble was – they abolished it too late. If it had been done twenty years earlier, we'd have long ago been as advanced as the rest of Europe.

MARKOV. Add to that all the seditious work begun by the Decembrists in 1825, the likes of Belinsky and Herzen in the 'forties . . . And all those other damned intellectuals . . . Mikhailovsky . . . the Uspenskys . . . the Shchedrins and Klyuchevskys – the harm they did was immeasurable . . .

KORNILOV. One off the cushion and straight into the pocket. And add to all that the Tsar's abdication at Berdichev. That place should be wiped off the face of the earth and a jungle made to grow on the spot.

MARKOV. Why a jungle? Why not just thistles?

DENIKIN. We're being swamped by a tidal wave . . . and anyone who can't or won't swim with it simply flounders and sinks. I remember a railway carriage, packed with troops in the big retreat, and there was a tall thin civilian, poor, wearing a threadbare overcoat, standing in the aisle between the seats . . . It was unbearably stuffy, he'd been standing for hours, the crowding was torture and tempers were flaring all round. Suddenly he shouted hysterically: 'Damn you all! I believed in the Russian soldier, prayed to God for him – but now, if I could, I'd strangle the lot of you with my bare hands!' The funny thing was they left him alone, nobody touched him . . .

LUKOMSKY. Even so, the February Revolution gave Russia a chance to . . .

MARKOV. February was the start of Russia's slow crucifixion . . . Cannon off No. 8 into the pocket . . .

LUKOMSKY. Excuse me, Markov, but I must disagree! Have we really got such short memories? Have we forgotten all the stupidity, all the incompetence – to put it mildly – of our revered monarch and his régime? Disaster in the supply system, chaos in the transport system, and as for the factories – we know perfectly well that it wasn't just something the socialists invented. Everybody knows about the incompetence on the home front, but you and I are only too well aware of the government's incompetence in military matters that we experienced every minute of the day. What's the balance-sheet of the war so far? Eight million Russian dead against four million Germans. Isn't that a verdict on the whole system? Two Russians for one German – only a bloody fool fights a war like that. Thanks to Rasputin the Romanovs were doomed, and they got what was coming to them. And the February Revolution was a blessing to the whole country. It's no wonder that all the generals with any brains welcomed it. Remember what Brusilov – probably our best general – said: 'If I have to choose between Russia and the Tsar, I prefer Russia.' And Kornilov here supported the February Revolution wholeheartedly.

KORNILOV. Yes, I was taken in by it at first.

LUKOMSKY. It's not our fault that the liberals couldn't steer the ship and they ran her aground.

KORNILOV. To this day I feel ashamed that I went along with it and that I . . . personally . . . arrested the Tsarina Alexandra . . . She behaved with great dignity . . . no tears, no hysterics . . . 'I hope, general, that you appreciate our situation. You were, after all, a prisoner of war yourself . . .' Aren't we going too far, gentlemen, by throwing mud at the imperial family?

DENIKIN (*to* LUKOMSKY). Look, Alexander Sergeyevich – let's tot up the results of the February Revolution . . . The army destroyed, industry at a standstill, no one wants to work, total irresponsibility . . .

MARKOV. Conferences, political meetings and speeches all over the country – but there's nothing to eat!

LUKOMSKY. At this moment, there's no freer country in the world than Russia.

DENIKIN. Russia has proved to be unworthy of the freedom she won.

LUKOMSKY. And that is exactly why we tried to seize power.

MARKOV. Yes – and as a result, Kerensky is in the Winter Palace and we're here.

DENIKIN (*to* MARKOV). No one is ever insured against treachery.

MARKOV. I warned you, I begged you not to trust that two-faced scoundrel Kerensky!

DENIKIN. Kerensky's agreement with us was quite clear: we would advance on Petrograd with the cavalry corps in order to kick out the Soviet, while he . . .

KORNILOV. Declared us traitors to the revolution. No, no,

gentlemen – it's entirely our own fault. We showed our hand, and that whole rabble – from the extreme left to the most moderate centrists – sank their differences and closed ranks against us, for the first and probably for the last time. The only question that we have to face now is – do we try and go on, or do we abandon the attempt altogether?

DENIKIN. The country is on the verge of falling apart. Who will forgive us if we accept this situation? Can we ever forgive ourselves?

LUKOMSKY. I'm not interested in ideology, only expediency. We should leave the dirty work – knocking Kerensky on the head – to the Bolsheviks.

KORNILOV. You're right. Our boundless love for suffering Russia bids us stay at our posts and snatch the country from unsafe hands. Pass the message to General Headquarters that in the case of a Bolshevik coup the army will not intervene. We shall not repeat our mistake. I don't like joking. Let them devour each other – let the extreme leftists smash the moderates and vice-versa.

KERENSKY (*leaps up from his seat, shouts*). There! There! You all heard that! Stop the clock – I demand to be heard! They've given themselves away! I was the tragic victim of the struggle between two extreme factions – Lenin's and Kornilov's! (*To the* GENERALS.) *They* are the ones who ordered the army not to help me when the Bolshevik attack came!

STRUVE. You idiot! You brought it on yourself! How could you have been so insane as to declare Kornilov a traitor and throw away your last chance of using the army to smash the Bolsheviks?

KERENSKY. By raising their hand against me, the generals were threatening democratic rule in Russia!

DENIKIN. You might at least admit now, when it's all in the past, that you never thought about Russia but only about yourself. All right, so we would have thrown you out of the Winter Palace and put Kornilov there instead, but our Russia would have been saved. But you ran for help to the Bolsheviks, who armed the workers and pushed the country leftward ... by calling in the Bolsheviks, you put the noose around your neck with your own hands, yet here ... now ... you're lying shamelessly to try to exculpate yourself.

KERENSKY. This is unheard-of! Forgive me, I can't go on . . . I feel unwell . . . (*Sits down and relapses into silence.*)

BUKHARIN. As a famous judge once said: 'The case should be closed, since both parties have decided to batter each other insensible.' Let the generals go on . . .

LUKOMSKY (*continuing*). Having the Bolsheviks throw out Kerensky presents no danger to us. Their triumph will not last long, because it will only aggravate the country's collapse and produce anarchy. We shall need only three weeks to liquidate the Bolsheviks, no more.

KORNILOV. What the country needs is an efficient system of military dictatorship, which will guarantee the restoration of law and order. I don't like joking . . . And if we unfortunately have to burn half of Russia to the ground and even if we have to spill three quarters of her blood . . . we didn't make that choice. It was forced on us. Tomorrow we will prepare a detailed operational plan. Gentlemen, I give you a toast! (*All the* GENERALS *stand.*) To Company Sergeant-Major Tsepura!

MARKOV. God . . . I can't wait to start stringing them up!

KERENSKY (*to the* GENERALS). Don't you think, gentlemen, that your three weeks have lasted rather a long time?

Scene Four

THE WINTER PALACE
06.30 hours October 24th 1917

The office of ALEXANDER KERENSKY, *prime minister of the Provisional Government.* KERENSKY *is seated at the desk.*

Enter Colonel POLKOVNIKOV.

POLKOVNIKOV. Colonel Polkovnikov, Commandant of the Petrograd Military District, reporting, sir.

KERENSKY. Good morning, Georgii Petrovich.

POLKOVNIKOV. The night passed without incidents. No food supplies were brought into the city during the past 24 hours, and stocks are at two thirds of the normal level.

KERENSKY. We'll discuss that in a moment. What are the Bolsheviks up to?

POLKOVNIKOV. If one disregards rumours, we are in full control of the situation.

KERENSKY. What about the three regiments' refusal to leave Petrograd and go to the front – was that a rumour?

POLKOVNIKOV. The Bolshevik Military Revolutionary Committee have issued an instruction that no orders issued by us are to be regarded as valid without their approval.

KERENSKY. What?! Why didn't you tell me before? You stand there reporting God knows what, while . . .

POLKOVNIKOV. I held talks with the MRC about cancelling that absurd instruction. The very fact that the Bolsheviks were prepared to discuss it with me is a sign of their weakness.

KERENSKY. But that's tantamount to insurrection . . . it's a call to mutiny . . . it's a challenge, and I shall respond to it. (*Gets up and paces around the room, thinking aloud.*) I've made too many concessions . . . Yes, I can be accused of weakness and excessive tolerance, but no one can say that I had recourse to harsh measures – until the state was threatened with overthrow . . . Yes, yes . . . I only wish I had died five months ago. I would have died in the belief that it *was* possible to govern this country without the whip and truncheon. Was Milyukov right after all, when he said that a free Russian state was nothing but a state of rebellious slaves? I'm often told that I'm too trusting and too much of a dreamer. We are accused of being more like a puddle of slush than a government . . . Well, then . . . I shall try to be less trusting – to put less trust in people, in their inherent goodness, in their conscience, their reason. I shall turn my heart to stone, banish my dreams of a free people, dreams which they all laugh at, despise and trample on. I am going to trample on *them* from now on! They shall not have their way! . . . God, what an impossible task I've taken on!

POLKOVNIKOV. Why is that, Alexander Fyodorovich?

KERENSKY. Because I know all too well the power of human ignorance – the ignorance not just of our wretched peasantry but of the whole of Russian society: they don't need freedom . . . they need a clenched fist! A clenched fist – not freedom! There is no coming to terms with the Bolsheviks, postponing the clash any longer is dangerous, so we must use an iron hand to force the Bolsheviks to submit ... Of course, if we weren't so averse to deploying the methods used by the Tsarist government, we should provoke the Bolsheviks into an armed uprising *now* ...

POLKOVNIKOV. They won't do it. They have arranged their move to coincide with tomorrow's Congress of Soviets. The Congress will pass a resolution calling for the transfer of power to the Bolsheviks, who will then go into the attack ...

KERENSKY. I only wish to God they would try and stage their uprising sooner, but unfortunately we can't rely on them doing that ... Very well, let them wait ... But *we* are not going to wait any longer. We must forestall them, strike first and prod them into showing their hand before they're fully ready ... Now, colonel – these are my orders: close all the Bolshevik newspapers immediately for incitement to rebellion against the Provisional Government. And to show we're even-handed, close down two extreme right-wing newspapers too – 'New Russia' and 'The Living Word'. Find Lenin immediately – I sense he is here, in Petrograd! – arrest him and haul him up in front of Alexandrov, the Public Prosecutor. By this evening I want you to have made all necessary operational plans for the army to seize the Smolny Institute and arrest the Bolsheviks and their allies, the Social-Revolutionaries. The troops from Northern Army Group, who will be in Petrograd at any minute, are placed under your command. As for the Congress of Soviets ... even your present forces will be sufficient to prevent the delegates from assembling. These orders are to be put into immediate effect.
(POLKOVNIKOV *salutes and exit*.) The die is cast, gentlemen!

Scene Five

SMOLNY INSTITUTE
08.15 hours, October 24th 1917

SVERDLOV, KAMENEV *and* STALIN *are waiting for* TROTSKY *to finish a telephone conversation.*

TROTSKY (*into the receiver*). Yes ... a confrontation is inevitable, and the pretext will be Kerensky's order to send all the troops of the Petrograd garrison to the front. Last night was critical, none of us slept.

DZIERZINSKI *strides on in a state of excitement.*

DZIERZINSKI. Half an hour ago a detachment of officer cadets occupied our printing works and none of the Bolshevik papers have appeared today!

STALIN. We know that.

TROTSKY (*into the receiver*). I'll bear all that in mind. We'll keep Lenin fully informed . . . Thanks. Yes . . . Goodbye. (*Replaces the receiver.*)

DZIERZINSKI (*excitedly*). I assure you – closing the printing-works means Kerensky is starting to act! We can't just protest! We must seize the moment, arrest the government immediately – our armoured cars are already positioned around the Winter Palace – and press on from there.

TROTSKY. Out of the question! The arrest of the Provisional Government as an isolated action is not on our agenda for today and cannot be. It would be a mistake to use our armoured cars for that, but to kick the cadets out of the printing works and publish our newspaper is another matter . . . Incidentally, I am going to propose that in a few minutes to the meeting of the Central Committee; in fact I've already issued the necessary preliminary orders.

KAMENEV. Running ahead too fast is one of the most typical mistakes of a revolutionary party.

DZIERZINSKI. So are you again proposing that we should trail along behind events? I'm sick of hearing that. If you keep on waiting, the workers will get fed up with us and act on their own.

STALIN. Cool down, Felix. The Central Committee will be meeting shortly, and then we'll decide what to do.

TROTSKY. It's so simple, Felix Edmundovich: everything depends on the Congress of Soviets and the resolution it's going to pass.

DZIERZINSKI. Are you so sure it will? I'm not.

TROTSKY. That is precisely why we must make every possible effort to ensure that it does. Tomorrow the Congress will vote for transfer of power to us . . .

DZIERZINSKI. And supposing it doesn't? Supposing it can't get a majority and hesitates? So far we have only 300 delegates out of 670 . . .

TROTSKY (*firmly, with conviction*). The majority will vote for us. Kerensky, of course, won't submit to that resolution, and then liquidating his government simply becomes a police matter, and not a political issue any longer. By this simple tactical move – taking power at the request of the Congress of Soviets – we shall solve a problem of world-wide historic significance without bloodshed. Simply and elegantly.

STALIN. If there are vital questions that can be decided by a simple show of hands, why decide them on the street?

DZIERZINSKI. So everything that we are doing now is . . .

TROTSKY. Is planning a defensive operation, Felix – defence and nothing more. But that certainly doesn't mean that all our units don't have to be fully mobilised and ready for action. If you like, you can call it 'active defence'.

DZIERZINSKI. How the hell can you talk about 'defence', when Kerensky has already ordered the arrest of the entire Military Revolutionary Committee? (*To* SVERDLOV.) Andrei, why don't you say something?

TROTSKY. If the Provisional Government takes it into its head to arrest us then we shall mount machine-guns covering all the approaches to Smolny. I'll give the order directly. But frankly I don't expect Kerensky to be so quick on his feet. His government is paralysed. It is just sitting there and waiting to surrender power at the moment when our broom sweeps them into the rubbish-bin of history.

DZIERZINSKI. We need Lenin. We need his advice. Let's send a reliable company of Red Guards to escort him here in safety . . . he should have been with us long ago.

STALIN. Not yet. That would be premature. We can't risk his life.

TROTSKY. First we shall seize power, and then Lenin can arrive at Smolny escorted by a guard of honour (*Smiles.*) and on a white horse! . . . So, we shall not allow ourselves to be provoked into premature action; we shall simply respond to what the other side does and . . .

STALIN. Wait for the Congress to open. (*Going off.*) I'll be back in a minute.

TROTSKY. Precisely. We will wait for the Congress.

DZIERZINSKI (*sitting down beside* SVERDLOV). Why don't you say something?

SVERDLOV. I can't get out of my head what Lenin said in his last letter: 'A defensive posture is death to an armed insurrection'.

Scene Six

FOFANOVA'S APARTMENT

08.25 hours, October 24th 1917

FOFANOVA *and* LENIN *are having breakfast, surrounded by newspapers.*

FOFANOVA. I couldn't find the Bolshevik papers at a single kiosk. I even took a tram to the news-stand at the Finland Station, but there wasn't one there either. They hadn't been delivered, they said, but no one knew why.

LENIN. Funny. What's happening on the streets?

FOFANOVA. The usual. People going to work.

LENIN. Did you see any troops?

FOFANOVA. No, I don't think so . . . Don't worry, Vladimir Ilyich, it'll work out . . .

LENIN. A situation as favourable as today only comes once in a hundred years . . . We agreed that we'd start today . . . But if the people at Smolny are still determined to wait for the start of the Congress, it's either total idiocy or absolute treachery.

FOFANOVA. Oh come, now – treachery? How can you talk like that?

LENIN. I'm nervous. Do you think it's easy for me to be in such isolation when *everything* has been wagered on one card? Why don't they want me to be at Smolny?

FOFANOVA. Because you're bound to be caught on your way there.

LENIN. But once I was at Smolny I couldn't be caught . . . The whole point is that a revolution doesn't tolerate delay. One must always be pushing ahead . . . forward all the time . . . not running too fast, but not dawdling either . . . The one golden rule is: *never stop* . . . always press onward . . . onward . . . onward . . . as Goethe said: '*Weiter, weiter, immer weiter* . . .' What time will you be back this evening?

FOFANOVA. By eight.

LENIN. On your way, please be good enough to give this letter to my wife.

FOFANOVA. Vladimir Ilyich, I know that when you're nervous or preoccupied you start pacing about the room. You have a man's heavy footsteps, and the neighbours down below know quite well that I live here alone . . .

LENIN. All right, I'll try . . . if I must walk, I'll go on tiptoe . . .

FOFANOVA. When I come back, I'll ring the bell three times as usual . . .

Scene Seven

SMOLNY INSTITUTE
11.30 hours, October 24th 1917

STALIN. I have been asked to describe the situation in Petrograd as it has developed up to the present hour. The Military Revolutionary Committee is divided between two views. The first is for an immediate armed insurrection. The second calls for a further concentration of our forces until they are absolutely ready and until the All-Russian Congress of Soviets is in session. I have to tell you that the Central Committee of our Party has opted for the second course – to continue with concentrating our forces. We are counting on popular pressure to influence the Congress of Soviets and thus to swing the votes at the Congress into calling on us to take power. The Provisional Government is all the more likely to hand over power to us peacefully if the masses express their will in strong and politically organised terms through the Soviets . . .

STALIN *steps aside from centre-stage and takes up a position on one side of the set.*

But now I wish to make a categorical protest at the hostile, anti-Bolshevik method that the author of this play is using here. He is making out that I, along with a majority of the Central Committee, agreed with Trotsky's plan to postpone the uprising. I could *never* have shared a joint position with Trotsky. This is grotesque: we are being treated like puppets and being made to say God knows what, simply to support a highly dubious interpretation of events and we are forced to submit to this! I protest!

DZIERZINSKI. The author is not to blame, Stalin. He is only quoting your own words, which exactly reflect your position at the time. It was all published in the journal, *The Proletarian Revolution*, in 1922, and you didn't protest then. Why not, I wonder? Was it because we were all alive then and were witnesses to what you actually said?

STALIN. I don't like the way the author is so very fond of rummaging among the dirty linen of the past, looking for subtle nuances of meaning in our opinions and our relationships with each other. Now the real motive force of history is the people, the masses. Why aren't we being shown the masses? Why isn't the stage filled with the crowds, the people who *made* history in October 1917? A play about the revolution without the Russian people? I'll swear that didn't happen by chance – there's a sinister motive behind it.

SVERDLOV. This play is about something else: in great historical events, and in revolutions in particular, so much depends upon who was standing on the captain's bridge. It's something that interests everyone.

BUKHARIN. Except those who were on the bridge.

Scene Eight

[*Although this scene begins with* LENIN *still impatiently cooped up in* FOFANOVA's *apartment, the author immediately starts to juggle with time, place and action in a manner that can be bewildering unless the date and location of each section of the scene is made clear to the audience.*]

LENIN, *clearly uneasy, is pacing up and down. Below, in the space occupied by the semicircle of chairs, spotlights pick out* PLEKHANOV *and* MARTOV, *who get up and approach* LENIN.

PLEKHANOV. I want to talk to you, on the strength of having been the first exponent and teacher of Marxism in Russia.

MARTOV. And I claim that right as an old . . . well, a former friend.

LENIN (*brusquely*). Right now I haven't the time for idle talk. We have long since defined our positions, the barricades are up, we each know by heart exactly what the others will say, so what is the point in starting the arguments all over again?

MARTOV. The point is that now we have been able to see all the results of your actions, we can analyse them calmly and draw the necessary conclusions for anyone who might want to follow in your footsteps.

LENIN. But why should I listen to you *now*, when my nerves are stretched almost to breaking-point?

PLEKHANOV. Because, young man, we are socialists, dammit! We may have disagreed with you about the ways of putting the socialist idea into practice, but we still share that same idea! Any tragedy that *you* suffer is our tragedy too, and vice-versa. Anyone who doesn't feel someone else's misfortune as keenly as if it were his own – is no socialist!

MARTOV. To me, the Bolsheviks are and always have been my comrades – admittedly comrades who made a terrible mistake, but still my comrades.

LENIN (*to* PLEKHANOV). Your hatred of us, which is so violent as to be positively indecent, has by now made you into the very symbol of anti-Bolshevism.

PLEKHANOV. I don't deny it.

LENIN. And tomorrow . . . ?

PLEKHANOV. You know perfectly well what will happen tomorrow! Tomorrow that vicious turncoat, Savinkov, will come to me and propose that as the most authoritative figure in Russian socialism I should head a new government, which will smash the power of your 'Council of People's Commissars' with fire and sword. And you know what my answer to him will be: 'I have not given forty years of my life to the working class to start gunning it down the moment it makes a mistake!'

LENIN. Yes, I know about that.

PLEKHANOV. And *I* know what will happen to you in five years' time: how the colleague who was supposed to help you in your fight against the effects of a crippling wound will in fact become your prison guard. And *that* tragedy, which will overcome you at the end of your life, allows me to hope that you will listen to me now.

LENIN. What do you mean – 'my prison guard'? It was a great deal more complex than that.

MARTOV. Since the publication of the day-by-day diaries kept by your secretaries, in which they noted every conversation they had with you, the whole world knows what a struggle you had in the last months of your life, the winter of 1923, to assert your right to convey your 'political testament' to the Party. How you had to use cunning to steal a few extra minutes of dictation time beyond the limited period allowed to you, how you were tormented by the denial of newspapers and other sources of information. You think he wasn't your 'prison guard'? But *he* knew well enough that you perceived his guardianship of you as a personal deprivation of freedom; after all, Fotieva, your principal private secretary, was meticulously reporting everything to him. *He* knew that the therapeutic regime – total isolation from the outside world – which he had created around you was perceived by you as the outcome of *his* instructions to them. If he saw and understood how much distress and suffering he was causing you, why didn't he refuse to go on with it, why didn't he step down and relinquish the task of supervising the conditions under which you were being kept?

STALIN. I tried to relinquish that responsibility, but my request was not granted.

MARTOV. An ailing, silent, inactive Lenin suited you, Stalin, but a Lenin who could dictate letters and instructions did not. If on one day he could demand your dismissal as general secretary after the incident with Krupskaya, what might he not demand tomorrow? Hence the ever stricter regime; the ever more complete isolation, the increasingly severe punishment for anyone who dared to infringe the rules you had laid down.

Lighting-change: the spotlights dim on the group of LENIN, PLEKHANOV *and* MARTOV; *two spotlights pick out* STALIN *and* KRUPSKAYA, *who stand facing each other.*

STALIN. Listen, Krupskaya, I want to talk to you. How is the patient feeling today? What's the news on that front?

KRUPSKAYA. Tolerable, but no more.

ACT ONE 193

STALIN. I sent him some grapes and some pears, which a Georgian comrade brought me from Tiflis. They were very good grapes.

KRUPSKAYA. Thank you.

STALIN. Tell me, Krupskaya, are you aware of the Politburo's orders concerning the medical regime for comrade Lenin?

KRUPSKAYA. Of course I am. Why do you ask?

STALIN. At the last plenary meeting of the Central Committee we discussed the foreign trade question, an issue that has worried our patient a great deal.

KRUPSKAYA. What worried him was the fact that you, Bukharin and some other Central Committee members could have made such a mistake.

STALIN. He sent Trotsky a letter from which it is quite obvious that Lenin is fully informed about this matter.

KRUPSKAYA. Well, what of it?

STALIN. Who gave you the right to disobey instructions issued by the Politburo?

KRUPSKAYA. Is that question meant seriously?

STALIN. Who gave you the right to inform Lenin about current political matters? Don't you realise the nature of his illness? The slightest excitement could end in disaster. You cannot play fast and loose with the fate of the Party.

KRUPSKAYA. I'm sorry, I don't quite understand you.

STALIN. You don't understand me? Do you think there are two standards of Party discipline – one for all ordinary members and another for Lenin's wife? What would the Party become if there were two disciplines – one for ordinary mortals, another for the few elect? I'm telling you straight: we won't stand for it! As General Secretary of the Party, I forbid you to talk to Lenin on political matters!

KRUPSKAYA. I know better than any doctor . . .

STALIN. No you do not. No one has, and never will have, a monopoly on Lenin – not even his wife or his sister . . . When he recovers and gets on his feet again, then you may say what you like to him.

KRUPSKAYA. *What* did you say?!

STALIN. Otherwise, despite all my respect for you, I shall be forced to order you to appear before a disciplinary hearing of the Party's Control Commission. And you need have no illusions about the Control Commission's verdict on you! Lenin's health is not your private, family possession. It is a treasure that belongs to the whole Party.

KRUPSKAYA. A wife knows better than anyone . . .

STALIN. Just because you sleep with the leader, it does *not* mean that you know what's best for him!

KRUPSKAYA. How dare you!

Lighting-change: the spotlight on STALIN *dims: spotlights pick out* LENIN *and* KAMENEV.

LENIN (*to* KRUPSKAYA). What's the matter, Nadya? Has something upset you?

KRUPSKAYA. No, no, I just ran upstairs and I'm out of breath. (*Spotlight dims on* LENIN. KRUPSKAYA *turns away and walks over to* KAMENEV.) Oh, Lev Borisovich!

KAMENEV. Yes, Nadezhda Konstantinovna . . .

KRUPSKAYA. Because of a short letter that Vladimir Ilyich dictated to me – with the doctors' permission – Stalin has allowed himself . . . to make an extremely rude and personal attack on me.

KAMENEV. Please don't upset yourself.

KRUPSKAYA. I've been in the Party at least as long as Stalin! In all my 30 years as a member, not one comrade has ever uttered a rude or indecent word in my presence.

KAMENEV. Nadezhda Konstantinovna . . .

KRUPSKAYA. The interests of the Party and of my husband matter to me quite as much as they do to Stalin!

KAMENEV. But of course, of course!

KRUPSKAYA. I know better than any doctor what I may and may not discuss with Vladimir Ilyich . . . I know what upsets him and what doesn't – and I *certainly* know it better than Stalin does!

KAMENEV. I beg you, Nadezhda Konstantinovna – calm yourself!

KRUPSKAYA. I must ask you to protect me from such rude, insulting interference in my personal life, and to stop him from using threatening and indecent language to me! I have no doubt whatever that the Control Commission, which Stalin has threatened me with, would be unanimously on my side, but I haven't the strength or the time to waste on this idiotic row. I'm only flesh and blood too, and I'm near the end of my tether!

KAMENEV. I would only implore you not to say anything about this to Vladimir Ilyich. I'll smooth it all over.

Lighting-change: spotlight dims on KAMENEV, *another picks out* LENIN.

LENIN. Nearly three months have passed – has Kamenev patched it up between you and Stalin?

KRUPSKAYA. How did you know about that?

LENIN. What did Stalin say to you?

KRUPSKAYA. How did you find out?

LENIN. That doesn't matter. What did he say?

KRUPSKAYA. He didn't say anything. I don't know what you've heard, but you seem to have got it all mixed up.

LENIN. All right, I'll tell you. I overheard you talking to my sister Manya when you both thought I was asleep.

KRUPSKAYA. This morning?

LENIN. Yes.

KRUPSKAYA. And you waited until Manya had gone out before opening your eyes?

LENIN. What did he say to you?

KRUPSKAYA. Get into bed and lie down *this minute*. Look at your face . . .

LENIN. To hell with that!

KRUPSKAYA. Take your medicine!

LENIN. Damn my medicine! What did he say to you?

KRUPSKAYA. You must not excite yourself, or you'll bring on another attack . . .

LENIN. Tell me at once. I will not for one second tolerate my wife being insulted. They warned us forty years ago that a Russian Revolution would only give people one right – the right to behave like beasts. So what are we to do? Admit they were right? Disregard it? A Bolshevik without honour . . .

KRUPSKAYA (*interrupts him sharply*). Do you want to pay for this with your life? It's too high a price!

LENIN. Honour has no price! . . . What did he say to you?

KRUPSKAYA (*realising that she has no way out, as every evasive remark of hers only increases* LENIN's *anger and agitation*). Very well, it was about the letter to Trotsky, which you dictated to me.

LENIN. Well – what?

KRUPSKAYA. He swore at me. But I've already told you I've forgotten his exact words.

LENIN. Swore at you? How?

KRUPSKAYA (*pause*). He said something vile.

LENIN. What?

KRUPSKAYA. Isn't that enough for you?

LENIN. Give me a chair . . . help me . . .

KRUPSKAYA. Volodya . . . Volodya, darling . . . Volodya, it was nothing, I've already forgotten . . .

LENIN. Give me your arm . . .

KRUPSKAYA. Volodya! Volodya! Don't close your eyes!

LENIN. Don't worry . . . I'll be all right . . . in a moment . . .

KRUPSKAYA. I'll call the doctors!

LENIN. Don't you dare! This is our private affair . . . If you call the doctors, they'll immediately inform Stalin. I'll be all right in a moment . . . I'll just lie down for a bit . . . shut my eyes, everything has gone blurred and hazy . . . I'll be better in a moment . . . I must pull myself together, must write another letter . . . Take me by the arm, Nadya, sit down beside me. If I pass out, it'll only be for a moment, so don't be afraid . . . I'll pull myself together . . . In a moment I'll dictate to you . . . what needs to be said in a case like this . . . (*Falls silent.*)

Lighting-change: two spotlights pick out PLEKHANOV *and* MARTOV.

MARTOV. Vladimir Ilyich, forget about Stalin, for heaven's sake . . .

PLEKHANOV. We have serious matters to talk about, we need you in fighting form . . .

LENIN. I am listening to you with all my attention. And I'll even give you my word that I won't interrupt.

PLEKHANOV. Vladimir Ilyich, the dough doesn't yet exist from which a socialist cake can be baked in Russia: our Russian peasant simply isn't ready for socialism yet. When you wrote that administering a state was so simple that any cook could do it, did it ever occur to you to think how many pots would be broken while she was learning how to run the country? It's no good diving into the water if you can't swim – that way the socialist idea will simply be drowned.

LENIN (*making an effort to be calm*). But who will educate the people, Georgii Valentinovich? Who will teach them how democracy works? Should it be those who know quite well that the political education of the masses means the end of *their* power? But what if the people themselves take power and on the basis of that power they set about acquiring education and culture? It's no good diving into the water if you can't swim, you say? Of course, Georgii Valentinovich. But on the other hand – if you don't venture into the water, you'll never learn to swim.

MARTOV. What worries me is something else: a nation of ignorant, drunken peasants can only be kept obedient by using a big stick. I also wonder whether you – who have never sought personal power and have always shunned the trappings of political leadership – whether you, in fact, aren't going to find yourself engaged in liquidating the revolution by the methods of terror, or – if that doesn't happen – whether *you* may not end up by being its victim? All right, all right, I can already sense that deadly irony of yours building up! But don't listen to me, listen to your friend and disciple, the woman you respect so much . . .

LENIN (*puzzled for a moment, then guesses*). Ah, you mean Rosa? Rosa Luxemburg? Of course – her *Letters from Prison*. Certainly – with pleasure! And even though she did change her mind about some things when she was released from prison, that doesn't matter – Rosa as always, has some well thought-out and serious warnings to give us! But take care – she is a woman of strong convictions and can be prickly. That doesn't worry you, does it? Rosa, come and join us!

ROSA LUXEMBURG. First let me say how very glad I am to appear on the Russian stage for the first time – until now my face didn't fit. Secondly, I shall say things that I did *not* change my mind about – the socialist principles that I was born with and died with.

MARTOV. Rosa, keep your voice down a bit if you're going to talk about the Party oligarchy.

ROSA L. (*sharply*). I shall decide, Julius, what I say and when I say it. (LENIN *sniggers to himself*.) . . . Having made the revolution in Russia, the Bolsheviks were the first among us to become men of action, and thus they saved the honour of international socialism. Thank God they found the courage to throw overboard the doctrinaire attitudes of their Mensheviks and our pedantic Marxists, who insisted that Russia had no right to a proletarian revolution because she was so backward. Thank God there proved to be men among us who showed the world that they didn't prefer congresses, conferences, speeches and dissertations about revolution – they preferred revolution itself!

LENIN. Bravo, Rosa!

ROSA L.. Of course, as a fanatical supporter of democracy, I was often shocked by the Bolsheviks' methods, but I always sought and found mitigating circumstances. They were more than right to use the mailed fist to suppress all opposition, but such methods should not be allowed to become the general rule in the long term.

LENIN. Bravo, Rosa!

ROSA L.. However – if the country's normal political life is suppressed . . .

MARTOV. This is it! This is the crux of the matter!

ROSA L.. (*ignoring* MARTOV). . . . the Soviets themselves will inevitably be gripped by a progressive paralysis. Without multi-party elections, without freedom of the press and of assembly, without the free interplay of opinion, then any political institution starts to rot. It becomes the mere semblance of a living organism and the bureaucracy becomes the only functioning element of that organism. Political life is gradually paralysed: the state comes to be governed by no more than a few dozen energetic Party activists. The effective leadership is concentrated in the hands of those few people, while the workers' representatives are summoned from time to time simply in order to applaud the leaders' speeches and to vote unanimously for ready-made resolutions drafted in advance, so that in effect the system of government becomes an oligarchy – the rule of a clique. Obviously this form of government is not the dictatorship of the proletariat, but the dictatorship of a handful of politicians. As I see it, the dictatorship of the proletariat should be the broadest and most unfettered form of democracy. Socialism without political freedom is not socialism. Without freedom there will be no political education of the masses and thus they will be prevented from taking part in the political life of the country. Freedom, if it is only for active supporters of the government, if it is only for members of the Party, however numerous they may be, is not freedom at all: freedom can only ever be freedom for those who think differently – freedom to disagree. The great danger for the Bolsheviks will begin when a temporary, unpleasant necessity, required by the turmoil of a revolutionary situation, is allowed to harden into a permanent virtue.

LENIN. Bravo, Rosa! (*To* MARTOV, *calmly, in a friendly tone.*) You, Julius, wrote somewhere about a five-year reign of terror that is bound to come when we take power. But I will go further: I tell you that unless we can work out the right relationship between the industrial workers and the peasantry, then you can be sure that we won't have just five but twenty, even forty years of counter-revolution and terror! Unless we draw the people into the administration of the state we shall remain a government *for* the people but not *of* the people, we shall hand over the country to the tender mercies of the bureaucrats, and politics will be replaced by intrigue and deals made behind closed doors. If we shy away from democracy; if the working class is replaced by the Party; if the Party is replaced by its permanent staff of paid officials and those officials do nothing but hang on the words of the leader; if any original thinking that differs from the leader's ideas is prosecuted as high treason; if the healthy turbulence of real life is suppressed by fear and replaced by a regime of the barracks and the prison – *then* we shall be faced by the most terrible question of all: 'What was it all for? If the old tyranny is simply replaced by a new tyranny – why did we have a revolution?' This is a very real danger that threatens us and the possibility of it developing most certainly exists – Rosa is right! – but such an outcome is by no means inevitable, it is *not* programmed into our system! Of that I am absolutely convinced. Every single person who can read and

think will, I hope, be able to see for themselves the true programme of the October Revolution and distinguish it from any errors and distortions that could discredit it. I absolutely agree with Rosa: the danger for us lies in the temptation to elevate a temporary necessity into a virtue. (*Looks at* MARTOV *and* PLEKHANOV, *who remain silent.*)
All right, now let's go back to October 24th . . . Petrograd is seething, but our role, I assure you, is purely secondary: events are leading the Party, not vice-versa. Soon the people will come pouring into the streets and they will act without us – and that, you may be sure, will mean the triumph of anarchy and elemental chaos. So we must head this movement, channel it, ennoble it, give it sense and direction. A bloody dictatorship by Kornilov – or an organised proletarian revolution and a socialist democracy. That is the choice. What would *you* do?

PLEKHANOV. The first thing to do, of course, is to damp down any surge toward spontaneous, elemental anarchy . . . extinguish it by every possible means. Let's just hope to God that you don't provoke a move by some new Kornilov, some would-be Napoleon. Then let the bourgeois revolution settle down and establish itself. The natural process of its democratic development will in any case create the conditions for a socialist revolution, and meanwhile . . .

LENIN. That's just it – meanwhile . . . meanwhile *what*?

PLEKHANOV. Slowly, gradually, step by step . . .

At this point LENIN *laughs, interrupts* PLEKHANOV *and starts singing a song that was written by* MARTOV *in the very early days of the Party, when those who later split into Bolsheviks and Mensheviks were all members of a single, united party. The song wittily satirizes the gradualist, 'step-by-step' approach to revolution of the kind advocated by* PLEKHANOV. MARTOV *joins* LENIN *in singing the first verse, then all the others – Bolsheviks and Mensheviks alike – pick up the song; it takes them all back to their young days when they were all together, and ends in a mood of general hilarity and good humour.*

LENIN (*to* MARTOV). Now there's an irony of history: who would have thought you were writing a satire on yourself . . . (*Sits down next to* MARTOV.) You and I died at almost the same time in January 1924. When I read about your last illness . . . believe me, Julius, I felt keenly how much we missed you. All right, enough of that . . . (*Stands up; to* PLEKHANOV *and* MARTOV.) So what is to be done, gentlemen – you who call yourselves our comrades? What is to be done on this 24th day of October, 1917? There is a crisis; we're in a blind alley such as we've never been in before. And the situation gets worse every day. So can a people that finds itself in such a desperate, hopeless situation . . . does a people have the right to hurl itself into the struggle and make a dash for freedom even if the odds are a hundred to one against it? Even if it thereby breaks the rules laid down by the pedants and the theoreticians? Answer, Mr Plekhanov!

PLEKHANOV. Why do you dislike me so much, Lenin?

LENIN (*after a pause*). I never loved or worshipped anyone in my life as much as I loved you at one time . . . Blinded by my admiration for you, I behaved toward you and your writings like a slave toward his master – and to be a slave is an unworthy thing. For a long time I forced myself not to see . . . your arrogance . . . your desire to exercise unlimited intellectual domination . . . your insincerity . . . your treatment of us as pieces on a chessboard. And so what could remain of my devotion to you? . . . Nevertheless, we have done what you taught us to do . . .

Lighting-change: all lights dim, except for two spotlights, one on LENIN, *one on* KRUPSKAYA, *who are back in the 1923 situation caused by* STALIN's *rudeness to* KRUPSKAYA.

LENIN *is recovering from a temporary lapse into unconsciousness.*

KRUPSKAYA. How are you, Volodya? Are you feeling better?

LENIN. Yes, yes, much better . . . Take a sheet of paper . . . It's not just a matter of his insults to you, this business goes much further . . . Write what I dictate.

KRUPSKAYA. No, Volodya, you mustn't . . . I implore you . . . you don't have the right . . .

LENIN. No, I must. Whatever it costs me . . . even my life . . . (*Almost shouts.*) But no one has the right to treat a Party comrade dishonourably! No one!

KRUPSKAYA. All right . . . all right . . . Only don't shout. I'm ready.

LENIN (*summoning up his strength with an effort*). 'Strictly secret and personal. To Comrade Stalin: I am not a person who easily forgets a wrong done to me personally, and needless to say I regard a wrong done to my wife as also directed against me . . .

I would therefore ask you to consider carefully whether you will agree to take back what you said and to apologise for it, or whether you prefer all relations between us to be broken off. Sincerely yours, Lenin. March 5th 1923.'

KRUPSKAYA. But why? Why are you doing this, Volodya? . . . These were almost the last words you spoke in your life . . . Afterwards your condition got worse than ever before . . . and on the 10th you had another stroke.

LENIN. Did he apologise?

KRUPSKAYA. Yes.

LENIN. This note and my 'Letter to the Party Congress' should have given him serious cause for reflection . . .

KRUPSKAYA (*sighs deeply*). Ah, the 'Letter to the Party Congress' . . . yes . . . much later it became known as your 'political testament' . . .

Lighting-change: spotlight dims on **KRUPSKAYA**; *other spotlights pick out the various characters who take part in the following section of the scene:* LENIN, ZINOVIEV, KAMENEV, BUKHARIN, KERENSKY.

ZINOVIEV (*to* LENIN, *with difficulty*). The fact is, Vladimir Ilyich, that when Nadezhda Konstantinovna handed us your letter containing your personal comments on all the leading comrades in the Party in May 1924, on the eve of the first Party Congress to be held since your death, we were shattered . . . It was a bombshell, which completely upset the applecart . . .

LENIN. What do you mean?

ZINOVIEV. A certain disposition of forces had already emerged among the leadership of the Central Committee . . . for more than a year the work of the Politburo had been under the direction of Kamenev and myself, and partly of Stalin. This three-man group acted as a reliable barrier against the dictatorial ambitions of Trotsky. Your letter upset the equilibrium. Stalin was so offended that he immediately offered his resignation, and we had great difficulty in persuading him to withdraw it.

LENIN. I wrote in my letter to the Party Congress that the relations between Stalin and Trotsky constituted a good half of the danger of a major split that was threatening the Party, and that if steps were not taken to prevent it, the split might occur suddenly and unexpectedly. I wrote about Stalin's rudeness and disloyalty – faults that are quite intolerable in a person occupying the post of General Secretary of the Party. I warned you that these characteristics of Stalin's were not a trifling matter, or rather that they were the kind of trifle which could too easily come to be of decisive significance for the whole future of the Party. A decisive trifle. Did you give serious thought to what that could mean . . .

ZINOVIEV. Of course, we did . . .

KAMENEV. Our only consideration was how to keep Stalin in his post of General Secretary.

LENIN. Why? Aren't there other people with good organising ability, more tolerant, more loyal, people who pay more attention to the feelings and legitimate concerns of other Party comrades? I've already mentioned Frunze to you as a possible candidate . . . And what about Dzierzynski? There are other interesting jobs that Stalin could do – after all, I wasn't talking about dismissal but merely a re-assignment.

KAMENEV. The fact is . . . (*To* ZINOVIEV.) I'm going to tell him everything.

ZINOVIEV. Go ahead.

KAMENEV. We had agreed between ourselves that at the Twelfth Congress the political review, which you always used to give at Party congresses, should be given by Zinoviev – not by Trotsky, but specifically by Zinoviev. This was very important: whoever gives the political review would be looked upon by the Party as your successor. Stalin willingly supported this proposal, and we in turn undertook to keep him in the post of General Secretary. At that time the General-Secretaryship was not a key position, Stalin himself had no pretensions to the role of leader, and it thoroughly suited us to have him in that job. You see, Vladimir Ilyich, in those days there was absolutely no question of Stalin reaching for any kind of dictatorial, autocratic power in the Party – on the contrary, he was a declared supporter of collective leadership. Believe me, it was *Trotsky*'s ambitions and his potential urge toward dictatorship that we saw as a far greater threat *in those days* than Stalin's personal failings . . . And if I am to be absolutely frank, we felt that Stalin – precisely because of his personal limitations – was no danger to us and to the Party.

ZINOVIEV. Nowadays, of course, all this sounds like a naked, unprincipled struggle for power, but at the time we were concerned about the way the revolution would develop in the future: on Lenin's lines – or on Trotsky's. It was that objective that determined the methods of the struggle.

LENIN. For the moment I shall not deal with the content of what you are saying. I shall leave aside its substance and your choice of alternatives – on the one hand my ideas, on the other hand Trotsky's ideas – but you, Grigory Yevseyich, you cannot avoid responsibility for the fact that, in what was a vital *ideological* dispute, all of you – you and Stalin, Kamenev and Trotsky – were guilty of turning it into a matter of sheer intrigue, cabals and backstairs politicking. (*To* KAMENEV.) Well, what happened next?

KAMENEV. When the three of us had read your 'Letter to the Party Congress', we decided that at all costs Stalin must remain as General Secretary. It was comparatively easy to get the Central Committee to agree to this. I was much more worried about the Party Congress. In my view, the chief thing was to avoid having your letter read out and discussed at a plenary session of the Congress: there the situation might have got out of control. So I proposed that the document should be read to each delegation separately – 'for information only', as the saying goes – and that would be all: no public reading, no general discussion. Where the biggest delegations were concerned, the two of us went together: I read out the letter and Zinoviev gave a commentary on it. He said that the Plenary Central Committee had already taken the decision to keep Stalin as General Secretary, that while Lenin's word was law for us this was one matter on which Lenin's misgivings had fortunately not been justified. there was *no* danger of a split in the Party; our General Secretary had taken good note of the remarks made about him and had earned the confidence of the Party. These tactics were successful. (*Pause*.) I'm sorry – 'success' is perhaps not the right word.

BUKHARIN. I was one of those who had no objections to this move and the way it was done.

LENIN (*after a long pause*). We all know the Russian people – their strengths, their weaknesses, and – I fear – the fact that they are still downtrodden and ignorant . . . an arrogant national pride is not something that afflicts us. But what is the *consequence* of that, what action should follow from it? That is the question of all questions, which divides people into political parties, into opposing philosophies; it is the question that determines our politics, our morality and all the rest. And even we Bolsheviks, who all belong to one Party, are, in the final analysis, divided by our attitudes to *the people* . . . on the rostrum we swear in the name of the people to do this or that, but then behind closed doors in our offices or committee-rooms we do exactly as we please. We prefer the state of affairs in which 'the few' issue imperious orders and 'the rest' obediently accept them. Major problems of Party policy and structure are decided within the inner circle of Party bosses, but never – God forbid! – by the delegates to a Congress, and still less by the Party rank and file, whom we both fear and despise. And *people* become a means and not an end. That is what all of you have in common . . . So, that being the case, is it socialism that we are creating or something that is completely foreign to socialism and which, I'm afraid, the people are going to find nauseating? . . . I said to Martov: 'If ' – and '*if* things go wrong, then we could find ourselves in the disastrous situation that you, Martov, predict'. But *you two* – and your colleagues in the Party leadership – you yourselves must be aware of the part that *you* have played in creating the situation where those dangerous but by no means unavoidable possibilities, of which Martov and Rosa Luxemburg warned us, become reality. And what happened later? What happened when you then flung yourselves into Trotsky's embrace and led the attack against my New Economic Policy in favour of 'super-industrialisation', oblivious to the fate of the peasants, oblivious to the fate of millions of living human beings? How much of that was Bolshevism and how much of it was made up of fundamental delusions that Bolsheviks should *never* have? How much of it was unprincipled ambition and wounded *amour-propre*? Yes, comrades – those mistakes of yours will turn out to have consequences far worse than the mistake you made when you leaked the planned date of our uprising in October 1917.

Looking guilty and dispirited, ZINOVIEV *and* KAMENEV *are silent.*

KAMENEV. We are prepared to accept any blame from you . . . The only thing that's unbearable is the thought that someone may interpret it as conferring your approval on what happened later – Stalin's purges and fabricated show-trials of which we were the principal victims.

LENIN. Who conducted your trial?

KAMENEV. Vyshinsky.

LENIN. Which Vyshinsky was that? Not the one who was a Menshevik?

ZINOVIEV. Yes, that's the one; in 1917 he was chairman of the Yakimanskaya district administration in Moscow and he obediently followed Kerensky in signing the warrant for your and our arrest as German spies. Well, what Vyshinsky failed to do in 1917 he succeeded in doing exactly twenty years later.

KERENSKY. I must admit that I experienced a certain satisfaction when I read about that.

LENIN (*to* KAMENEV *and* ZINOVIEV). What happened?

ZINOVIEV. Acting on behalf of the Central Committee, he demanded that we agree to take part in an open trial as the accused – 'in the interests of the Party'.

LENIN. In the interests of the *Party?*

KAMENEV. 'You led the opposition to Stalin and the Party did not follow you. In order that your supporters should lay down their arms and prove that they have genuinely rejected your ideas and returned to the true Party faith, you must show them all where the opposition has taken them, how Trotsky, Kamenev and Zinoviev have taken them into a political swamp . . .' – something of that sort.

ZINOVIEV (*ironically*). We didn't have to admit very much: simply that on Trotsky's instructions we had organised the murder of Kirov and plotted to kill Stalin, Voroshilov and other Party leaders.

KAMENEV. And that if we agreed to admit all this, then our lives and the lives of our wives, children and friends would be spared.

ZINOVIEV. By then, Vladimir Ilyich, we were morally and physically broken.

KAMENEV. We told Yagoda, the head of the OGPU, that we would agree to the proposal, but only on condition that Stalin confirmed all these promises in the presence of all the members of the Politburo.

ZINOVIEV. When we were escorted under guard into Stalin's office in the Kremlin, the only Politburo members present were Stalin and Voroshilov.

KAMENEV. We stood in the middle of the room. They were seated, we were standing. Nobody said a word. Finally, Stalin motioned us to sit down on a couple of chairs.

Lighting-change: the spotlight on LENIN *fades; a spotlight picks out* STALIN, *who joins* KAMENEV *and* ZINOVIEV *in re-enacting the scene.*

STALIN. Well, what do you say to my proposal?

KAMENEV. We were promised that our case would be examined at a full session of the Politburo.

STALIN. You see before you a sub-committee of the Politburo, which is empowered to hear whatever you may have to say.

ZINOVIEV. Over the past two and a half years several promises have been made to Kamenev and myself, but not one of them has been kept. How can we trust you now? When Kirov was killed, we were forced to say that *we* bore the moral responsibility for his murder, and Yagoda gave us your personal assurance that this was the last sacrifice we would have to make. Yet now you are planning another mockery of a trial that will fling mud not only at us but at the entire Party, at the revolution itself, and which will discredit the very nature of Bolshevism in the eyes of the whole world.

STALIN. Don't waste your time trying to frighten us. We don't scare easily.

ZINOVIEV. Then let me appeal to your good sense . . . I beg you to cancel this trial. It will bring the Soviet Union into utter disgrace with world opinion. It will be a blow to the whole concept of socialism. If all you want to do is kill us, then kill us without any fuss and without this public farce of a trial, which is simply being staged to make us – two of the most senior and best-known Bolsheviks – admit that we were nothing but a gang of murderers. Just think: you intend to put on this show simply to demonstrate that members of Lenin's Politburo and personal friends of Lenin – yes, we had our disagreements! Yes, we argued with him, but that was because we were so close to him and he trusted us! – were nothing but a bunch of unscrupulous crooks and that our Bolshevik Party was no better than a snakes'-nest of traitors and spies . . . If Lenin were alive, if he could have seen all this . . . (*Breaks down, sobbing.*)

KAMENEV. Don't you see that if we, Old Bolsheviks, are no

more than terrorists – it means that we must renounce all the principles of Bolshevism?

STALIN. Would it be for the first time? This raises a legitimate question: are you really so attached to your principles, your views, your convictions? No one else in history has ever switched so easily from one set of principles to another, no one else ever changed their views with quite such ease as you two. First you were with Stalin and against Trotsky, then you were with Trotsky against Stalin. If you renounced your convictions so easily in the past, will it be so very hard for you to renounce them once again? I don't think we're asking very much of you – at least it's something you must find quite familiar. All that howling and weeping and desperation over such a trifle: you abandoned your principles often enough before, why can't you do it one more time?

KAMENEV. And you wouldn't allow that we were with you as long as you were following Lenin's principles? That as soon as you set off on a course that Lenin would never have accepted and put the principle of personal loyalty to yourself higher than any . . .

ZINOVIEV *(terrified, to* KAMENEV*)*. Lev Borisovich!

STALIN. You were going to say something, Kamenev? We're listening . . . (KAMENEV *remains silent.*) I think the members of the Politburo put it absolutely correctly when they said: We thank Kamenev and Zinoviev for their effective work for the Party in the past and for the successful part they have played in the fight against Trotskyism, which proved instructive to many Party members. But it is their misfortune that they have rejected what was good in their past record. This has caused us great concern; we have tried by every possible means to keep them in the Party leadership, but it is they themselves who have done everything to break all the strands of friendship that united us in the past. They were annoyed, it seems, because they no longer called the tune in the Party; because they were no longer in a position to dictate their will to the Party; because they were no longer, metaphorically speaking, mounted on horseback and giving the orders. And instead of accepting this with a good grace, instead of curbing their pride, instead of crawling on their bellies with words of repentance on their lips, they compounded their misdeeds by throwing in their lot with Trotsky. What did the great Lenin say about the way to deal with treason by the leaders? I am a pupil of Lenin too, and my interpretation of his thinking on this subject is – either they must capitulate, totally and unconditionally, or they must resign. And if they won't resign, we shall kick them out.

ZINOVIEV. We are guilty of many mistakes in the past and now that we are on the brink of the grave we don't intend to whitewash ourselves. But it never entered our heads to . . .

STALIN (*interrupting*). Who said of me at a plenary session of the Central Committee: 'No matter what difficulties may have been caused by this clique of pushy Stalinites, we shall fight them and all other gravediggers of the revolution to the bitter end.' Who said of me that our Party Congresses represented the ultimate triumph of stage-management by Stalin and his cronies? Who took such pleasure in repeating that I was a 'genius of mediocrity'? I never forget anything. You are a couple of pygmies who imagined you were going to save the revolution . . . In 1917 you both betrayed the cause of the revolution, claiming that you were saving it.

KAMENEV. You didn't think so in 1917. You opposed Lenin's suggestion that we should be expelled from the Party after that incident.

STALIN. Yes, and I was well and truly bawled out by Lenin for my pains. (*To* ZINOVIEV.) It's too late to weep now. You should have thought twice before trying to oppose the Central Committee. You were warned more than once that the line you were taking would end lamentably. You didn't listen, and in lamentation it has ended indeed. Even now we say to you – submit to the will of the Party and your life will be spared, along with the lives of all those you have led astray. But you still won't listen. So you have only yourselves to thank if your case ends even more lamentably – as badly, in fact, as can be.

KAMENEV. And what guarantee do we have that you won't cheat us again?

STALIN. Guarantee? What sort of guarantee can there be? That's simply ridiculous! Perhaps you want an official agreement, certified by the League of Nations? You obviously forget that you're not in some village market-place, haggling over a stolen horse, but in the Politburo of the Communist Party. If the Politburo's assurance is not enough for you, then I can see no point in continuing this conversation. Voroshilov here has said that if you two still have an ounce of common sense between you, you should go down on your knees in front of comrade

Stalin and thank him for saving your lives. And if you haven't any common sense, then to hell with you, you will have to die! What do you say to that, Zinoviev? Do you still have an ounce of common sense?

ZINOVIEV *(after a long pause)*. Yes, I do.

STALIN. There was a time when you two were distinguished by your clear thinking and your ability to tackle a question dialectically. Now you argue like a couple of blinkered, hair-splitting, small-town lawyers. You seem to have convinced yourselves that we are organising your trial merely to send you to the firing-squad. That's not very intelligent. As if we couldn't have you shot without a trial of any sort if we thought it necessary! You forget three things: the trial is not aimed at you but at Trotsky, the sworn enemy of our Party . . . Secondly, if we didn't have you shot when you were actively opposing the Central Committee, then why should we shoot you now that you are helping the Central Committee in its fight against Trotsky? Thirdly, you also forget that we Bolsheviks are the disciples and successors of Lenin, and that we don't intend to shed the blood of long-standing Party members, however many grave sins against the Party they may have committed.

Long pause.

KAMENEV. We agree. But we want it made quite clear once again that none of the oppositionists, nor their wives, nor their children, will any longer be persecuted for having belonged to the opposition, and that they will not be subjected to the death sentence.

STALIN. Of course; that is part of the arrangement.

KAMENEV. Then on those terms we agree.

Lighting-change; spotlights dim on **KAMENEV** *and* **ZINOVIEV**; *a spotlight picks out* **SVERDLOV**, *who approaches* **STALIN**.

SVERDLOV. Stalin, at that moment you knew you were planning to have them shot anyway . . .

STALIN *(furiously)*. I only ever knew one thing: all those Zinovievs, Kamenevs, Bukharins and Rykovs did nothing but get under my feet, hinder me, grab my arms and prevent me from doing the work that the great Lenin had bequeathed to us. I had sworn an oath over his coffin and I had carried out that oath, whatever all of you may say!

Lighting-change: spotlight on **STALIN** *alone. Funeral march.*

STALIN (*solemnly*). Comrades! We communists are people cast in a special mould. We are made of special stuff. We are those who make up the army of that great proletarian strategist, the army of comrade Lenin. There is no higher honour than to belong to that army. There is no higher calling than to be a member of the Party whose founder and leader was comrade Lenin. It is not given to everyone to be a member of such a party. It is not given to everyone to withstand the storms and adversities that are bound up with membership of that Party.

Before he departed from us, comrade Lenin enjoined us to hold high and keep undefiled the great vocation of being a member of our Party. We swear to you, comrade Lenin, that we will keep your commandment with honour.

For twenty-five years Lenin cherished our Party and moulded it into the most powerful and battle-hardened workers' party in the world. The unity and cohesion of its ranks has been forged by our Party in the heat of battle. By that unity and cohesion it has won victory over the enemies of the working class.

Before departing from us, comrade Lenin also enjoined us to guard the unity of our Party as the apple of our eye. We swear to you, comrade Lenin, that we shall keep this commandment, too, with honour!

A spotlight snaps on to **LENIN**, *who leaps to his feet, unable to restrain himself.*

LENIN. Stop! I can't listen to this any longer!

Scene Nine

THE WINTER PALACE – KERENSKY'S OFFICE
00.30 hours, October 25th 1917

Colonel **POLKOVNIKOV** *is reading his report on the situation to* **KERENSKY.**

POLKOVNIKOV. All the army's officer-cadet schools in Petrograd have been put in a state of instant combat readiness. The cadets who arrived from Peterhof have been assigned to the Winter

Palace. We have intercepted a radio signal from the cruiser *Aurora* with a call from the Bolshevik Military Revolutionary Committee to act with caution, but firmly and decisively.

KERENSKY. With caution . . .

POLKOVNIKOV. According to the police department, Lenin's whereabouts have been established. He will be arrested shortly. Bearing the strategic situation in mind, I consider it necessary to deprive the Bolsheviks of freedom of manoeuvre and to prevent them from operating freely throughout the city.

KERENSKY. I agree. Raise the lifting bridges!

Curtain

ACT TWO

Scene One

SMOLNY INSTITUTE
13.20 hours, October 25th 1917

TROTSKY (*advancing to the fore-stage*). People are asking us whether we are intending to stage an armed coup. That will depend on Kerensky and his tottering government, who want to break up the All-Russian Congress of Soviets when it meets. If the government chooses to make use of the short time – the 24, 48 or 72 hours that still separate it from extinction – to disperse the Congress and attack us, then we shall respond by a counter-attack: blow for blow, steel for iron!

Kerensky and Co. think that history is made in drawing-rooms and ministerial offices, where new-born bourgeois 'democrats' rub shoulders with titled liberals, where jumped-up provincial lawyers soon learn to kiss the hands of counts and princes. Fools! Gasbags! Blinkered idiots! History is made in the trenches, where a soldier, drunk on the ghastly fumes of war, first plunges his bayonet into an officer's gut and then, riding on a carriage roof or astride a buffer, travels back to his native village 'to make the red cock crow' – his graphic image for setting fire to the landowner's roof . . . Perhaps such barbarism isn't to your taste? Can't be helped, says History: as ye have sown, so shall ye reap. Can anyone still seriously believe that history is made in the Winter Palace? Nonsense, rubbish, fantasy, cretinism! This time, gentlemen – as you are shortly to find out – History has chosen for her experimental laboratory the Smolny Institute – until a few weeks ago the boarding-school for Young Ladies of the Nobility. Here, History is preparing her final extinction of that suppurating obscenity – the rule of Russia by the landowners and the bourgeoisie. They are coming to this place, to Smolny, in a steady stream: the grimy delegates from the factories; the uncouth, the grey-clad, the louse-ridden emissaries from the trenches. And from here they will carry far and wide the prophetic message: 'Long live the socialist revolution of workers and peasants!' (*Moves to one side, addressing both the auditorium and those on stage.*) I now wish to protest against the blatant bias in the script of this play. It is high time, comrades, to abandon the lying account of events purveyed in Stalin's *Short Course on the History of the Bolshevik Party*. I wrote on several occasions after the October Revolution that our declared policy of waiting for the opening of the Congress of Soviets was nothing but an intentional tactic to confuse Kerensky, a manoeuvre to blunt his vigilance, a kind of camouflage. To organise an insurrection under the barefaced slogan of seizing power by the Bolshevik Party is one thing, and is hardly likely to bring us the broadbased support that we need; but to plan and carry out an insurrection in order to defend the democratic rights of the Congress of Soviets is quite another matter. Surely that is clear enough, isn't it? Why must we once again parrot the lies of the Stalinist school of falsification?

MARTOV. Listen, Trotsky, that's not true and you know it. Whether we were at Smolny, as you and I were, or in the Winter Palace, like Kerensky, none of us at the time really knew what was going on. We were all being drawn along in the wake of events. You really were waiting for the start of the Congress, and you had your reasons. But all that theory about 'camouflage' and 'confusing Kerensky' was something you read later in the book written by our – Menshevik – historian Sukhanov, who wrote it two years after the revolution, and which you, with hindsight, adopted as having been your idea. You needed that theory in order to justify the contradiction between your position and the position taken up by Lenin, who was convinced that to wait for the start of the Congress of Soviets was sheer lunacy. I assure you that if the Congress *hadn't* assembled against the background of the insurrection, then neither we, the Mensheviks, nor the Right Social-Revolutionaries would have walked out; the resolution inviting the Bolsheviks and the Left S-Rs to take power would not have been passed, because we would have voted it down, and thus the Bolsheviks would not have been given *carte blanche* by the Congress. But if it hadn't been for Lenin arriving at Smolny at midnight on that night, the 25th, and persuading you to bring the insurrection forward, you would have become, as they say in English, 'the man who missed the bus.'

Scene Two

BYKHOV

14.40 hours, December 25th 1917

The GENERALS *are discussing the plan of action drawn up by* GENERAL LUKOMSKY.

MARKOV. Kollontai.

KORNILOV. Definitely.

LUKOMSKY. Maxim Gorky.

DENIKIN. Martov and Plekhanov too.

KORNILOV. Bronstein . . . Kamenev . . . Stalin . . . And that other one, what's his name – Yoffe.

MARKOV. Where the Bolsheviks are concerned, it's quite clear – they must all be strung up.

DENIKIN. All the same, it would be a good idea to put them on trial, at least the ringleaders.

MARKOV. Why? The main thing is not to stand on ceremony and not to get bogged down in legalistic formalities.

LUKOMSKY. There is one trial that we must organise. The leading Bolsheviks must be tried on the well-founded, documented charge of paid espionage for Germany – that will have a much more powerful effect than simply shooting them. It will be execution for high treason.

KORNILOV. There can be no question about all those extreme leftist revolutionaries. The country will understand that and accept it. I propose another aim: we must put the whole country in a state of shock, of paralysis, so that no other filthy rebel of whatever colour will dare to raise his head. Understand? A state of clinical shock! Will we achieve that by putting Lenin up against a wall alongside some workman? Never. But if all those snivelling liberals – the Rodzyankos, the Milyukovs, the Struves and the Berdyaevs – are seen dangling from lamp-posts, then . . .

MARKOV. Don't forget Kerensky!

DENIKIN. But Struve? That's going too far.

KORNILOV. What we have to fear, Anton Ivanovich, is not

'going too far', but not going far enough. We will only paralyse the malcontents if we don't cast our net wide enough. I don't like playing around with half-measures. All the chattering, thinking, theorising classes – the cause of all our troubles! – must be rooted out in one fell swoop! And if all Russia is convulsed with horror, then you can reckon we've won . . . Look – I'm not a bloodthirsty man, my proposals are based on realistic expediency. You and I have got to save Russia. We are not the ones who brought her to the brink of the grave, but it is we who must save her.

LUKOMSKY. Only by first inducing a convulsion can we put our plan of an efficient system of military dictatorship into effect. The entire population will be formed into three armies – one army at the front, one to man the transport and supply system, another in the factories. The Soviets will be abolished, all mass organisations and trade unions will be disbanded, and the press, except our newspapers, will be closed down . . .

DENIKIN. Why must we do that? We're a civilised European country. The country's had enough of harsh censorship.

LUKOMSKY. I agree; that will only be for the short term. Meanwhile all political parties are to be abolished. All political activity will be controlled through a single party headed by Kornilov.

DENIKIN. I'm not so sure about that either. We need to create the impression that we are in the shadows, out of sight. We are soldiers, men of action. We'll always find plenty of chatterers to run a political party.

MARKOV (*laughs*). We'll keep a few of them for our own purposes – on a short leash!

KORNILOV. Where the army's concerned, add this: immediate disbandment and dispersal of all units that have been infected with revolutionary propaganda. Troops from those units to be put into concentration camps on the strictest possible regime and with reduced rations. Field court-martial and the death penalty for civilians throughout the country. I don't trust either Petrograd or Moscow, so we will start off by sending in the cossacks and giving them a free hand.

LUKOMSKY. What about the structure of a future Russian state?

MARKOV. With Russia's historical traditions and given the

character of the Russian peasant, he needs one thing: a monarchy, and nothing else.

LUKOMSKY. It would be advisable to install a Tsar five years later, rather than five minutes too soon.

DENIKIN. We shouldn't prejudge that question. The first step is to install ourselves in the Winter Palace. But once that's done, I wouldn't rule out the idea of a military dictatorship.

LUKOMSKY. What about the Constituent Assembly?

MARKOV. Abolish it after its first session, if it rejects our dictatorship.

KERENSKY (*leaps to his feet*). Wait! Stop! Did you hear that? Can't you see the similarity between two forms of Russian extremism? On January 5th 1918 the Bolsheviks dispersed the Constituent Assembly because it rejected a Bolshevik regime. The Constituent Assembly was the only truly representative body, elected by secret ballot and universal adult suffrage, in the whole of Russian history! And what did the generals do with the elected deputies of the Constituent Assembly? No, not these generals, but their twin brothers – Kolchak and his ilk. I regard it as my duty to tell the world about that incident. The Social-Revolutionary deputies, who had a majority in the Constituent Assembly, moved to Omsk, where they attempted to reassert their democratic authority. Kolchak arrested them and threw them in jail. The Bolsheviks raised a revolt, released all the prisoners, but, alas, they were unfortunately unable to hold out against a counter-attack by Kolchak's White troops, who proposed to the arrested deputies that their lives would be spared and their safety guaranteed if they returned to their cells. So those good comrades, the deputies of the Constituent Assembly, as befits honourable democrats, went back into prison. And what happened? That same night the elected representatives of the people were all dragged out of their cells and bayonetted to death. The Whites did not even deign to waste bullets on them. It is time the world knew about this. I'll say more: I always believed that if the generals had won, it would have produced in Russia a form of military-fascist dictatorship. And that would truly have been the way to the tomb!

KORNILOV (*to* KERENSKY). Stop that drivel! It is now three o'clock in the afternoon of October 25th. You'd do better to tell us what you did to crush the Bolsheviks. Did you start to act decisively, or did you still continue to hesitate and dither in your usual cowardly fashion?

DENIKIN. The justification for the line we took, Mr Kerensky, was proved by subsequent events and the lessons of history: it was precisely our methods which enabled Stalin, like Peter the Great, to raise Russia to the ranks of the world's great powers. Churchill is supposed to have said that Stalin made two mistakes: when he showed Europe to Ivan – the ordinary Russian soldier – and when he showed Ivan to Europe. I absolutely disagree with that, which could only have been said by someone who wasn't Russian. The fact that Europe was shown to Ivan was a blessing; it made the Red Army aware of the nation's great strength. And there can be no doubt that it was no mistake on Stalin's part to have shown our splendid Ivan to Europe: it cured Europe once and for all of any urge to threaten us with the sword.

STALIN. General, if you are such an apologist for my methods, why weren't you among the group of émigrés, headed by Maklakov, a former Russian ambassador, who in the spring of 1945 came to Bogomolov, my ambassador in Paris, and announced that they recognised my government as the legitimate national government of Russia?

DENIKIN. While admitting the efficacy of methods that we were merely proposing to use, and which you used successfully, I nevertheless categorically deny your right to the throne of Russia. In my view, the person who sits on the Russian throne, no matter what his name may be, should be a *Russian*.

STALIN (*stung by this remark*). So all the Russian Tsars were Russians, were they? Catherine the Great was pure German, as were all her descendants down to and including Alexander II. The last Tsar, Nicholas II, was the son of a Danish mother and married to yet another German. You're a chauvinist, General! Making that suggestion about such a multi-national country as ours is positively immoral!

DENIKIN. I'm a plain-spoken man: there are things about you that I like, and there are other things . . .

STALIN. In his book about Moscow in 1937, Leon Feuchtwanger recalled the reply made by Socrates when he was asked about certain obscurities in the teachings of Heraclitus. The great Socrates said: 'That which I have understood is excellent. From that I conclude that the rest, which I have not understood, is also excellent.'

Scene Three

FOFANOVA'S APARTMENT
15.00 hours, October 25th 1917.

LENIN *is pacing about the room, grim and preoccupied. A spotlight picks out* STRUVE, *who gets up from his chair.*

STRUVE. Vladimir Ilyich, I want to talk to you.

LENIN. Please do.

STRUVE. It is now three o'clock in the afternoon. You're thinking that your place is not here, but at Smolny. I want to prove to you that if you stay here, it will be a blessing for Russia. It is only three o'clock; there is still time to change the scenario . . .

LENIN. Pyotr Bernhardovich, is it worth wasting our time? After all, I know you so well; would you like me to predict, verbatim, exactly what you are going to say? 'The Russians still have the mentality of serfs, for which there are a dozen historical reasons . . .'

STRUVE. I'm not in the mood for jokes. The Russians indeed still do have the mentality of serfs, for which there certainly are a dozen historical reasons. Both you and we want to see them free men. You believe that in order to do that you have to change the external conditions, the social and political structure, in other words – what's needed is a revolution. Our reply to you is that however often you may alter conditions in Russia, even if you include your planned October Revolution, the Russians will still not change – slavery has been so thoroughly hammered into their souls. Why won't they change? Because the innermost essence of a man doesn't depend on outside circumstances, on the social structure, but on whether or not a spiritual principle exists in him – 'the kingdom of heaven is within you'. As long as people themselves don't possess a sense of inner freedom, no revolutions are ever going to *make* them free. Starting with the Decembrists and ending with you, all Russian revolutionaries have been the spiritual allies of the terrible latent Russian propensity for anarchy, violence and hooliganism. Because in rousing the Russian people by your bold ideas and desperate actions, you revolutionaries have brought Russia nothing but misfortune; because revolutions have only ever given rise to bloody rebellion followed by bloody repression. *There* lies the historic crime of the Russian intelligentsia, *that* is what should make them repent and refrain, once and for all, from inciting the Russian people against their rulers. The true calling of the Russian intelligentsia is not rebellion and revolution! Forgive me for using the words of a religious thinker, I know they're not your kind of language, but the great good sense contained in them may be revealed even to you: 'It is better to light a single candle than to curse the darkness!'

LENIN. How is a man to rise from his knees? That, in the final analysis, is what our revolution is about. How? How is a frightened onlooker, a passive victim, to be turned into a fighter for his own cause? It's a terrifying prospect. Fear has a thousand aspects. How are they to be overcome? I am convinced that a man creates and fulfils himself by action, by deeds, and not by spending centuries on his knees in front of an ikon. But when he does rise from his knees in order to utter the truth, to act on the truth, to hold fast to the truth – that is the moment when he changes the social and political conditions that have kept him on his knees . . . and he changes *himself.*

STRUVE. No, Ulyanov, that was all dreamed up by a German Jew and garbled into Russian terms.

LENIN. As a half-German and a one-time Marxist, aren't you ashamed of yourself, Pyotr Bernhardovich?

STRUVE. No, I am not. There was indeed a time when I toyed with Marxism, so I know what I'm talking about. None of Marx's ideas suit Russian soil; Russian soil longs to be planted with other seeds that are native and unadulterated. Surely we can think up some better, more worthwhile ideas than that second-hand claptrap, can't we? Have we no sense of national pride, when all's said and done?

LENIN. Yes, we have. But it lies elsewhere. The Russians have proved that they *can* stand up and fight for the right – think of the war of 1812 against Napoleon. Russia is not only the country of pogroms, of the gallows, of prisons, of hunger-strikes and of servility to the powers that be. And we feel a profound contempt for those members of the Russian intelligentsia who encouraged those reactionary gangs, the Black Hundreds, who terrorised the Russian people.

STRUVE. I didn't expect you to say anything different.

LENIN. So is this argument worthwhile?

STRUVE. I'm thinking of the people out there who are listening to us. Let *them* consider what we are saying.

LENIN. Indeed, let them.

STRUVE. And let them give an answer to my chief question: Do you, Ulyanov, believe in what you're saying? Do you believe in the revolution, when in fact your plans will amount to the negation of that revolution if you put them into effect? You promise the people democracy, although you know perfectly well that you will turn the so-called 'dictatorship of the proletariat' into a monopoly of power for one party; that you will abolish all other parties; that you will suppress all newspapers except your own; that you will unleash your own terror and put everyone who doesn't share your politics in front of a firing-squad . . .

SPIRIDONOVA. Stop! Just a minute! I must speak! No one here will suspect me of being sympathetic to the Bolsheviks, but to keep silent at this moment would be positively immoral. Mr Struve has a very short memory. Lenin never thought of the dictatorship of the proletariat as a one-party system and never spoke of it as such. What's more, when proposing an electoral system of proportional representation to us in December 1917, he said that the Soviet system would enable the workers, if they were dissatisfied with their party, to elect new delegates to the Soviets, to give power to another party and to change the government lawfully and without violence. And you are well aware of that . . . The Bolsheviks demanded only one thing from all the other parties: to acknowledge and respect the basic decrees of the October Revolution and to abstain from any armed attack on the Soviet regime. And what was the response? The measure of freedom granted to those parties was only ever used by them for what lawyers call attempts to subvert the existing order. I ask you: what government would tolerate that? Would you? Would *we* have put up with it? Never! One can only marvel that the Bolsheviks' patience lasted as long as it did. The October Revolution was the pure well-spring: what muddied it was the civil war that began six months later. And so, Mr Struve, there is no call for you to depict yourself as some kind of holy innocent. You're a man of considerable political experience: you shared a table with Lenin in your younger, Marxist days; you were also a minister in Baron Wrangel's 'White' government of Southern Russia during the civil war – and now you tell us fairy-tales about immaculate conception. We all share the responsibility for having thrown away Lenin's offer of constitutional machinery for changing the party in power. Well, when the Kronstadt mutiny took place in 1921 and all the opposition parties supported that rebellion, the Bolshevik response was predictable – those parties were abolished. Even so, in 1922 Lenin again considered the idea of legalising the Menshevik Party.

STRUVE. And you can still say all that – after the Bolsheviks put a bullet in the back of your neck in 1941?

SPIRIDONOVA. Not in the back of the neck, Mr Struve – in my face, without a blindfold and with my eyes open. (*To the auditorium.*) Yes, it seemed to all of us at the time that when we opposed the Bolsheviks we were doing it for the sake of Russia's future, whereas in fact we were only motivated by narrow, petty, immediate party interests. It was *we* who destroyed the chance of a constitutional political opposition in Russia and created an intolerable situation for the Bolsheviks, which made coexistence between the parties impossible. Power exerted without a framework of constraints will corrupt even a saint. Without giving up one iota of my party's strategic, long-term programme, I wish to condemn its tactics. I was even reflecting on our fatal mistakes as I took my last steps on earth . . . But still, I ask you not to judge us harshly. Our beliefs were sincerely held – and our mistakes were the errors of sincerity. We loved Russia to the point of heartache and we died, in spite of everything, as men and women of principle with a profound and undiminished belief in socialism.

STRUVE. Astounding!

LENIN. You could never understand that, Pyotr Bernhardovich.

STRUVE. No doubt. Nevertheless, I shall put my last argument . . . What will happen as a result of your revolution? You will unleash the Beast that lurks in the Russian mob.

LENIN. A moment ago you were talking about your beloved Russian people.

STRUVE. Yes, the Beast. No political concessions, such as your New Economic Policy, will keep it on a leash. What to do about the Beast: that is the chief political problem for any government of Russia. Only those bent on suicide can contemplate democracy on Russian soil, still less socialist democracy. To drive the Beast back into its stall, Stalin will have to erect a rigid state structure that will be indistinguishable from the Russian Empire of the Tsars. He will create a great world power; he will *not* create the first phase of a true communist society. And because Bolshevism will thus be discredited, people will start to look for a substitute in Great Russian nationalism, which is the only idea capable of replacing Bolshevism. Marxist socialism is doomed to extinction. So is the game worth the candle, Vladimir Ilyich?

LENIN (*ironically*). In school I always got top marks for scripture. I will answer you in the words of St Paul the Apostle from his First Epistle to the Corinthians, Chapter 15, Verse 21: 'For since by man came death, by man came also the resurrection of the dead.'

Lighting-change. STRUVE *and* SPIRIDONOVA *return to their seats. Place and time revert to* FOFANOVA's *apartment in the afternoon of October 25th 1917. The front door-bell rings three times. Enter* FOFANOVA.

FOFANOVA. It's me! They've raised the lifting bridges across the Neva! Kerensky gave the order, apparently. As soon as I heard the news, I made an excuse and came home. Have you eaten? Look – I bought the 'Workers' Voice' on the way. (*Hands the newspaper to* LENIN.) It seems the officer cadets occupied the printing-works this morning, but our people threw them out and today's issue was published after all . . .

LENIN (*absorbed in the newspaper*). What did my wife say to you?

FOFANOVA (*laying the table*). The Central Committee won't let you go. Patrols are out looking for you.

LENIN. What's happening on the streets? Has it started yet, or not?

FOFANOVA. How shall I say . . . Everything seems quite normal. Lots of people on the streets, the shops are open, queues everywhere . . . If it has started, you wouldn't notice it . . .

LENIN (*looking through the newspaper*). What?! What's this?!! They're out of their minds! They've decided to wait for the start of the Congress of Soviets! That means disaster!

FOFANOVA. What's the matter, Vladimir Ilyich?

LENIN. So that's why they're keeping me cooped up here . . . Have you read what Stalin has written in the leading article? No insurrection today, but wait for the Congress tomorrow. I see it all now . . . they're supposed to be my brothers-in-arms, my friends . . . Yesterday it was Zinoviev and Kamenev who blew the gaff . . . today it's Stalin and Trotsky . . . Margarita Vasilievna, please don't go out again for a while. I must have time to write a letter which I would like you to deliver for me . . .

Lighting-change. LENIN *goes over to* STALIN *and* TROTSKY, *who stand up.*

LENIN (*to* STALIN *and* TROTSKY). What does this mean?

TROTSKY. Events are developing according to plan. Our people wouldn't let them raise the lifting bridges, now we are planning to take control of the central telegraph office.

STALIN. We decided on this policy because . . .

LENIN (*furiously*). This isn't a policy – it's a piece of shit! Stop telling me fairy-tales! I'm asking you straight out: it is now three o'clock in the afternoon – is the insurrection under way or not? Or are you again trying your delaying tactics of waiting for the Congress?

TROTSKY. You'll see how neatly it will all be done . . . By a simple show of hands . . .

LENIN. And what if we don't have a majority?

STALIN. If . . .

LENIN. And what, pray, are your answers to a thousand other 'ifs'? You haven't any. In other words, we are to construct a tactical plan based on unknown quantities, based on hot air, are we? But that's not a policy, it's gambling! Today a majority of the people are behind us; we have a chance to seize power virtually without bloodshed – and you are gambling on things that should never be left to chance. Both of you keep glancing in the mirror of history to see how you look: 'What splendid fellows we are,' you say, 'with a simple tactical move we shall achieve great strategic objectives.' And what if it goes wrong? How will you then justify yourselves to the Russian people? By groaning and sighing and making idiotic apologies?

TROTSKY. But look, Vladimir Ilyich, you know that . . .

LENIN. Yes, I know! In five months' time, at Brest-Litovsk, it will be a gambling game again and not a policy! It's absolutely amazing! All of you – Zinoviev, Kamenev, Trotsky and Stalin – all of you have the right to be in the Bolshevik headquarters, you have each played a huge role in the revolution so far, but your qualities, pushed beyond a certain limit, turn into God knows what! If you keep on as you are going, you won't only damage or obstruct our cause – you will ruin it completely! Why won't you let me come to Smolny?

STALIN. Out of concern for your safety.

LENIN. Drop it, Stalin! You know perfectly well that the moment I turn up at Smolny it would put an end to your game of waiting for the Congress, and that's why you're forcing me to take a back seat. My safety! Don't you and Trotsky realise that in the end I shan't give a damn for your refusal to give me an escort and I shall come alone . . . across the whole city, where there are people waiting around every corner to catch me and bump me off . . . still, it's useless to talk to you now, you only listen to yourselves . . . (*Addresses the other Bolsheviks.*) Comrades, I want to talk to all the members of the Central Committee who are present at this moment . . .

SVERDLOV, KAMENEV, ZINOVIEV, DZIERZINSKI *and* BUKHARIN *get up from their seats and approach* LENIN.

LENIN. Comrades, what is going on? We must thrash this out. I insist on a clarification. For the past two months something odd has been happening between the Central Committee and myself. I obeyed the Central Committee and went over to Finland, where I went underground and bombarded you with my ideas and proposals. You read them and politely pushed them to one side . . .

KAMENEV. Now, Vladimir Ilyich, that isn't . . .

LENIN. You, Lev Borisovich, are something of an expert where my letters are concerned. Wasn't it you who suggested that the letter I wrote in September, in which I raised the matter of an insurrection, should just be burned?

KAMENEV. No, it wasn't me.

LENIN. Well, at any rate, it wasn't entirely without your participation. You didn't even give my proposals the careful consideration they deserved. You simply didn't reply to any of my suggestions of that nature. Who corrected and edited my articles, who crossed out of them all my references to your glaring mistakes? Was it you, Stalin?

STALIN. Why should I have done that?

LENIN. Because at that time you and Kamenev were running *Pravda*. What am I to make of all this? I see it as a subtle hint that the Central Committee doesn't want to discuss this or that issue, a subtle hint that I am to shut my mouth and keep out of the way . . .

ZINOVIEV. Vladimir Ilyich . . .

LENIN. I insist that we – all of us – speak frankly and like grown men, not like naughty children! You are forcing me to offer my resignation, which I will do, retaining the right to put across my views in the rank and file of the party and at the Congress of Soviets. I am far from believing that my opinion is never mistaken and should always be accepted as a matter of course. But let us please *discuss* it instead of passing it over in silence, let us please argue instead of making moves behind my back like a cheating chess-player. Let us accept *your* conclusions – but let it be politics and not backstage horse-trading!

STALIN. Why are you so furious? We're all on your side.

LENIN. When I saw that the Central Committee was hesitating and that the defeatist mood represented by Zinoviev and Kamenev might gain the upper hand, without waiting for your permission I left Finland and came back to Petrograd on my own initiative. We gathered together, we immediately found a common language, we were united, we had a democratic discussion and we took a decision about the insurrection. Zinoviev and Kamenev were trying to shoot us in the back. I demanded their expulsion from the party, but the Central Committee did not go along with me.

SVERDLOV. Those differences of opinion were very soon forgotten.

LENIN. That is quite true. I am not doubting the Central Committee's right to take decisions, but nor can anyone deprive me of the right to have doubts about a particular decision, even though I may have accepted it . . . Now let us continue. Only yesterday we agreed that we would launch the insurrection today. Today comes, and Trotsky starts playing his game of chess behind my back. It is now three o'clock in the

afternoon, and I ask comrade members of the Central
Committee: is the insurrection on its way, or are we simply
engaged in planning moves to make in response to what
Kerensky may do? What are we doing – are we making a
revolution, or are we merely talking about it like a lot of
communist windbags? If I haven't convinced you, then kindly
make your objections, argue – I don't mind how heated you
get, only don't just sit there in silence! (*No one speaks.*) Once
again you're forcing me to act over your heads . . . I will
shortly send Fofanova to you with a letter demanding that the
matter be decided this evening or tonight at the latest. As I
suspect you may still hesitate, I shall personally appeal to all
district party organisations and all regiments requesting that
they put the utmost pressure on you. I categorically demand
that you bring me to Smolny at once! (*Gives the letter to*
FOFANOVA.) Off you go, Margarita Vasilievna, and don't
come back without their agreement for me to leave here and go
to Smolny.

FOFANOVA. You'll send me there and back another three times
and each time the answer will be the same: no, he is not to go.

LENIN. I don't believe it . . . (*Sits down, utterly exhausted.*) Though
by now I'm getting used to their cavalier attitude to my
requests and recommendations.

TROTSKY. Come now, Vladimir Ilyich, you're just tired and in a
bad mood.

LENIN. A bad mood? (*He clearly lacks the strength for further
discussion, but overcomes his weakness with an obvious effort.*) In
December of 1922, realising that I am dying, I will dictate a
letter to the Party Congress, asking that it be read out to the full
Congress. What could be simpler, you might think? And how
was my request treated? What was done instead?

TROTSKY. I had no part in that.

LENIN. Oh yes, you did! And how you did! Silent, with your
arms crossed, watching disdainfully as a vile act was committed
before your eyes – is that what you call having no part in it?
How could you have refrained from protesting against that
jesuitical manoeuvre: a reading of the letter to each delegation
separately, with comments by Zinoviev which made nonsense of
my letter? (*To* BUKHARIN.) How was your silence ensured? (*To*
DZIERZINSKI.) And yours? . . . It didn't occur to one of you
to give any thought to that most decisive but apparently trifling

matter which became the cause of the greatest tragedy for the revolution and for socialism. (*To* STALIN *and* TROTSKY.) A simple move, a shift in positions, a swing in a different direction would have saved both of you for the revolution – saved the revolution itself.

TROTSKY. Is that really how you see it?

LENIN (*furiously*). Do you think it wasn't your position in the 'twenties that destroyed the October Revolution? And do you think your calls from Mexico to set up an underground party, to stage an uprising, to start another civil war were part of the aims of the October Revolution? (*Paces nervously back and forth.*) It was then, in the 'twenties, that we should have changed the system which allowed one man to concentrate limitless power in his own hands. But no – having rejected one of my recommendations, you rejected the other one too. I warned you that in 1922 the proletarian policies of our party were not being determined by the party membership – we had lost the flower of the membership in the civil war and a mass of rubbish had taken its place – but by the enormous monolithic authority of that thin layer that we called the party's 'old guard'. All it needed was a slight internal clash or disagreement within the 'old guard' and its authority would be, if not undermined, then so weakened that it could no longer influence vital decisions. And you all fed the flames of that internal quarrel. One way of to some extent forestalling your quarrels and no doubt of defusing them would have been to bring a hundred workers from the factory-floor, real proletarians, into the Central Committee. They wouldn't have taken a single word of yours on trust; they wouldn't have uttered a single word that didn't square with their conscience; they wouldn't have been intimidated by any 'authority' when it came to calling a spade a spade. Thirty full-time party functionaries and a hundred workers: a watchdog body of workers like that wouldn't have allowed you to split up into squabbling factions as you did.

STALIN. At the 12th and 13th Party Congresses we increased the membership of the Central Committee by 17 and 15 respectively.

LENIN. And who were those extra members? Not a single worker, not a single peasant. And (*To* STALIN.) do you know why you increased the numbers, and why (*To* TROTSKY.) you approved the increases? Because you both subscribe to the

same authoritarian creed: for both of you, the masses are
simply the object, the dumb beneficiaries of your good deeds,
and not the subject, the initiators of creative political action. I
always sought the solution of problems by an *extension* of
genuine democracy, but you did so by the opposite means.

STALIN. Why do you say that, Vladimir Ilyich? I never uttered a
single word against democracy.

TROTSKY. I always fought for more democracy.

LENIN. We all know well enough what sort of 'democracy' was
favoured by those like you who advocated 'tightening the
screws'. It's the kind of 'democracy' which regards the people
as a herd of cattle, but in whose name a self-appointed élite can
decide those people's fate. I can hear you now: 'How could
mere workers make sense of the issues discussed at Politburo
meetings? The old man must be off his head . . .' What – you
didn't think that? Oh yes, you did! At all events, they would
certainly have made sense of the ideological battles that went
on between you; they would have seen the personal issues that
were bound up with them and which poisoned them by turning
them into naked struggles for personal power. *They* wouldn't
have let you split up into warring factions.

STALIN. That is pure illusion, Vladimir Ilyich.

TROTSKY. I agree. It's an illusion.

LENIN. I dedicated my life to that illusion, as you call it – and
which I would call faith in the Russian worker, his potential, his
common sense – and I never once had any reason to regret it.

STALIN. What occurred was a fierce ideological struggle, and
that, fundamentally, is always a struggle for power. How are
your workers supposed to decide which blow in that fight is
right and necessary and which is not? Your idea is an illusion.

LENIN. An ideological struggle within the Party, comrade Stalin,
differs from a vulgar brawl in that it is not supposed to result in
scoring points off each other but in mutual agreement and
cooperation. Why do you have to see every differing opinion as
nothing but malice or a counter-revolutionary plot? Why do
you have to inject personal malice into every such argument, as
you so often did? Why didn't you ever learn that in politics it
always has the worst possible consequences?

STALIN. When it was a case of maintaining the unity of the Party, *you* were never at a loss for words. Remember the 10th Congress and your resolution on Party unity and the outlawing of factional groupings. In the final analysis, it was *that* which enabled us to forge the ranks of the Party into a steel-like unity.

LENIN *(after a pause)*. At critical moments, when internal Party strife is more dangerous than Denikin and all his White armies, there is no room for factions and oppositions. Of that I am profoundly convinced. But *then* we were talking about a specific moment in time and about specific disagreements – not about general principles. If we were to forbid altogether the clash of opinions and tendencies within the Party, to deprive the Party and the Central Committee altogether of the right to appeal to the Party at large when the issue is a fundamental one, an issue of principle – how then could we ever achieve unity? Yes – unity is the strength of the Party, but a blind unthinking unity based on the unquestioned will of the leader, on personal devotion to him, on the absence of argument or the clash of opinions – that would fatally weaken the Party. And supposing the leader were to take the wrong course? In that case the Party, constricted by a dogmatic, servile conception of loyalty, would be unable to make use of its rights and duties; it would be silent, although its duty should be to cry 'halt'; it would simply approve everything that the leader said or did. Was the resolution on Party unity an instrument of unity, or was it a weapon to shut people's mouths and thrust aside anyone who was independent enough to have some awkward views of their own? Unity from conviction – or unity from fear? And if you have the latter, aren't you then perilously close to Bonapartism, disguised with a scrap of communist camouflage? Aren't you getting close to genuflection and deification? There's as much socialism as there is democracy in it – none at all!

STALIN. Are you questioning my role in the struggles of the 1920s?

LENIN. No. When you were leading a principled fight to defend the legacy of the October Revolution, I was with you. But when your glaring lack of principle was cloaked in a patchwork of pseudo-marxism, then even the dead felt bitterly ashamed of you. For instance, that cult of idolatry that you organised . . .

STALIN. I see what you have in mind. I put up with all that nonsense, that chorus of hosannas, because I knew how much naive pleasure it would give to our people. But you can't complain: thanks to that, your name was always held in honour and affection, your portrait hung everywhere, people bowed down to your memory . . .

LENIN. There is no better way of killing a politician than turning him into an ikon. And by the way, talking of holding me 'in honour and affection' . . . When General Vedenin, the commandant of the Kremlin, was touring the premises at his take-over, he found a pile of books covered with a filthy dust-sheet under a staircase in some dark passageway. It turned out that these books were the contents of my library. My former apartment had been turned into a typing-pool on your orders, and the books had just been stacked in a heap.

STALIN. What should we have done with them? Opened a museum?

LENIN. I should think giving them to the Rumyantsev Library would have been better than chucking them under the stairs.

STALIN. Well . . . perhaps I am a bit rough round the edges . . . No one has ever complained, though, except . . . But it's true I am rude to enemies of the Party . . . The people gave me a mandate to complete the work that you had begun . . . No one else in world history had ever had such a responsibility . . . And when I said I was no more than the faithful disciple of Lenin, that wasn't hypocrisy on my part . . . I really did nothing but take your methods and adapt them to new historical circumstances.

LENIN. That is not true and you know it! To take the methods meant purely for use in conditions of a long and ruthless civil war and to claim them as the universally valid methods of building socialism – that is the worst possible crime against socialism!

DZIERZINSKI. How can you open an antique pocket-watch by using a sledgehammer and an axe?

LENIN (*to* STALIN). And if you and your ilk call yourself disciples of Lenin, Leninists or whatever, then I am most certainly not a Leninist!

STALIN (*barely restraining himself*). You always used to say to us: 'Marx is no longer able to revise Marxism, so you and I have to do it'. Does that only apply to you, or to us ordinary mortals as well? Who said: 'One must break and bend obsolete ideas if the interests of the people require it'? Does that mean only you can do it, or can we too?

LENIN. Had the New Economic Policy become an obsolete idea by 1929? Why did you abolish it, when I intended it for the long term?

STALIN. Because you were mistaken in your plans and predictions for it. The N.E.P. had already ceased to work by 1928. We were left without bread. I went to Siberia myself to supervise the requisitioning of grain and I saw it with my own eyes: there was plenty of grain but the peasants were not handing it over. What do you think our comrades felt when, after one of them had spent two hours persuading them to deliver their grain, some fat pig of a peasant would stand up and say to him: 'Now you, my lad, can dance for us – then maybe I'll let you have a little wheat.' What would you have had us do, comrade Lenin? Dance? Or grab them by the throat, so that the towns didn't starve, so that the Red Army could get its rations, so that the factory chimneys would keep smoking?! Once in 1918 you sent me to Tsaritsyn to get wheat and save the revolution. I didn't give way to the moaners and snivellers, and I delivered that wheat. So why should I have backed down ten years later, in 1928? The peasants had declared war on us. We had no alternative: we had to win that war too.

DZIERZINSKI. That's not true. The peasants didn't declare war on us.

STALIN (*to* DZIERZINSKI). What business is it of yours? You departed this life as an honest Bolshevik, so you can shut up!

DZIERZINSKI. I died defending the New Economic Policy against the efforts of Trotsky, Kamenev and Zinoviev to smash it. And I would have dealt with your attack on it in the same way.

BUKHARIN. The N.E.P. was, above all, a system of civil peace between countryside and town, a close alliance between workers and peasants. It was a highly complex mixture of individual, group and state enterprise aimed at getting the country's economy functioning again after *8 years* of world war, revolution and civil war – and it worked. It was also a proof that the Party could run this vast country in times of peace as well as times of strife and upheaval: it proved that the Party had changed from being the Party of civil war to the Party of civil peace. Might there be crises? Of course there might – largely due to our own mistakes and our lack of flexibility. How could they be overcome? On the basis of N.E.P. and in the conditions of a mixed economy. And what did Stalin offer as a solution to the grain crisis?

STALIN. I will describe my proposals, if you like.

BUKHARIN. Excuse me, but they have heard and studied your version millions of times. They were never once allowed to hear my ideas on the subject.

STALIN. Luckily for them! Consequently you weren't able to paralyse their will, you didn't muddle their brains, you didn't put out the fire of their determination with your liberal claptrap. They had to win another war. We struck the right note in 1929, which we called the year of the great turning-point. We changed from ousting the elements of capitalism from the towns and villages by economic methods to booting those elements out by direct compulsion. Why? Because a war was brewing on our doorstep, because we had no time to wait for milder, slower methods to succeed. We destroyed the old system of farming, we made the peasants pay tribute and forced them to provide the capital needed to expand and modernise our industry. And the big farmers, the kulaks, we liquidated as a class; we shot the obstinate ones and sent the rest to Siberia. Throughout the country we imposed the system of collective farms and state farms as the basis of socialism in the countryside.

BUKHARIN. That was just the trouble: you *imposed* the system. After centuries of serfdom, the October Revolution had given the land to the peasants. Of course they wouldn't stand for having it taken away again, so you had to drown their resistance in blood. The result was that instead of Lenin's civil peace we got Stalin's police state.

DZIERZINSKI. Everything that Trotsky, Zinoviev and Kamenev proposed we should do in 1926, their suggested methods, their ideas on how to raise the capital funds to industrialise the country, all tended towards the same system that you applied – which basically involved robbing the peasants.

STALIN. You don't understand, Dzierzinski. A new generation had grown up who hadn't seen the revolution or the civil war. I gave them something to fight for. What we are doing, comrades, I told them, is *your* revolution, *your* civil war. Be bold! Our great slogan 'Catch up and overtake the West!' which the heroic Soviet working class made a reality, wasn't dreamed up in comrade Stalin's study. We only put into words what the nation was thinking.

BUKHARIN. But Marxists are not interested in just *any* progress. Socialism isn't only tons and metres, dams and factories; above all else it is human beings and the relationships between people. If there is nothing socialist in those relationships, if we don't give a damn about *people*, then what on earth are we doing?

STALIN. We are building – we *have* built – a great power, and nothing whatever in this world can now happen without taking us into account.

BUKHARIN. In that case, idiots that we are, why didn't we simply follow Stolypin? In the years before the Great War, he made Russia into a great power, too. Wasn't it because we wanted another kind of greatness – a socialist kind? No one will argue against industrialisation and transforming agriculture along socialist lines; all that is absolutely necessary, there is no other way. The whole question is – how? That is what divided us.

STALIN. No wonder Trotsky called you Johnny Head-in-air. None of you leaders of the right wing understand our Bolshevik tempo of development; you don't believe in it and you never will accept anything other than gradual development, anything faster than mere drifting. You really aren't a dialectician, you know; for you, the category of time doesn't exist. We're not going to wait for History to dispense charity to us: we're going to force her to give it to us. Otherwise we shall be crushed from outside. (*Pause.*) All right, then – what does your programme consist of? What are you advocating?

BUKHARIN. I'm advocating a slow advance into socialism, lasting perhaps decades, through the planned growth of industry; through co-operatives; through a thousand and one variants of the co-operative principle, from the lowest to the uppermost levels of the economy. I advocate a change of slogans: not 'Who is against Whom?' but 'Who is with Whom?' I am for overcoming difficulties primarily by economic means – by incentives rather than by force and terror. I want the economy to exist for people, not people for the economy. I want the Soviet state to obey its own laws, not to rule by arbitrary, secret decrees which can change every time the leader has a stomach-ache or a hangover. I favour a free, pluralist culture, and not one that is uniform, monotonous and servile. I favour the political dictatorship of a Party which never forgets what Lenin said to it: 'If you exclude or persecute everyone who is less than slavishly obedient, you will end up by being surrounded by disciplined fools – and then you will most certainly destroy the Party'! I am for the firm rejection of any form of nationalism, whether it be the crass nationalism of the fascists or the subtler pseudo-socialist kind – another demand that Lenin made. Finally, I am for the primacy of conscience, which applies in politics as much as in personal conduct – despite what some people seem to think; and I want us never to forget that just as there is no such thing as dry water, so there can be no such thing as inhumane socialism.

STALIN. And how many years do you want for all that to come about?

BUKHARIN. I don't know . . . twenty or thirty, but all of it to be applied seriously and for the long term . . .

STALIN. And what if there is war tomorrow?

BUKHARIN. If there is war tomorrow we shall fight, undivided by any mutual disagreements or grudges. But so long as you don't encourage the onset of war by your stupid blunders, there will be no war – provided you don't inflame the Western working class by your assertions that social democrats are simply fascists. Provided you really build up a strong Red Army and don't fatally weaken it by purging all its best leaders, so letting the fascists think your forces are so weakened they can strike with impunity . . . and so on . . .

STALIN. We had ten years at the most before they struck, and in that time we had to make the leap from nothingness into socialism. That is why I whipped the country into action.

BUKHARIN. All right, so all we had was ten years. But why couldn't we have done what we did with human decency, in Lenin's way? Think how many human tragedies we would have avoided, how many millions we would have kept alive! Did you ask those millions of men and women who accomplished that leap from 'nothingness' into your brand of socialism whether they wanted to be consigned to *real* nothingness, sent to unknown graves, slandered, humiliated and crushed, labelled as 'enemies of the people'? What was your response to their selfless enthusiasm, the like of which has never before been seen in human history? *You murdered them by the million* . . . The October Revolution, which they accepted with such fervour, never offered the murderous alternative that *you* chose to force upon them. What would have become of our Party if in October 1917 we had proposed to the Congress of Soviets not Lenin's programme – peace, bread and freedom – but comrade Stalin's future programme instead?

STALIN. Yet no one took up *your* ideas, Bukharin, and no one followed *you*. Not even your little friends of the left opposition; that should have given you cause to think. Trotsky made that quite clear in 1928 . . .

TROTSKY. I don't take back a word of what I said! With Stalin against Bukharin? Yes! With Bukharin against Stalin? Never!

BUKHARIN. It wasn't I who had cause to think, but you, Stalin, when even your enemy Trotsky declared himself ready to join forces with you against me. Trotsky – the man for whom the people and the revolution were never anything but raw material for building monuments to himself, and whose talk of 'Leninism', lacking any understanding of its spirit, its meaning or its essence, was simply a cover for his own longing for primacy and power. In your politics you two were poles apart, but in your contempt for the masses, for ordinary people, you were a perfectly matched pair.

LENIN (*to* BUKHARIN). Nikolai Ivanych, when my letter to the Party Congress was read to each delegation separately, why weren't you disturbed by that 'decisive trifle' – the dangerous flaws in Stalin's character – that I was trying so hard to warn the Party about?

BUKHARIN. I didn't understand it at the time. When I did understand it, Stalin was in an apparently unassailable position and I had become just another card in his sinister game; it was too late.

STALIN. The Party gave no support either to you, to Rykov, or to Tomsky.

BUKHARIN. The Party at large knew nothing of what was really going on in the months that led up to those purge trials. It was Lenin, after all, who taught us that the unity of the Party was the supreme good. So we didn't break ranks and appeal to the Party – that was our greatest mistake. We became the seemingly dumb victims of a behind-the-scenes struggle among the Party's leaders and senior officials, a game at which you, Stalin, had no equal.

LENIN. No, Nikolai Ivanych, you can't reduce it all to that. It's too simplistic. In my 'Letter to the Party Congress', despite my serious reservations about Stalin's character I also called him one of the most outstanding members of our Central Committee, and I still think I was not mistaken in saying that. Nor can you ignore his quite remarkable organising ability and other political skills.

BUKHARIN. And nor can I ignore *our* ability to compromise, which made us into his victims. When the clashes between us and Stalin were raging behind closed doors, I used to wonder at night whether we had the right to keep silent about what was going on. After all, the fate of the country was at stake. So wasn't our silence simply cowardice? And if we didn't communicate our misgivings to anyone beyond the innermost leadership, weren't our rows and fights with Stalin simply a kind of political masturbation? Yet we *still* kept silent about them, and so to all my other transgressions I added that one, which was perhaps the worst of all. We painted ourselves into a corner, as it were, because we were too afraid of breaking the rules of Party unity which we ourselves helped to make.

STALIN. Once again I must say I don't like the tendentious direction this scene is taking. In the play proper, by the way, the Winter Palace hasn't been taken yet.

BUKHARIN. What are you afraid of?

STALIN. I can sense which way the argument is going. Questions like these can't be decided in a theatre.

DZIERZINSKI. But the theatre is an excellent means of bringing them out into the open! To cure a disease properly, the precise diagnosis can only be reached when consultants can hold a free and frank discussion. And these three hours in the theatre are our contribution to that task. Go on, Nikolai Ivanych.

BUKHARIN. I admit it's probably true there was a great deal that Rykov, Tomsky and myself had failed to learn, hadn't considered or had underestimated. The Party did not support us. We capitulated. The mood in the Party favouring the methods of 'war communism' proved to be too strong for us. Too few Party members realised just how much that mood ran counter to their own and the people's fundamental interests. Obviously, pulling out a revolver and saying to an unarmed peasant: 'Hand over everything you've got!', is much easier than organising a flexible price-system, setting reasonable rates of taxation and teaching good husbandry on the farm. Party members came to realise all this in 1937, when tens of thousands of them found themselves in Siberia or looking down the muzzle of a cocked revolver, but by then it was too late.

KRUPSKAYA. By then *nothing* could be done – except to intercede for individuals . . .

LENIN. Did you try?

Lighting-change.

KRUPSKAYA (*to* STALIN). Joseph Vissarionych . . .

STALIN. I'm listening, Nadezhda Konstantinovna. How are you feeling? I hear you were upset because you weren't allowed to speak at the Moscow City conference. Please don't stand on ceremony, but always call me at once. We won't tolerate such behaviour to our senior Party members.

KRUPSKAYA. I want to ask you a favour again.

STALIN. What's it about? Is it about Pospelov's comments on your memoirs? I think you'd do better to approach comrade Pospelov himself.

KRUPSKAYA. No, it's not about that. He took me to task in his review in *Pravda*, telling what I should say about Lenin and how I should say it. I suppose he knows what he's doing; he will always have it on his conscience.

STALIN. I can appreciate authors' touchiness about their work – I suffer from the same thing.

KRUPSKAYA. Fritz Platten has been arrested, Joseph Vissarionych. He saved Lenin's life, you remember, on the 1st of January 1918, the first time he was shot at. Schotmann, Rahiaa and Gorbunov have all been arrested too . . . I'm only concerned about those who were very close to Lenin, whom we knew well . . . And now Yemelyanov has been sentenced to the firing squad too . . .

STALIN. You shouldn't really ask me about these matters, Nadezhda Konstantinovna. I don't take these decisions.

KRUPSKAYA. Wait, Stalin! I implore you! Yemelyanov took Lenin in and hid him in Finland when Kerensky ordered his arrest in July 1917. I'll vouch for him as if it were myself! Arrest *me* rather than him! He loved Lenin . . . he saved his life! What will his children think? And what will become of them?

STALIN. All right, Nadezhda Konstantinovna. Your assurances are quite good enough for me. I'll send word to the appropriate quarters . . . But you must forgive me, too, for not having returned your call straight away. And for the future, let's arrange things like this: if anything is worrying you, get in touch with me without fail – either straight to me or through 'proper channels', it doesn't matter how you do it; just be sure to get in touch.

Lighting-change.

KRUPSKAYA (*to* LENIN). I wanted to speak at the Party Congress.

LENIN. And did you?

KRUPSKAYA. No. I died ten days before the start of the Congress. February 26th 1939 was my 70th birthday and I died on the 27th, probably from over-excitement. He spared Yemelyanov's life; the death sentence was commuted to 25 years imprisonment, for which we must be grateful.

BUKHARIN. In 1929 I ridiculed Stalin's declaration that an intensification of the class struggle would be inevitable for our future development, but I still failed to imagine what that phrase was actually going to mean for the Party and the people.

STALIN. I wanted to spare your life . . . I gave you a chance, but you didn't take it . . . In the spring of 1936 I sent you abroad: why on earth did you come back? You knew quite well how it would end . . .

DAN. He knew. And we all knew. I and several other Mensheviks were living in Paris, where I had several talks with Bukharin. I tried to persuade him not to go back; why return to certain death? 'No', he said, 'I could never be an émigré.'

BUKHARIN (*to* STALIN). Koba, there's no one to touch you when it comes to cunning, but that little idea of yours was very clumsy – your intention stuck out a mile, even a blind man could have seen it. I can just imagine what a pleasure I must have deprived you of when I failed to stay in Paris! Forgive me.

STALIN. You deprived me of one pleasure, but you gave me another when we had you shot – who's counting? So you came back; but we knew exactly what you were thinking while you were away, because you let it show in your lecture on Goethe. When you quoted Engels on the dilemma that faced Goethe, you were actually sending a message to your supporters about yourself: 'He was forced to exist in an environment which he must have despised, and yet he was bound to it as being the only one in which he could function . . .' That's right, isn't it? I haven't misquoted it? (*Smiles*.) I don't think you can accuse me of not being perceptive. That being so, it seems legitimate to ask the question: which of us is guilty of duplicity, which of us is the double-dealer?

BUKHARIN. If you want to oversimplify everything like that . . .

STALIN. Not oversimplify, but reduce matters to the basic truths that can be understood by ordinary, simple people, whose interests I represent. And now take a look at your portrait as seen by an unbiased observer: your thinking can barely be called Marxist, you never did understand dialectics – and those are not my opinions, they are Lenin's. To that I would add: you were a yes-man to the kulaks. And a double-dealer: in 1928 you rushed to embrace Kamenev, whom only the day before you had been kicking up the backside. Why, one wonders? In order to form a bloc against me. 'A damnable cross between a fox and a pig' – it wasn't Vyshinsky who thought up that insult to throw at you during your trial; I told him to call you that. Is it surprising, therefore, that our Party preferred a tough-minded practical politician to such a miserable pygmy as you, a tearful humanist always whining on about conscience and morality while you were trying to give more land to the kulaks? Didn't you once say about yourself: 'I am the worst organiser in Russia'? When the Party preferred me to you, I don't think that was a careless or an unthinking choice. I think the Party made the right choice.

BUKHARIN (*looks at* STALIN *in silence, then turns to* LENIN). Every day for almost six months before my arrest, Yezhov the secret police chief and Vyshinsky the state's prosecutor sent me, on Stalin's orders, copies of statements made under interrogation by the purge victims, in which I was described as either a British or a German spy; an agent of Trotsky's; as having plotted to kill you, Vladimir Ilyich (and, of course, Stalin) and so on and so forth – it's all too boring to repeat. This jesuitical device was meant to wear me down, like a soldier being reduced to a bundle of nerves from the constant fear of snipers. I was a wreck; every night I expected to hear the door-bell ring, but Stalin had decided to prolong his pleasure for as long as possible. On November 7th I·was watching the Revolution Day parade on Red Square from one of the ordinary spectators' stands. Up came a Red Army soldier, saluted, and said: 'Comrade Stalin asked me to tell you that you shouldn't be down here. He invites you to come up and stand beside him at the saluting-base on top of Lenin's tomb' . . . Tomsky had the courage to shoot himself; Rykov and I couldn't do it. He wanted to, but his family wouldn't let him. I realised the end had come, and I wrote my testament. It began: 'I am leaving this life . . .' I asked my wife to learn it by heart and tear it up. Once a month she was to write it out again, repeat it and tear it up again. In that way it has survived to this day. In early February of 1938, Sergo Ordzhonikidze managed to talk to Rykov and myself; he said that he and a number of other comrades refused to believe the pack of lies that was being circulated about us, and that he would speak up for us at the February Plenum of the Central Committee, when our case was due to be discussed. Sergo was our last hope.

Lighting-change.

STALIN. What's the matter, Sergo? What do you want? You've been phoning me at all hours of the night, not letting me sleep . . .

ORDZHONIKIDZE. The NKVD has searched my apartment.

STALIN. Well, so what? It's their job. They might search my apartment too. It's nothing special.

ORDZHONIKIDZE. Last night they arrested my deputies and all the departmental heads in my Commissariat of Heavy Industry. *(Barely able to restrain himself.)* What does this mean?

STALIN. I ought to be asking *you* what it means! I warned you at the Politburo meeting – your lenience towards enemies of the people, your playing along with out-and-out scoundrels like Bukharin and Rykov – none of this has gone unnoticed, and it's bound to reflect badly on your moral character.

ORDZHONIKIDZE. Cut out the 'moral' bit.

STALIN. What about that performance you put on at Voroshilov's birthday celebrations? The Politburo was walking up the aisle towards the stage, and comrade Ordzhonikidze has to push his way through the rows of seats for all to see and has to hug Rykov, whose neck was already practically in the noose. And the whole Politburo then had to stand on stage, looking like fools and waiting for comrade Ordzhonikidze to come and join them. What were you trying to prove? And to whom? To me? *Ushen mama dzaglo!* [*Georgian obscenity*].

ORDZHONIKIDZE. Why do you have to bump off Bukharin and Rykov? Haven't you drunk enough blood already?

STALIN. Who d'you think you're talking to?

ORDZHONIKIDZE. I'm talking to you. Now sit down! (*Rather to his own surprise,* STALIN *sits down.*) Did Lenin write about you that you were ' . . . the rightful favourite of the Party'? Did he write that about me? Or did he write it about Bukharin? He wrote it about Bukharin. Whose arms did Lenin die in? Mine? No. He died in Bukharin's arms. And is that why you want to put a bullet in the back of his neck? What proof have you that he is guilty of all the absurd charges against him?

STALIN. Haven't you read the testimony of all the witnesses?

ORDZHONIKIDZE. If you gave Yezhov the order to do so, he would produce witnesses to testify against *you*.

STALIN. I don't need any proof. Let *him* prove he hasn't been harbouring hostile and disloyal thoughts. He's been blabbing everywhere, as usual, a lot of crap about the NKVD getting up to dirty tricks and practically hatching a plot against the entire Party. (*Smiles.*) We'll send him along to the NKVD so that he can check it out . . . personally!

ORDZHONIKIDZE. He's sitting at home, helping to look after his newborn baby, and everybody knows you've already passed sentence on him before he's even been arrested, let alone tried. So why call a plenary session of the Central Committee to be held in four days' time? Just so that you can tighten the noose around his neck with your own hands? I saw Pyatakov just before his trial and I didn't recognise him. What did you do to him? Are you having our people tortured just because the fascists are torturing communists in Germany and Italy? We're not fascists, for God's sake! Why put yourself in the same league as those brutes? Lenin united us by the power of reason – you're trying to do it by fear, blood and violence.

STALIN. What's the matter with you, Sergo? Why so faint-hearted? We're in the middle of a vicious fight – the fight which you and I warned the Party about more than once. We're engaged in rooting out our enemies, something which you and I also foresaw long ago. So what's worrying you, old friend?

ORDZHONIKIDZE. What worries me is *you*.

STALIN. What?! Tired of life, Sergo? Do you *want* to die?

ORDZHONIKIDZE. Yes, I do.

STALIN (*sensing danger*). What's all this about, old friend? Are you really so upset by that house-search? I'll tell Yezhov to call his stupid dogs off . . .

ORDZHONIKIDZE. Why have you been arresting mere boys – Andrei Sverdlov and Dmitry Osinsky?

STALIN. They're free-thinkers. Getting dangerous ideas . . .

ORDZHONIKIDZE. And do you have a monopoly of thinking?

STALIN (*jokingly*). Get away, you old son of a bitch! Call yourself a friend!

ORDZHONIKIDZE (*commandingly*). Sit down!

STALIN. Why get so excited, old friend? Surely you and I can settle your problem? Who else do you think was wrongly arrested?

ORDZHONIKIDZE. Am I supposed to plead for your own wife's brother? Does it mean nothing to you that he was your son's teacher? Prison as a mark of your gratitude?

STALIN. All right, we'll release him . . . But what is this? Why are you so wound up about my family? Who else is on your list?

ORDZHONIKIDZE. All the people who are on *your* list . . . in the Party . . . in the army . . . my men who were taken last night . . . I see it now: you have a plan – you won't be satisfied until you've grabbed them *all*, will you? . . . I'm asking you to spare them all. Would you like me to get down on my knees?

STALIN. Calm down, Sergo, old friend . . . You're fundamentally naive and trusting, you believe everyone, you love everyone. (*Suddenly furious.*) Why do I prefer those who support me from fear and not from conviction? Because people can change their convictions like putting on a new pair of gloves! If you're so wise and compassionate, if you're so humane, where were you until now? Why didn't you stand up and warn me sooner? Why didn't you grab me by the arm? There was a time when you and I did everything together, I couldn't take a single step without you. So what's happened? Scared of the responsibility? Wasn't it you and I together who attacked and destroyed all those punks of the opposition? You're not frightened of this new bunch, are you? They're nonentities! Not one of them has the will-power or the guts to see their ideas through to the bitter end! They're weaklings! They're not men at all!

ORDZHONIKIDZE. I have just realised, only now, that you purposely caused the grain shortage and all the other crises. You consciously didn't want them solved by normal, peaceful means . . . You needed another civil war . . . You needed the country in flames – then you could act like a general on a white horse and no one could argue with you because you were handling an emergency.

STALIN. Tell me straight: who has put you up to this? Who has dared to raise their hand against the friendship between you and me? Do you remember who saved you when your beloved Lenin proposed throwing you out of the Party? Or don't you know the meaning of gratitude? You'd better take advantage of the moment – I'm feeling kind and well-disposed, so ask my pardon . . .

ORDZHONIKIDZE (*not hearing*). Aren't you afraid of retribution? It will come, you know, even if death saves you . . . You're afraid – I can tell, because every night you use a flashlight to look under the bed you're going to sleep in. Yes, you're afraid. I often wondered why you had that funny habit. How could you destroy yourself like this, Koba? You have nothing: no friends, not even a woman who loves you . . . Your only passions are power and cruelty. Tell me – what pleasure is there in making wives and children weep, even men weep? What is pleasant about it? Or do you get pleasure from the power to kill or pardon at your whim?

STALIN. You swine! I had your oldest brother shot and I promise you – not one Ordzhonikidze will be left alive! Not one! That I guarantee to you.

ORDZHONIKIDZE. The kindest, the most forgiving people in the world are the Russians; it isn't in their nature to bear a grudge. Even so, they remember the centuries of Tartar rule with hatred. And they will remember you in the same way.

STALIN. Now, as you will realise, there is only one way out for you. I grant it to you for old times' sake.

ORDZHONIKIDZE. I took that decision this morning. I only regret that I lack the strength to shoot *you* now. We ourselves made you the symbol – no, the idol – of the October Revolution. Now that you are swatting us like flies, one after another, we can't raise a hand to stop you. For that we can't be forgiven – myself least of all. You're right: we marched in step alongside you so firmly that we didn't notice when we suddenly found ourselves wading through blood. It's unforgiveable! I curse the day when I first trusted you and began to follow you.

STALIN. And don't imagine that your death will plunge a knife into my back. I'll say you died of a heart attack.

ORDZHONIKIDZE. Whatever happens, retribution will catch up with you. The Furies will come for you, alive or dead. And now get out!

Exit STALIN. *A burst of music almost drowns out the sound of the shot as* ORDZHONIKIDZE *commits suicide. Blackout, then a spotlight picks out* BUKHARIN, *who reads out his farewell letter.*

BUKHARIN. I am leaving this life. I bow my head, but not to the executioner's axe of the proletariat, which should be merciless but also chaste. I feel helpless in the face of an infernal machine which, by the use of the methods of the Middle Ages, exercises a gigantic strength, organises the fabrication of slander, acts boldly and confidently.

Dzierzinski is no longer with us; the splendid traditions of the Cheka have gradually become a thing of the past, when the revolutionary idea guided all its actions, justified harshness towards our enemies and preserved the state from all forms of counter-revolution. That is why the Cheka earned our special confidence, its special esteem, authority and respect. Now, the greater part of the so-called NKVD is a degenerate organisation of ideologically illiterate, rotten, well-paid bureaucrats who, exploiting the Cheka's erstwhile authority and pandering to Stalin's morbidly suspicious nature – to put it mildly – carry out their dirty work simply to earn medals and promotion – while failing to realise, incidentally, that they are simultaneously working for their own destruction; history does not tolerate the survival of witnesses to foul deeds.

That 'wonder-working organisation' can take any member of the Central Committee, any Party member and grind them into dust, brand them as a traitor, a terrorist or a spy. If Stalin were to harbour any doubts about himself, confirmation would be instantly provided. Thunder-clouds are hanging over the Party: my innocent head alone will drag thousands more innocent heads with it into the grave. Because it has been found necessary to create an organisation – a Bukharinite organisation

– which never existed in reality, not only now, when for the past seven years I have not had so much as a hint of disagreement with the Party, but which did not even exist back in the days of the Right Opposition. I know nothing of the secret organisations of Ryutin and Uglanov. Together with Rykov and Tomsky I made my views known openly. I have been in the Party since the age of eighteen, and the aim of my life has always been the struggle on behalf of the working class, the victory of socialism. Recently the newspaper that boasts the hallowed title of *Pravda* – 'The Truth' – has been publishing a foul lie, which alleges that I, Nikolai Bukharin, wanted to destroy the achievements of the October Revolution and restore capitalism. This is a piece of unheard-of effrontery, a lie whose equivalent in insolence, in public irresponsibility, could only be a lie such as this: it has been discovered that Nicholas II devoted his whole life to fighting capitalism and the monarchy and to struggling to bring about a proletarian revolution.

If I made a few errors in the methods needed to build socialism, let posterity judge me no more severely than it has judged Lenin. We were seeking the way to one and the same goal and seeking it for the first time, along an as yet untrodden path. It was a different time, when different customs prevailed. *Pravda* used then to publish a list of issues for discussion; we argued, sought ways ahead, quarrelled and made peace, and pressed forward together.

I appeal to you, the future generation of Party leaders, whose historic mission will include the duty of unravelling and exposing the monstrous tangle of crimes, which in these terrible days are growing to ever vaster proportions, are flaring up like a great flame and which will suffocate the Party.

I appeal to all members of the Party! In what are perhaps the last days of my life I am convinced that the cleansing force of history will wipe away the filth that has been heaped on my head. I was never a traitor; I would have unhesitatingly paid for Lenin's life with my own. I loved Kirov, and never organised anything against Stalin. I am asking a new, young and honest generation of Party leaders to read out my letter at a plenary session of the Party, to exculpate me and to reinstate me in the Party.

For you should know, comrades, that on the banner which you will carry in the victorious advance to communism there is a drop of my blood too. Signed: Nikolai Bukharin.

All lights come up. There is a long, uncomfortable pause.

LENIN. I am unquestionably guilty of failing to remove Stalin from his post in 1923 – my accursed illness prevented me . . . but that is no excuse, because I perceived the true state of affairs too late and did not reform the system in a way that would have prevented Stalin – or anyone else – from gaining absolute power.

SVERDLOV. Vladimir Ilyich . . .

LENIN. No, you don't have to spare me! I want everyone to know that I entirely accept the guilt and the moral responsibility for what happened. (*To* STALIN.) I would like to talk to you.

STALIN. I don't see any need for it.

LENIN (*restraining himself with an effort*). Marxism, communism, the October Revolution are all inconceivable without a definite, specific set of political and moral standards. It is the right and duty of every thinking Bolshevik to measure his actions against the yardstick of those standards. We are *all* subject to the jurisdiction of the court of history.

STALIN. You aren't going to deny that my ideas and convictions were *communist* are you?

LENIN (*explodes*). I most certainly do deny that!

STALIN. In that case, I don't see what we have to talk about.

LENIN. You have a different set of standards. I don't even want to waste words on discussing whether what you did was good or bad; it simply had nothing whatsoever in common with the aims of the revolution. It suited some people, it impressed some people . . . History will show us where your achievements end and your mistakes begin, where your mistakes end and your crimes begin. As for us, here and now, if we are concerned for the future of our cause, we must say loudly and clearly: socialism – yes! All the truly socialist measures that have been brought about – yes! Stalin's methods – no! Morality à la Stalin – no!

MARTOV. Milyukov, the liberal foreign minister in the first Provisional government who later edited a Russian daily newspaper in Paris, regarded Stalin as a major statesman – he compared him to Peter the Great. And if you were to place him in the succession of Russian Tsars, then perhaps he really was an emperor, a sovereign autocrat?

SVERDLOV. In 1917 we began quite a different line of succession; the October Revolution was the starting point of a new era.

PLEKHANOV. I regard Milyukov's opinion as dubious. If you consider Stalin's mistakes of the 1930s alone – astounding in their crass dilettantism and arrogance – you can be sure that no European people except the wretched, longsuffering Russians would have put up with a government like Stalin's. In fact he admitted as much himself, when he made his famous toast to the Russian people at the victory banquet in the Kremlin.

SPIRIDONOVA. When his Politburo colleagues came to him at the moment of the German invasion in June 1941, he was terrified; he thought they had come to arrest him, and all they wanted him to do was to address the nation on the radio. He was in such a state of nerves that he couldn't even do that, and Molotov made the official announcement instead.

DZIERZINSKI. It was the Soviet people who saved him – and what was his response? Before the war was even over, the conveyor-belt of arrests started up again.

PLEKHANOV. Given a total lack of Marxist principles, autocratic rule over such gigantic human resources as ours can only breed what it did.

MARTOV. I find the figure of Stalin totally alien and repellent. But one must be objective – one can't ignore an entire one-third of a century. He did create the modern Soviet Union.

SVERDLOV. 'Victorious generals are not court-martialled' is not one of our principles. We cannot be indifferent to *how* socialism was built in Russia and what sort of socialism it was – if it can be called socialism at all. The ways, the methods and the means concern us no less than the objective, no less than the results.

DZIERZINSKI. The modern Soviet Union was created. That is so. But should we not be asking the question: was it *thanks to* Stalin or *in spite of* him? How great was the potential of the October Revolution, if even under such nightmarish conditions it produced such results! But if the army had not been left leaderless by the purges; if our best economists and technicians had not been shot or imprisoned; if the peasants had been allowed to form voluntary co-operatives; if our thinkers and writers had been allowed to soar in freedom; if conscience and morality had been raised up and kept on a pedestal of honour – where might we not be today?

MARTOV. I think a lot of people are not going to like it if you pose the question in over-extreme terms.

SVERDLOV. Those people who shut their ears to the groans of millions of prisoners from behind barbed wire – they will certainly not like it. Those who admire 'the magic of the lash' and see the cudgel as the universal method of solving all problems – they won't like it. Those who served the system on the principle of 'anything you say, sir', the lackeys of ideology – they won't like it. Nor, of course, will those with the mentality of perverted slaves, who drool at the memory of the heavy hand of the master. But they, of course, are not the only ones . . . The real problem lies in ensuring that the millions of people who lived and worked honestly shouldn't think, from what we've been saying, that their lives were pointless, wasted.

MARTOV. I sympathise with your problem, and therefore I think you shouldn't be too hasty in dotting all the 'i's and crossing all the 't's. Moses led his people through the wilderness for forty years in order that the generation born in slavery should die out.

DZIERZINSKI. I doubt whether our country has so much time to spare. We must hope that the mounting sum of true facts will open the eyes of those whose eyes are still closed.

SPIRIDONOVA. The very stones will cry out. Aren't you frightened at that?

DZIERZINSKI. No. All future generations must recognise Stalin's hand-writing, hideous though it may be.

MARTOV. Khrushchev did his best.

SVERDLOV. Khrushchev was a product of the October Revolution. He was, of course, a man schooled under Stalinism, but still a man of October. He may have made mistakes, he may have been clumsy, he may have been inconsistent, but he started the process of bringing us back to the truth. At the time, and in those conditions, it was a real feat. We shouldn't forget that.

STALIN. Somebody once sent me a denunciation of Khrushchev as unreliable. I threw it aside. I was a fool to do so. Now Molotov, Kaganovich, Voroshilov – deep down they may have feared and hated me, but they would never have mounted a vicious attack on me. That's what comes of once showing tolerance and kindness . . . You think I had too many people shot? Don't make me laugh. We live in Russia – the land of the Tsars. And the Russian people will only acknowledge us when *one* man is running the country. And whatever you may say, however much you may prate about democracy, in the final analysis there will always be *one* leader. What serious politician ever voluntarily hands over the reins? And who is going to take them over? I'm not against democracy and self-government as subjects for discussion at evening classes. For a time. But we have to demonstrate a *real* love of the people in other ways, in ways that the people are capable of understanding and appreciating. Therefore don't boast about Khrushchev's denunciation of me in 1956, but think of what came after him. I can never be erased from the national memory. Many will go on defending me when they defend themselves. Until you tell people clearly and firmly what was the real result of my revolution from above: whether it was the flowering of socialist democracy; the harnessing of popular enthusiasm; the final and irreversible victory of socialism, as I mantain and as any who isn't blind can see – or whether it was millions of senseless deaths, as some slanderers maintain, quoting our enemies abroad – you will never make any progress. How will you look upon the years of heroic work by the Soviet people under my leadership: through the prison bars of the purge years, or in the light of Magnitogorsk and the Dnieper Dam? *That* is the question you must answer!

SVERDLOV. That is a false antithesis, and just another example of your favourite method of setting half the people at odds with the other half. Our method is different: to decide which part of our inheritance to reject (while never, of course, forgetting it) and which part to cherish and take forward with us. We shall take Magnitogorsk; we shall take the Dnieper Dam; we shall take our faith in socialism; every day that carries us further away from a nation of slaves – those we shall take and never reject!

STALIN. Let me give you a piece of friendly advice: if you don't want to have a mass of resentful people at your back, if you want to avoid a lot of extra, unnecessary trouble – leave me in peace. The house has been built, and it's habitable . . . But if you can't keep your hands off it, then give it some cosmetic refurbishment; change the wallpaper, put in some new furniture, but get on with tackling today's problems. There are more than enough of them.

SVERDLOV. If only you knew how much we *don't* want to have anything more to do with you! The trouble is, no matter which problems we tackle, we keep bumping up against you and your legacy.

STALIN. So what do you propose?

DZIERZINSKI. To get rid of all the evil you left behind. That's it: to save the baby, but throw out all the dirty bath water.

LENIN. Contempt for the masses and their interests on the one hand and piercing discontent among the masses with the existing order on the other hand are not enough to produce a revolution. Neither is the degeneration of the system of government and the loss of its authority. Either of them can only produce the slow and agonising decay of a country if that country lacks the strength to destroy the system. But it is a fact of life that the October Revolution sowed seeds which, sooner or later, will always germinate and send up shoots. October is not something that can be rooted out of people's souls. Even in the very worst years our people kept oil in their lamps. And that is precisely what ensures that we, who began it all, did not live and die in vain.

SVERDLOV. But for our people to have lamps that burn and give light we ourselves must first light them.

LENIN. Precisely. (*To the* BOLSHEVIKS.) So, comrades, shall we set the mechanism of revolution going at full speed, or shall we keep on marking time? Let's not fool ourselves, let's pluck up our courage and say it straight out: either we go onward or we slide back – and if the latter, then the Bolsheviks will disgrace themselves for ever and disappear as a serious political party.

DZIERZINSKI. You're right, Vladimir Ilyich, but we miss you badly here.

LENIN. I'm waiting for permission to go to Smolny.

KORNILOV (*to the* MENSHEVIKS). Ditherers! Go on – do something! There's still time!

DAN. Shortly before midnight I tried to do just that . . .

Scene Four

THE WINTER PALACE
23.20 hours, October 25th 1917

DAN *and* KERENSKY *approach each other from opposite sides of the stage.*

DAN. As acting chairman of the All-Russian Executive Committee of the Soviets . . .

KERENSKY. Forget the formalities! Tell me in plain Russian . . . do you support my government in its heroic fight against left-wing extremism?

DAN. We will support you, but only if you take certain firm political measures, which will cut the ground from under the Bolsheviks' feet.

KERENSKY. When I sent you a request for your support this morning, I thought I was appealing to Russian patriots. I felt sure you would not fail me. It seems I was wrong. Good day to you!

DAN. Wait, Alexander Fyodorych! I've come to you with a concrete proposal. The situation can still be saved. You must immediately – this minute – issue a decree on making peace with the Germans and giving all the land to the peasants. Notify this to the whole country by telegraph and put up posters to that effect overnight, throughout the city. Tomorrow you will see an immediate change in the mood of the population. With one stab you will let all the air out of the Bolsheviks' planned insurrection. Tomorrow morning every soldier, every worker and every peasant will know that the Provisional Government is the champion of their keenest hopes and their interests. What will the Bolsheviks have to offer them then?

KERENSKY. Have you finished? My cabinet is in session, and I'm late.

DAN. I'm talking to you about the way to save Russia . . . I implore you!

STRUVE. Alexander Fyodorych, wait – don't send him away! There is still just time to save everything . . . think, for God's sake! Have you taken leave of your senses?

KERENSKY (*to the auditorium*). What can I say? One must be self-critical. I was in a hurry at that moment . . . although, in my view, even if we had issued those decrees they wouldn't have helped us. They might perhaps have made life slightly more difficult for the Bolsheviks, but that's all. (*To* DAN.) The Provisional Government, Mr Dan, does not need to be lectured or given instructions. Now is not the time to talk, but to act. I dealt with Kornilov, and I will deal with Lenin. Good day to you.

DAN. Goodbye, Kerensky. (*To the auditorium.*) What could I do?

KERENSKY (*almost shouts*). And what could I do?

KORNILOV. Shut up! Bloody intellectuals, nonentities – you dropped Russia in the shit, and then you spent fifty years in Paris and New York arguing about who should have done what . . . Swine!

Scene Five

FOFANOVA'S APARTMENT
23.10 hours, October 25th 1917

Three rings at the door-bell. LENIN *dashes to open it. Enter* RAHIAA.

LENIN. I thought it was Fofanova. What's the news from Smolny?

RAHIAA. I don't know. I've been at my job at the factory all day.

LENIN. Supper's on the table, then we're going to Smolny.

RAHIAA. Has the Central Committee given you its permission?

LENIN. We're not going to wait for their permission, we're going anyway.

RAHIAA (*sits down at the table*). Once before I didn't wait for the Central Committee's permission, brought you here from Vyborg – and who got it in the neck?

LENIN. We both did. How far is it to Smolny?

RAHIAA. About ten kilometres.

LENIN. Can we make it in two hours?

RAHIAA. Vladimir Ilyich, you know me.

LENIN. And you know me. You do realise, don't you, that I *must* be there as soon as possible?

RAHIAA. Yes, I do. And do you realise what's happening out there on the streets? Supposing I lose you?

LENIN. Never mind. Eat your supper. You can say that I wasn't here when you arrived.

Picks up his overcoat from the chair, puts it on, takes a Browning automatic out of his hip pocket, checks the magazine, cocks the hammer, sets the safety-catch and puts the pistol into his right-hand overcoat pocket.

LENIN. Is it raining?

RAHIAA. A bit. Tell them that I shouted at you and tried to stop you going.

LENIN. I will.

RAHIAA. I'll go first, you walk behind me. If I have to shoot . . .

LENIN. We'll both shoot. Wait a minute . . . I don't want Margarita Vasilievna to be worried . . . (*Quickly writes a note.*) 'I've gone where you didn't want me to go'. Come on – let's go!

All three acting-spaces are blacked out, leaving only the characters sitting in the semi-circle of chairs. LENIN *and* RAHIAA *are the last to take their seats.*

DAN. When I saw him arrive at Smolny at midnight, I realised that all was lost, that the machinery of the armed insurrection would now be put into action at full speed. So everything happened as Lenin wanted it. But what can you do with a man who thinks of nothing but revolution for 24 hours a day?

KERENSKY. Everyone knows what happened next. We can all go now.

One by one, in the same order in which they entered, the characters – except LENIN *and* STALIN *– leave the stage.*

LENIN *gets up and stands centre-stage, looking into the auditorium; he wants to say something to us in private – something important, essential. He is waiting until he is alone. All the others have gone, except* STALIN. *The pause grows unbearably long.* STALIN *does not go. When the situation becomes absolutely intolerable,* STALIN *can contain himself no longer and breaks the silence.*

STALIN. I would like a word with you, to explain everything.

LENIN (*harshly*). You and I have nothing to say to each other. (*To the auditorium.*) We must go onward . . . onward . . . and onward!

They continue to stand in the same positions, a considerable distance apart. We are all longing for STALIN *to go. But he does not go . . .*

Curtain